Toward a New Public Diplomacy

Palgrave Macmillan Series in Global Public Diplomacy

Series editors:

Kathy Fitzpatrick, Quinnipiac University, USA
Philip Seib, University of Southern California, USA

At no time in history has public diplomacy played a more significant role in world affairs and international relations. As a result, global interest in public diplomacy has escalated, creating a substantial academic and professional audience for new works in the field.

This series examines theory and practice in public diplomacy from a global perspective, looking closely at public diplomacy concepts, policies, and practices in various regions of the world. The purpose is to enhance understanding of the importance of public diplomacy, to advance public diplomacy thinking, and to contribute to improved public diplomacy practices.

The editors welcome submissions from scholars and practitioners representing a range of disciplines and fields (including diplomacy, international relations, international communications, public relations, political science, global media, marketing/advertising) and offering diverse perspectives. In keeping with its global focus, the series encourages non-U.S.-centric works and comparative studies.

Toward a New Public Diplomacy: Redirecting U.S. Foreign Policy
  Edited by Philip Seib

Toward a New Public Diplomacy

Redirecting U.S. Foreign Policy

Edited by
Philip Seib

palgrave
macmillan

TOWARD A NEW PUBLIC DIPLOMACY
Copyright © Philip Seib, 2009.

All rights reserved.

First published in 2009 by
PALGRAVE MACMILLAN®
in the United States—a division of St. Martin's Press LLC,
175 Fifth Avenue, New York, NY 10010.

Where this book is distributed in the UK, Europe and the rest of the world,
this is by Palgrave Macmillan, a division of Macmillan Publishers Limited,
registered in England, company number 785998, of Houndmills,
Basingstoke, Hampshire RG21 6XS.

Palgrave Macmillan is the global academic imprint of the above companies
and has companies and representatives throughout the world.

Palgrave® and Macmillan® are registered trademarks in the United States,
the United Kingdom, Europe and other countries.

ISBN: 978–0–230–61744–5 (paperback)
ISBN: 978–0–230–61743–8 (hardcover)

Library of Congress Cataloging-in-Publication Data

Toward a new public diplomacy : redirecting U.S. foreign policy / edited
by Philip Seib.
    p. cm.
  ISBN-13: 978–0–230–61744–5 (alk. paper)
  ISBN-10: 0–230–61744–1 (alk. paper)
    1. United States—Foreign relations—Public opinion. 2. United
States—Foreign public opinion. 3. Public opinion—United States. I. Seib,
Philip M., 1949–

JZ1480.A5T69 2009

327.73—dc22   2008054999

A catalogue record of the book is available from the British Library.

Design by Newgen Imaging Systems (P) Ltd., Chennai, India.

First edition: September 2009

10 9 8 7 6 5 4 3 2 1

Printed in the United States of America.

CONTENTS

PREFACE

Those who make and implement American foreign policy say nice things about public diplomacy, which can be defined, in shorthand fashion, as reaching out directly to foreign publics rather than foreign governments. This is not merely a matter of being liked for its own sake. U.S. security interests require that peoples around the world not be hostile to America and Americans. Given the potentially devastating capabilities of rogue states, terrorist organizations, and even hate-driven individuals, the United States must define itself through deeds and words in ways that build global friendships or at least diminish enmity and so limit the scope and intensity of anti-Americanism.

Few in decision-making roles will disagree with this, but even fewer are willing to commit to a coherent, modern approach to public diplomacy. Too many U.S. public diplomacy ventures are rooted in cold war-era thinking and are most noteworthy for their lack of imagination. Not surprisingly, they are not accomplishing what needs to be done.

President Barack Obama has the opportunity to change all this. Those of us who have contributed to this volume hope that it will prove useful to the new administration by offering an array of approaches to public diplomacy that are worthy of exploration. Some current endeavors, such as cultural diplomacy, need to be fine-tuned and expanded, while others, such as the Middle East broadcasting projects, need to be blown up and rebuilt.

Beyond its hoped-for usefulness in policy making circles, the book is also designed to interest those who pay attention to U.S. foreign policy and find it lacking. Public diplomacy needs a constituency both within the government and among members of the broader public who are willing to assert that this must be made a more integral part of America's interaction with the global community.

According to the conventional wisdom of the twentieth century and the first years of the twenty-first, America owes its place in the world primarily to its muscle, and it makes no sense to jeopardize preeminence by altering its fundamental strategy of foreign affairs. Today, however, some policy makers recognize that the world is changing, that merely being a "superpower"—whatever that means now—does not ensure security or prosperity in a globalized society. When officials such as Secretary of Defense Robert Gates urge that more money be put into the State Department's budget and tell U.S. troops in the Horn of Africa that they must incorporate public diplomacy in their mission, as he did in late 2007, times are changing.

This book makes the case that America's diplomatic course must change even more. Public diplomacy should be elevated to become a truly integral part of the way the United States deals with the rest of the world. The stakes are enormous. Hostile publics constrain relationships even with friendly governments, making it difficult to achieve policy goals ranging from trade pacts to defense alliances. Beyond that, hostility provides an environment in which dislike can foster hatred, which may then become manifest in violence, including terrorism.

Although underlying policies matter most, failure to engage fully in public diplomacy neglects valuable American assets. Throughout the world, appreciation of American ideals and culture remains strong, even in many of the countries where U.S. policy is scorned. If such positive feelings could be built upon, then America's tenuous position in the world might be strengthened.

The need for greater attention to public diplomacy is partly a function of globalized communication. Proliferation of satellite television and the Internet means that people know more and know it faster than at any previous time. This can produce quick explosions, such as the Danish cartoon controversy of 2006 (which involved caricatures of the prophet Mohammed), and it has increased volatility among the denizens of "the Arab street," "the Chinese street," and other publics. This restiveness affects domestic politics in these countries and complicates the tasks of diplomacy. Less dependent on government-tied media for information, publics must be courted directly rather than exclusively through their governments. Further, a government concerned that large parts of its population are antagonistic toward the United States may be reluctant to cooperate with U.S. policy. Public diplomacy could help reduce this problem.

In the Middle East, for example, satellite television and Internet-based news providers have energized the public sphere to an unprecedented extent. Addressing this enlivened intellectual/political community has become essential for any country wishing to have influence in that region. In China, even a government well practiced in controlling its citizenry has frequently found itself facing unpredictable tides of public opinion generated by pervasive new media. Similar circumstances exist elsewhere in the world, and newly curious populations may be receptive to thoughtful public diplomacy approaches.

In this evolving global political environment, public diplomacy should be viewed as an increasingly important tool of foreign policy. The United States has acknowledged this with much talk but little effective action. Public diplomacy has been conducted episodically and superficially, with ill-conceived stunts outnumbering thoughtful long-term projects. Despite the good intentions of some practitioners at individual embassies or in the warrens of the State Department, using substantive public diplomacy is usually only an afterthought among principal policy makers. While America's standing in international public opinion polls has plunged, corrective responses have been plagued by aimlessness.

How much attention the Obama administration will pay to public diplomacy remains open to question, but Obama's past statements about foreign policy indicate that he is sensitive to the need to reinvigorate America's standing in the world. Proclaiming one's country as "the most powerful nation" means little if that power is grounded almost entirely in military capability. International influence in the twenty-first century will be rooted in the ability to cooperate with state and non-state actors on matters such as preserving the environment, adapting to the expanding number of economic powers, protecting against global pandemics, and ensuring that access to nuclear, chemical, and biological weaponry is tightly controlled.

Fostering goodwill among peoples and states is only part of the way to reach such goals, but it is an essential part, and that is why public diplomacy must become a more central element in a reinvented American foreign policy.

This book is divided into three parts. The first provides an appraisal of American public diplomacy as it stands today. Ambassador William A. Rugh lays out the case for "soft power" rather than "hard power," which in essence is the desirability of convincing rather than coercing. Nicholas J. Cull presents a capsule history of American public diplomacy, showing the many ups and downs in this field's past. Shawn Powers and Ahmed El Gody look at a key element of post-9/11 U.S. public diplomacy, Al Hurra television, the American-run Arabic-language broadcasting channel that has been so ineffective.

The second part comprises views from some of those to whom American public diplomacy is directed. Viktoria V. Orlova, Guolin Shen, and Hussein Amin present viewpoints from Russia, China, and Egypt respectively. Their analyses make clear that U.S. public diplomacy efforts face tough audiences that are skeptical, to say the least, of American motives.

The third part examines how American public diplomacy might become more imaginative and more effective. Amelia Arsenault considers ways that new technologies can be better put to work in public diplomacy. Kathy R. Fitzpatrick looks at the role of the private sector, which in partnership with the government could reach untapped audiences. Neal M. Rosendorf suggests ways that cultural public diplomacy could be expanded and made more effective. Jennifer A. Marshall and Thomas F. Farr scrutinize the often overlooked role of religion in public diplomacy. Given the importance of religion as a keystone of America's heritage and as a key element in the lives of audiences that many public diplomacy efforts are designed to reach, this topic merits far more attention from policy makers. Similarly, as Abiodun Williams points out, the U.S. military has become a player in public diplomacy ventures and this must be carefully considered because it involves a fundamental change in the military's tasks and, if handled badly, could distort the perceived purposes of public diplomacy.

Finally, I knot together all these threads to suggest elements of a public diplomacy agenda for the Obama administration and beyond.

I would like to thank my colleagues who so generously agreed to contribute chapters to this book. The roster purposely includes a mix of established leaders in the field and young scholars whose work will influence the course of public diplomacy for decades to come.

The book was born at the Center on Public Diplomacy at the University of Southern California. The center, along with USC's Masters program in public diplomacy, provides a home for those who are committed to treating public diplomacy with the seriousness it deserves. Geoff Wiseman, Nick Cull, Sherine Badawi Walton, Lisa Larsen, and an array of immensely talented students and fellows make this an interesting, lively place. We all enjoy the support of Dean Ernest Wilson.

At Palgrave Macmillan, Farideh Koohi-Kamali, Toby Wahl, and Asa Johnson have been supportive throughout the writing and editing.

Finally, a note of appreciation is owed to all the women and men who have been working tirelessly to advance American public diplomacy. They work for the government, private businesses, NGOs, and on their own to improve their country's standing in the world. Their commitment to the peaceful assertion of U.S. interests is an indication that public diplomacy can succeed if it is given the attention it merits.

PHILIP SEIB
November 2008

PART I

Growing Pains: American Public Diplomacy Today

CHAPTER ONE

The Case for Soft Power

WILLIAM A. RUGH

Development of the Concept

The term "soft power" was coined by Professor Joseph Nye, who first introduced it in a book he published in 1990, and in two scholarly articles that came out in the same year.[1] His concept was built on an idea discussed much earlier by two other scholars who talked about "the second face of power."[2] Then after 9/11, Professor Nye further refined his concept in several new publications. His book, *The Paradox of American Power,* which came out in 2003, fully developed the soft power idea, just at a time when the Bush administration was using hard power to bring about regime change in Iraq.[3] Nye quickly followed that in 2004 with another book on soft power that devoted an entire chapter to public diplomacy, and another scholarly article summarizing his thesis.[4]

The concept has gained support. A number of scholars have picked up Nye's term in their writings. One wrote on China's use of soft power.[5] Another wrote on soft power in Europe, saying European nations have used it effectively as a counterweight to American hard power.[6] One writer focused on the pop culture aspect of soft power, such as movies, television, pop music, Disneyland, and America's fast-food brands including Coke and McDonald's.[7]

Professor Nye has continued to write about soft power,[8] and most recently, several analysts including Nye have talked about the concept of "smart power" as a refinement. Joseph Nye and former Deputy Secretary of State Richard Armitage co-chaired a Commission on Smart Power at the Center for Strategic and International Studies (CSIS), that produced a report on the subject.[9] The University of Southern California Center on Public Diplomacy is carrying out a project on Hard Power, Soft Power, and Smart Power, directed by Professor Ernest Wilson.[10]

What Is Soft Power?

Nye begins by defining "power" as "the ability to influence the ability of others to get the outcomes one wants." He then distinguishes between three ways to affect the behavior of others: "You can coerce them with threats, you can induce them with payments, or you can attract them or co-opt them." The first and second are "hard power," that is, the use of military power or economic power, or "sticks" and "carrots." The third is soft power, which he defines as "the ability to affect others to obtain what one wants through attraction rather than coercion or payment."[11]

Nye explains soft power in this way:

> A country may obtain the outcomes it wants in world politics because other countries want to follow it, admiring its values, emulating its example, and/or aspiring to its level of prosperity and openness. In this sense, it is important to set the agenda and attract others in world politics, and not only force them to change through the threat or use of military or economic weapons. This soft power—getting others to want the outcomes that you want— co-opts people rather than coerces them. Soft power is the ability to shape the preferences of others.... Soft power is not merely influence, though it is one source of influence.... It is also the ability to entice and attract.

He says "soft power rests on a country's culture, values and policies."[12]

What Is Smart Power?

The CSIS Commission on Smart Power defines it as follows: "Smart power is neither hard nor soft—it is the skillful combination of both. Smart power means developing an integrated strategy, resource base and a tool kit to achieve American objectives, drawing on both hard and soft power. It is an approach that underscores the necessity of a strong military, but it also invests heavily in alliances, partnerships and institutions at all levels to expand American influence and establish the legitimacy of American action."[13]

Joseph Nye says, "A smart power strategy combines hard and soft power resources."[14]

Hard Power Is Insufficient

The case for soft power rests partly on the fact that hard power is insufficient to support American national interests adequately.

Professor Nye says, "The current struggle against international terrorism is a struggle to win hearts and minds, and the current overreliance on hard power is not the path to success"—adding that the Bush administration specifically has depended too much on hard power and not enough on soft power.[15]

The CSIS Commission on Smart Power argued that "maintaining U.S. military power is paramount to any smart power strategy" but it also concluded that "U.S. foreign policy has tended to over-rely on hard power because it is the most direct and visible source of American strength.... U.S. foreign policy is still struggling to develop soft power instruments."[16]

Military power used as a foreign policy instrument may not necessarily help us achieve our national objectives despite the fact that America has military capabilities that are unrivaled in the world. For example, on the military side, the United States in 1990 in its confrontation with Iraq over Iraq's occupation of Kuwait clearly had overwhelming military power that it threatened to use in attempting to persuade Iraq to withdraw. Saddam Hussein however refused to withdraw and the United States had to use that military power as a foreign policy weapon to force Iraq to do so. The threat failed, and although the actual use of force succeeded, the Iraq problem was not resolved. Then in 2003, the United States again threatened Saddam and again when the threat did not work, American troops entered Iraq and changed the regime by force. The military action however did not bring about democracy and stability in Iraq and the region, goals that the Bush administration has claimed to have, and one result of the U.S. military actions in Iraq has been actually to diminish respect for the United States as the failure to achieve our states objectives has damaged the prestige and reputation of our country. In other words, the potential positive "soft power" impact of American military action did not materialize, and the military action turned into a soft power negative, undermining respect for the United States.

America's economic power is not sufficient to protect United States national interests, despite the fact that the United States has by far the most powerful economy in the world. For example, between the 1990–1991 crisis in Iraq and 2003, the United States attempted to use the hard power of economic sanctions to persuade the Iraqi government to change its policies. Strict economic boycotts and controls were placed on Iraq in 1991 by the international community and the enforcement of them was led primarily by the United States from 1991 until 2003, using its superior military and economic capabilities. But these sanctions failed to persuade Saddam to change his policies. Moreover, as the years passed and it became increasingly apparent that these economic sanctions were not working, many people in other countries increasingly felt sympathy with the Iraqi people who were suffering from the impact of the sanctions, and they tended to blame the United States for causing the suffering of innocent civilians. Therefore the use by the United States of its economic (hard) power as a foreign policy tool against Saddam's regime tended to have negative soft power consequences, diminishing respect for American policy. Many people in other countries believed the United States was using its power for no good purpose but to punish innocent people.

Similarly, the United States is in a serious confrontation with Iran, over nuclear issues, Iraq and other matters. Washington has applied strict economic sanctions, and even implied threats of force, to achieve its objectives in Iran, but they have failed.

The Importance of Context

Nye says there are three sources of soft power: "In international politics, the resources that produce soft power arise in large part from the values an organization expresses in its culture, in the examples it sets by its internal practices and policies, and in the way it handles relations with others."[17]

The international context has changes in recent years with the information revolution and globalization, both of which have improved America's ability to project soft power.

But whether soft power results from any of these sources, and its impact, depends essentially on the context. Moreover, as Joseph Nye says, "Soft power can come from a country's culture in places where that culture is attractive to others"; it can come from a country's political values when these values are admired and when the country "lives up to them at home and abroad"; it can come from its foreign policies, when foreigners see these policies as "legitimate and having moral authority."[18] In all of these cases, as Nye argues, context is important in determining whether soft power results. Soft power is the power of attraction, but capabilities and policies can repel as well as attract others, depending on circumstances. Soft power depends even more than hard power on context, and especially "the existence of willing interpreters and receivers."[19]

As the impact of soft power, which can be positive or negative, depends so much on context, it is important to look at specific examples to see how circumstances at the time affect it.

Soft Power Derived from Our Culture

Soft power can derive from American culture if that culture is admired and respected abroad. "Culture" in this sense means literature, art, performing arts and music, including both "high culture" and popular culture—and education.

Hollywood films and American popular music are well known throughout the world. Most people in foreign countries admire these achievements and respect them as evidence of a vibrant and innovative culture. For those people, American culture means power for the United States. For some, however, America is a decadent, self-indulgent, and uncontrolled society which is immoral; therefore they do not admire or respect what they see in our films or hear in our music, but regard it as a negative influence in the world, so American culture for them does not constitute a power.

The most important sources of United States soft power are American films, television programs, music, and education. American art, theater, and religious practices, as well as American sports, are also important sources of soft power for some foreign audiences. Hollywood films are shown around the world and are popular for many reasons, including the quality of production. Many films are dubbed or subtitles into local languages. Many appear on local television screens.

Similarly, many foreign television stations acquire American television programs of many types, including especially entertainment shows, sports such as basketball, and documentaries. The foreign TV station managers who acquire them do so not only because the American programs are popular, but also because a full-service station has time to fill and the American TV industry can supply a wide variety of material.

Hollywood films and TV programs are however always reviewed by the local cinema owner or TV manager to be sure the content is suitable for local audiences and contains no material that would violate local laws or cultural taboos. The local review can result in rejection of the film or in deletions of the offending portions. In this way, the result tends to be to enhance the positive impact of this form of soft power. Even if the film does not happen to give the audience a balanced or accurate picture of American life, it may end up being a helpful addition to American soft power. On the other hand, in some countries, when an American film is shown that has passed local censorship because it fits within the dominant cultural norms, a conservative minority may still find the film offensive and regard it as evidence of American immorality.

American music, especially popular music, is well known throughout the world and is a significant source of soft power. American literature is less well known, to a large extent because of the language barrier limits access to English speaking-countries and well-educated elites elsewhere. American art and the performing arts (dance, theater, etc.) are even less well known and are not a major source of soft power.

American educational institutions are widely admired around the world. Large numbers of foreign students prefer to come here to study rather than to go anywhere else. More than half a million foreign students are studying at American universities here, and it is the preferred place for most foreign students who want to study abroad. Only cost and visa restrictions keep the numbers from being higher.

American universities located in foreign countries are also examples of soft power because they tend to have excellent reputations, attracting many foreign students, and enhancing by their high-quality standards local respect for American education. The American University of Beirut, established in 1862 (called at first the "Syrian Protestant College") and the American University in Cairo, established in 1919, became models of excellence in education for people of the region. Several institutions of higher learning that have been established recently in the Middle East, in Sharjah, Dubai, Kuwait and elsewhere, have put the word "American" in their names because American education has such great respect. Moreover, in the many countries where secondary schools with American-style curricula have been established, local parents are generally eager to send their children to study there because of their respect for American education. That is soft power.[20]

Soft Power Derived from Our Political Values

The most important sources of United States soft power derived from our political values are our democracy and our political system generally. Our electoral process, the accountability of our political leaders, transparency of government, the court system and the legal protections of our citizens, access to power by minorities, and guarantees of free speech. More broadly, America is seen as a land of opportunity where a merit system usually prevails and anyone regardless of race, religion, gender, or national origin has a chance to succeed in a profession or activity of his or her choosing.

The American political system and American political values are widely known throughout the world and widely admired. Democracy in America may seem to Americans to be flawed in a number of ways, but people who live in other countries where democratic rights do not exist or are circumscribed, or do not exist at all, tend to admire our political system. This is on balance a major source of our soft power. But not all foreign audiences approve of American political values.

American elections are followed closely by foreign media and because our campaigns are so long, stories about them are often in the news worldwide. These stories continuously remind foreign audiences of the American electoral process, which most of them admire. They provide many examples of the open nature of our political debates, and the underlying freedom to criticize powerful people in public without retribution.

This domestic political process enhances respect for American political values and American soft power. However, there have been other circumstances in which foreign audiences have had a negative impression of American political values. After 9/11 several developments that were widely reported around the world have undermined the respect that most foreigners have for by the American approach to politics.

On the other hand, when Secretary of Defense Donald Rumsfeld was required to appear before congressional committees to answer tough questions about Abu Ghraib, that enhanced American soft power despite the overall negative impact of the story. His appearance was seen as an example of American official accountability.

The security measures taken by the United States after 9/11 also have ended to diminish the soft power potential it had enjoyed as a country that defended individual rights and had a system of laws that did not discriminate. The new visa screening measures that the United States implemented immediately after 9/11 were widely regarded as discriminatory against Muslims and Arabs. New delays in visa processing caused study abroad students to miss enrollment deadlines and persuaded foreign businessmen to cancel their trips to the United States. Moreover, stories of harassment of Muslims and foreigners in the United States were picked up by the foreign press and had a negative impact. Although very few individuals were actually mistreated, their stories received wide circulation abroad and helped reinforce the impression abroad that the United States was abandoning its longstanding principles of political fairness.

Revelations about the American treatment of Iraqi detainees at Abu Ghraib, plus extended detentions without trial of detainees at Guantanamo, and media stories about torture being used by American officials, all have served to undermine the respect that most foreigners have had for the American judicial system and the humanitarian treatment of detainees.

Freedom of speech in America tends to create positive soft power, but sometimes statements by American citizens that are reported abroad lead to criticism. For example, the comments by a few prominent American Christian leaders such as Frank Graham criticizing Islam were widely reported in the Muslim world and caused a negative reaction that spilled over to the United States generally. Although these statements were made by private individuals, they were assumed by many people abroad to represent American thinking and some even assumed they were officially sanctioned.

Soft Power Derived from Our Foreign Policies

Since the United States is the world's only remaining superpower, and its foreign policies affect people all over the world, these policies constitute a major source of soft power. To know whether a specific American foreign policy generates positive or negative soft power however, one must look closely at the priorities and concerns of each specific foreign group, and whether that group regards the American policy as consistent with its interests or not.

American economic assistance programs, when they are known by people abroad who benefit from them, generally enhance America's reputation as a generous country that is carrying out its global responsibilities. And the prompt humanitarian efforts by the United States during the Tsunami crisis, and the earthquake disaster in Pakistan were widely reported around the world. These reports helped to enhance the respect foreigners have for American generosity. Many people expect that the United States should be generous because it is so wealthy and these effort help fulfill that expectation.

American policy toward the Arab-Israeli conflict has for sixty years caused most Arabs and many others to criticize the United States for unfair bias in favor of Israel. The general perception of the critics is that the United States bears considerable responsibility for actions of Israel that they disapprove of. They assume that because the United States is so powerful, and because its relationship with Israel includes the provision of substantial military assistance, that Washington could, if it wished, put pressure on Israel to comply with Arab requirements. So on the one hand foreign audiences watching the Arab-Israeli conflict have great respect for American political power but they are critical of Washington for not exercising that power in an even handed manner. Those two aspects of America's soft power therefore work in opposite directions.

Whenever the United States decided to use active and direct mediation as an honest broker between the parties in the Arab-Israeli dispute, that usually becomes a significant source of smart power. Arabs recognize that the United States firmly supports the existence and sovereignty of Israel, and the Arab states have not reconciled themselves to the continued existence of that state, but they also want Washington to exercise its influence over Israel to bring about a fair and balanced resolution of the dispute. As the CSIS Smart Power Commission stated, "In the Middle East and elsewhere, effective American mediation confers global legitimacy and is a vital source of smart power."[21]

Other foreign policy initiatives of the Bush administration have met with mixed reactions from foreign publics. His Global War on Terror is widely regarded as being fought with the wrong methods, and many suspect he has ulterior motives. Likewise the invasion that the United States led against Iraq has also been widely criticized for having failed to accomplish its stated objectives, and many people also suspect ulterior motives (e.g., control of oil) different from the stated ones. These aspects of America's current foreign policy are being followed closely around the world, and they affect America's reputation and standing as a major power, but their soft power potential has been generally negative on balance.

The Bush administration declared American support for democracy around the world as a high foreign policy priority. But some of its specific actions led many people to suspect that it was either insincere or ineffective in implementing that support. Since the United States is so powerful, foreign audiences expect that it has the ability to achieve what it proclaims are its goals. The United States invaded and occupied Iraq and openly helped the Iraqis set up a new political system, which turned out to be dysfunctional. The move was at first applauded by many people around the world, and it seemed that the United States was carrying out its political principles abroad. But as time went on, the Iraqi situation became violent and the political process was stalled, it seemed to many people abroad that the United States had in fact failed to support Iraqi democracy. And when Hamas won the election in Palestine, the Bush administration refused to support Hamas. Although the rationale for trying to isolate Hamas was the refusal by Hamas to recognize Israel, many people around the world began to doubt that the United States was sincere and this undermined its reputation as a supporter of democracy.

Joseph Nye argues that soft power works better in democracies. However as he points out, a foreign country which is democratic can pose problems for American interests. He cites the example of Turkey in 2003 refusing access to U.S. planes for the invasion of Iraq because the Turkish parliament was opposed to it and at the same time that the United States has been able to gain access in friendly authoritarian countries.[22]

How Does Soft Power Relate to Public Diplomacy?

Public diplomacy is a deliberate act designed to communicate with the public in foreign countries. It can—and often does—make use of soft power. But soft power exists whether anyone makes use of it or not, because American soft power derives from many different sources, not just our foreign policy.

To relate soft power to public diplomacy, we first need to define the latter term, because there is a newer definition alongside the traditional definition of it. Both definitions agree that the public diplomacy involves American communication with the public in foreign countries. But the traditional definition says that American public diplomacy is an activity carried out by the U.S. government, while the newer definition says that it can also be carried out by "international actors," meaning not only the government but also nongovernmental organizations (NGOs), commercial entities, and even individuals.[23] Whichever definition is used, soft power is involved.

In traditional public diplomacy, the U.S. government uses existing soft power potential as a resource to further American national interests. Public diplomacy programs can disseminate information through a variety of channels about aspects of the United States and its behavior, including the behavior of American citizens and organizations, which foreign publics regard as laudatory, with the result that America's reputation and prestige are likely to be enhanced. A state controls its foreign policy and that is one aspect of soft power, and if it is perceived by foreigners as beneficial to them it will be an asset, but if it is perceived as detrimental to them it will be negative. Other aspects of soft power are largely beyond the control of the state to any significant degree.

The role of soft power in public diplomacy is somewhat different if we define public diplomacy as an activity that can be carried out also by nongovernmental actors, to the extent that those nongovernmental actors communicate with and otherwise affect the perceptions of foreign audiences. That is, the activities and communications by American NGOs that are known by foreign publics, through a variety of means, are not coordinated centrally as are government public diplomacy efforts. If they originate from commercial entities, they are likely to be undertaken ultimately for a profit motive related to the goods and services those entities are trying to sell. If it helps sales to associate their "brand" with America because their customers have a positive opinion of the United States that can be related to their product, then they are making use of American soft power. Indeed this might change with circumstances, so that if a particular target audience is at the moment unhappy with the United States, for example over Washington's foreign policy, then the company might downplay its American connections to avoid negative soft power.

We will use the traditional definition of public diplomacy in the following discussion.

In any case, most elements of soft power exist regardless of what U.S. government policy makers do with respect to the rest of the world. Policy decisions on strictly or primarily domestic issues, such as the rule of law or human rights do affect soft power but they are usually taken based on domestic considerations, such as aspects of Bush's policy on security after 9/11, including immigration restrictions, surveillance, and interrogation of resident foreigners, Guantanamo and even Abu Ghraib. Other aspects of soft power such as the American domestic political system, social behavior, treatment of minorities, culture including popular culture, technology, and the economy basically exist regardless of foreign considerations but they affect America's soft power. Public diplomacy is related to soft power because it should be used to amplify those aspects of the existing soft power that are helpful to (1) explaining the United States, (2) countering distortions and misinformation, and (3) enhancing American prestige, all of which serve U.S. national interests and foreign policy.

Joseph Nye, who uses the traditional definition of the term public diplomacy, says:

> In international politics, the resources that produce soft power arise in large part from the values an organization expresses in its culture, in the examples it sets by its internal practices and policies, and in the way it handles relations with others. Public diplomacy is an instrument that governments use to mobilize these resources to communicate with and attract the publics of other countries, rather than merely their governments. Public diplomacy tries to attract by drawing attention to these potential resources through broadcasting, subsidizing cultural exports, arranging exchanges, and so forth. But if the content of a country's culture, values and policies are not attractive, public diplomacy that "broadcast" them cannot produce soft power. It may produce just the opposite.

He illustrates that by saying that Voice of America (VOA) extolling virtues of a foreign policy that is disliked will be seen as propaganda, meaning it will not be credible or effective. He concludes, "Public diplomacy's task is to try to attract foreign publics by drawing attention to appropriate aspects of its society and policies."[24]

Nye says, "Public diplomacy has a long history as a means of promoting the country's soft power and was essential in winning the cold war.... Public diplomacy is a tool in the arsenal of smart power, but smart public diplomacy requires an understanding of the roles of credibility, self-criticism, and civil society in generating soft power."[25]

The CSIS Commission on Smart Power said, "Although a number of independent commissions have criticized the U.S. government for problems implementing public diplomacy, it remains a critical part of U.S. smart power."[26]

Finally let us look at the three main sources of soft power—culture, political values, and foreign policy—and ask how a public diplomacy program carried out by the U.S. government can take advantage of them to further American interests.

Cultural soft power derived from Hollywood films, television, education, music, literature, and the performing arts, all originates from the

American private sector, with few exceptions. Foreign audiences have access to much of this through private commercial channels. An official U.S. public diplomacy program therefore focuses on attempting to help disseminate more widely examples of these products that represent the best of American culture and are appropriate for given foreign audiences. Public affairs professionals at field posts look for ways to facilitate the distribution of appropriate cultural materials that otherwise would not reach the audiences they are working with in their particular countries. Thus cultural affairs officers arrange for visits of performing artists, exhibits, and so on when they can, and they promote translations of appropriate American book into local languages. U.S. government broadcasting carries American music. Willis Conover who had a regular jazz program on VOA for many years was the most popular American in Eastern Europe during the cold war. Radio Sawa, the Arabic language radio station, devotes most of its air time to American pop music because it is so well liked. As for education, the U.S. government has spent billions of dollars over the years for scholarships to bring thousands of foreign students and professionals to the United States who otherwise would not have come here.

Likewise most of the *soft power derived from our political values* exists beyond the control of U.S. officials. American politics, including election campaigns and statements by politicians, as well as the actions of our courts and most of the regulations and circumstances affecting American freedoms, all take place outside the direct control of government officials. Therefore the task of official public diplomacy professionals in this area is to help explain the American political system and the values behind it to foreign audiences who may have an insufficient or distorted picture of these subjects. The best way to do that is to bring foreign visitors to the United States to see our political system for themselves, but public diplomacy professionals also work to disseminate information about the system through all available means.

Soft power derived from U.S. foreign policies is at least theoretically subject to influence by American officials. Foreign policies however are decided by the president and his advisors based on a number of factors, which may include some consideration of foreign public opinion, but that is often a minor reason for the policy. Strategic, domestic, and other considerations often dominate the policy making process. It is one important function of public diplomacy to report to policy makers on foreign opinion and point out possible consequences of policy decisions that are being considered, but policy makers do not always give foreign opinion much importance.

Criticism of the Soft Power Thesis

Some analysts have criticized Nye's soft power thesis. One of them is Brian Hocking. Hocking says that there is an underlying logical inconsistency in the argumentation about public diplomacy and soft power. Hocking's argument is this: "If people want to do what you want them to do through cultural affinity, why expend so much energy on public diplomacy? The answer lies partly, of course, in the fact that few actors possess soft power in the form presented by Nye in the U.S. context. Indeed, it is precisely the lack of soft power of hegemonic proportions that energizes the public diplomacy strategies of many governments."[27] Hocking's observation may apply to small nations that possess little weak in hard power, but for the United States the situation is quite different. The United States, because of its size and its preponderance of hard power, and its involvement in matters around the world, is a tempting large target for criticism. Also because there is so much interest in and information about America, it is natural that misinformation abounds, especially because of the IT revolution. In those circumstances, a systematic public diplomacy program is appropriate to convey information about America's soft power to foreign audiences.

Ernest J. Wilson has a different criticism. He says, "What is 'smart' in one context may not be smart in another." Smart depends on time and place, what is smart in one place or time may not be smart in another. It also requires awareness of the target audience, the global context, and the right tools.[28] And Y. Fan asserts that the soft power concept is ethnocentric, based on an American point of view. Because it assumes that power is based on a nation's attractiveness, he says, it is confusing because a country has many different actors and some may be attracted while others are not. Therefore whether attractiveness is important depends on which groups are affected and how much influence they have on policy. He also says policy making at the national level is complex, and unlike relations on a personal level that are affected by emotions and attractiveness.[29] These comments however do not invalidate the basis thesis but only elaborate on it, adding some nuance. It is an important point that the existence of soft power varies with the size and prominence of the country, and since the United States is arguably the most prominent country in the world today in terms of awareness by the global public of what the country is doing domestically and in foreign affairs, it naturally has the most soft power.

Historian Niall Ferguson is another critic. He dismissed the concept of soft power because it was "soft," and seemed to rely only on popular commercial products. But Nye responded saying, "Of course, the fact that a foreigner drinks Coca-Cola or wears a Michael Jordan T-shirt does not in itself mean that America has power over him. This view confuses resources with behavior. Whether power resources produce a favorable outcome depends upon the context."[30]

Joseph Nye and has published an essay that responds to criticisms and discusses misunderstandings of the concept that he says others have fallen into.[31] He says it is untrue that soft power is the same as economic power, that it cannot be measured, that it is more humane than hard power, and that the military produces only hard power not soft, and that soft power is irrelevant to the current terrorist threat. He does agree with those who say that some goals can be achieved only through hard power, and that soft power is difficult to use.[32]

Conclusion

The concept of soft power is useful in understanding an important dimension of international relations that had often been overlooked. American public diplomacy programs depend heavily on the existence of American soft power. American soft power exists, whether anyone makes use of it or not in public diplomacy. And because American soft power is so abundant, that is one reason to justify investing money in American public diplomacy; the potential is there to be exploited.

The United States spends relatively little on public diplomacy, missing opportunities to take advantage of our soft power. Hard power is much better understood by the American public and by the Congress, and as a result it is much better funded. The Pentagon has a budget of nearly three hundred billion dollars and employs more than three million people, while the State Department, which is responsible for public diplomacy, has a ten billion dollar budget and less than $1.5 billion of that is allocated for public diplomacy.[33] The Bush administration's effort to resolve Middle Eastern problems by the use of hard power (the invasion and occupation of Iraq, threats against Iran, and military and economic assistance programs to Israel and selected Arab countries) seem not to have achieved what was intended, and that has to some extent encouraged a discussion in America about soft power and public diplomacy. Even Secretary of Defense Robert Gates has spoken about the importance of improving our nonmilitary capabilities, and used the term soft power.[34] Others in the Pentagon are talking about "strategic communications" programs that look a lot like public diplomacy.

Pentagon officials are interested in these efforts essentially as an adjunct to war fighting and there is little coordination between the Pentagon and the State Department on these matters.[35]

Meanwhile the term soft power has entered the public discourse to the extent that prominent Americans are using it regularly. In a panel discussion by five former secretaries of state, for example, three of them pointedly argued for expanding its use.[36] The idea has been planted, yet the United States still has much to do to take full advantage of its soft power assets.

What are the implications for the future of public diplomacy? The United States is blessed with enormous potential soft power. One of the tasks of public diplomacy is to take advantage of that potential by helping to project it in support of American national interests. There are several ways in which more might be done in the future to build on this natural advantage.

First of all, public diplomacy professionals have a wide selection of instruments and means at their disposal through which soft power can be projected. The U.S. government has used radio broadcasting through the VOA and surrogate stations like RFE and RL for decades, and now uses television. It disseminates official texts and commentaries, as well as other printed media such as pamphlets to foreign individuals and foreign newspapers and other publications. It sponsors libraries and cultural centers that make information available to students and others around the world, and it undertakes translations of American books into foreign languages. It supports cultural presentations as appropriate in foreign countries. It promotes personal contact between Americans and foreign peoples in a number of ways, by sponsoring student and professional exchanges, sending American speakers abroad, holding press conferences and conducting face-to-face discussions with key foreign opinion leaders. All of that has been done for decades, but recently the U.S. government has also made use of Web sites, blogs, and text messaging, as well as videoconferencing, so that the United States can participate fully in the ongoing global dialogue and projects its soft power.

The point is, there is no one single means by which soft power should be projected, but we should make use of all available channels to do so. It is not enough to rely on one or two of the available means to project soft power, we should make more effort to use them all. The effort should especially stress the personal element that is sometimes forgotten in this high-tech information age, since the personal experiences of foreign students in America and the personal encounters of Americans with foreigners abroad are the most powerful tools we have.

Second, America's leaders should be much more aware of the benefits of soft power and smart power than they have been in the recent past, so that they can take advantage of its full potential. Congress and the administration have found it easy to support our hard power assets, but they have been slow to give sufficient attention and support to our soft power. Our leaders should be aware that our foreign policy decisions, and even our domestic policies, have an impact on foreign public opinion and that in turn has an impact on our ability to accomplish our goals. They should appreciate the importance of making use of our soft power and enhancing its instruments.

Third, the American public diplomacy program would be much more effective if it were better coordinated. The new concept of smart power argues that we should combine soft and hard power assets in a deliberate way. That concept recognizes and seeks to remedy a fundamental problem that our public diplomacy effort has fallen into, namely that separate agencies of government and separate private interests have been using American power abroad largely in parallel but in largely uncoordinated channels. The State Department, which is ostensibly responsible for our public diplomacy, conducts its programs with a relatively modest budget and limited staff. But the Pentagon has lately devoted significant personnel assets and large financial resources to activities that resemble public diplomacy, and USAID and other government agencies also have become involved. These programs by different arms of the same government are poorly coordinated. At the same time, business leaders and others in the American private sector are more involved than ever before in the international arena, and some of them are talking about doing public diplomacy or even "privatizing" it. This discussion sometimes ignores the fact that extensive cooperation has quietly taken place for a long time in public diplomacy between the U.S. government and private entities.

For decades, under the U.S. Information Agency (1953–1999) and then under the State Department, the U.S. government worked very closely with many elements in the private sector as partners in a locally coordinated public diplomacy efforts around the world. The U.S. government, for example, has funded and managed the Fulbright exchange program for many years but it has been carried out with extensive support and participation by private American organizations like the National Council of International Visitors, the Institute of International Education, and America-Mideast Educational and Training Services (AMIDEAST). Partnerships between the government and private sector entities should continue and to be expanded, to the extent that NGOs and other private sector organizations are willing to be involved. A comprehensive plan should be developed that includes all of these elements that are now busy separately projecting soft power abroad. This does not require creating a single entity that has sole control over all American public diplomacy efforts. But they should agree on a common purpose and a clear understanding of responsibilities. In short, no matter how "public diplomacy" is defined, the private sector is important to the effective use of American soft power, and there should be some basic agreement on how we can do this together.

The U.S. public diplomacy effort has been facing new challenges because of the information technology revolution and rapid growth of the global market. But if it manages the response carefully, the natural soft power advantages America enjoys can be of great benefit to the national interest.

Notes

1. Joseph S. Nye, Jr., *Bound to Lead: The Changing Nature of American Power* (New York: Basic Books, 1990); "The Changing Nature of Power in World Politics," *Political Science Quarterly* 105, no. 2 (1990); and "Soft Power," *Foreign Policy* 80 (1990).
2. Peter Bachrach and Morton Baratz, "Decisions and Nondecisions: An Analytical Framework," *American Political Science Review* 57 (1963): 632–642.
3. Joseph S. Nye, Jr., *The Paradox of American Power: Why the World's Only Superpower Cannot Go It Alone* (New York: Oxford University Press, 2003). He also published an op-ed at that time "Propaganda Isn't the Way: Soft Power," *International Herald Tribune*, January 10, 2003.
4. Joseph S. Nye, Jr., *Soft Power: The Means to Success in World Politics* (New York: Public Affairs Press, 2004), see Chapter 4, "Wielding Soft Power," 99–126; also "The Benefits of Soft Power," *Compass*, Harvard Business School, August 2, 2004.
5. Joshua Kurlantzick, *Charm Offensive: How China's Soft Power Is Transforming the World* (New Haven, CT: Yale University Press, 2007).
6. John McCormick, *The European Superpower* (New York: Palgrave Macmillan, 2006).
7. Matthew Fraser, *Weapons of Mass Distraction: Soft Power and American Empire* (New York: St. Martin's Press, 2005).
8. Joseph S. Nye, Jr., "Public Diplomacy and Soft Power," *Annals of the American Academy of Political and Social Science* (March 2008): 94–109.
9. Richard L. Armitage and Joseph S. Nye, Jr., *CSIS Commission on Smart Power: A Smarter, More Secure America* (Washington DC: Center for International and Strategic Studies, 2007).
10. Ernest J. Wilson III, "Hard Power, Soft Power, Smart Power," *Annals of the American Academy of Political and Social Science* (March 2008): 122.
11. Nye, "The Benefits of Soft Power," August 2, 2004.
12. Nye, "Public Diplomacy and Soft Power," 94–95.
13. Armitage and Nye, *CSIS Commission on Smart Power*, 7.
14. Nye, "Public Diplomacy and Soft Power," 94.
15. Ibid.; Joseph S. Nye, Jr., "Think Again: Soft Power," *Foreign Policy* (March 1, 2006).

16. Armitage and Nye, *CSIS Commission on Smart Power*, 7–8 and 62.

17. Nye, "Public Diplomacy and Soft Power," 94–95.

18. Nye, "Think Again: Soft Power," *Foreign Policy* (February 2006), *http://www.foreignpolicy. com/story/cms.php?story_id=3393*

19. Nye, "The Benefits of Soft Power," August 2, 2004, 2.

20. See for example, Rasmus G. Bertelsen, "The Soft Power of the American University of Beirut, the Universite St. Joseph in Beirut and the American University in Cairo," unpublished thesis, Harvard Kennedy School (2008).

21. Armitage and Nye, *CSIS Commission on Smart Power*, 12.

22. Nye, "Public Diplomacy and Soft Power," 99.

23. Nicholas J. Cull, *The Cold War and the United States Information Agency* (Cambridge: Cambridge University Press, 2008).

24. Nye, "Public Diplomacy and Soft Power," 95.

25. Ibid., 94.

26. Armitage and Nye, *CSIS Commission on Smart Power*, 47.

27. Brian Hocking, "Rethinking the 'New' Public Diplomacy," in *The New Public Diplomacy: Soft Power in International Relations*, ed. Jan Melissen (New York: Palgrave Macmillan, 2005), 35.

28. Wilson, "Hard Power, Soft Power, Smart Power," 122, fn.3.

29. Y. Fan, "Soft Power: The Power of Attraction or Confusion," *Place Branding and Public Diplomacy* 4, no. 2 (2008).

30. Nye, "Think Again: Soft Power" (March 1, 2006).

31. Ibid.

32. Ibid.

33. Wilson, "Hard Power, Soft Power, Smart Power," 116.

34. Secretary of Defense Robert Gates, address, Kansas State University, November 26, 2007.

35. Wilson, "Hard Power, Soft Power, Smart Power," 117–121.

36. Remarks by former secretaries Baker, Christopher, and Powell during a CNN television broadcast September 20, 2008, CNN.com/transcripts.

CHAPTER TWO

How We Got Here

NICHOLAS J. CULL

There is an irony at the heart of U.S. public diplomacy. Although America's mass communications and popular culture have transformed the world, neither the people of the United States nor their Congress have been truly comfortable with a government role in communication at home or abroad. The U.S. government has deployed public diplomacy—the conduct of foreign policy through engagement with foreign publics—principally only in such times of dire need as the Revolution, the Civil War, or World War I. When the crisis passed, Congress closed down the apparatus of international propaganda. The present apparatus of U.S. public diplomacy survived its origins in World War II only because advocates of the international information program succeeded in persuading legislators of that such a tool was necessary to counter Soviet propaganda. When that threat ended in the early 1990s, the impetus to reduce the mechanism of U.S. public diplomacy returned; a marked reduction in the U.S. capability in the area followed. The post-9/11 period has seen a steady attempt to rebuild U.S. public diplomacy and to create an interagency structure. As momentum builds for another great reorganization of American public diplomacy, it makes sense to review the past. Since the dawn of the cold war the mechanism of public diplomacy has been through a number of transformations. The structures created by these reorganizations in—1947–1948, 1953, 1974–1978, 1983, and 1999—all bore the marks of political compromise and none was truly based on the necessities of the case. The need is to do better is indisputable, and understanding the forces that have distorted the process in the past and the models that have been tried or suggested is a precondition for success.

The Elements of Public Diplomacy

Although the term public diplomacy is relatively new—dating only from 1965—the practice is ancient. The term draws together five venerable elements of statecraft. The foundational element is listening. The first duty of a public diplomat must be to listen. This function is traditionally conducted via a combination of desk and leg work at diplomatic posts and ideally introduces an awareness of international opinion into the making of foreign policy. The second element is advocacy: the creation of a public voice for foreign policy by which decisions and events are explained to foreign publics to mobilize their consent or blunt their criticism. The third and fourth elements are cultural and exchange diplomacy: foreign policy through the export of culture and exchange of people and ideas. The fifth element is international broadcasting, which by its nature requires a distinct set of resources and skills. While it is possible to see broadcasting as an extension of both advocacy and cultural diplomacy, the special ethical considerations associated with journalism have often set international broadcasters on their own path, and in any case provide a formidable centrifugal force toward some form of independence or autonomy. Military aspects of communication—strategic communication, information operations, and psychological warfare—operate in a space perilously close to that of public diplomacy and present a challenge to the integrity of the civilian process. The maintenance of the firewall between the civilian/overt and military/covert needs to be a major concern in the structuring of any nation's public diplomacy.

The structuring of public diplomacy is made more difficult by the fact that each element of public diplomacy has its own source of credibility and requires a slightly different relationship to the ministry of foreign affairs and head of state. The listener needs to be able to feed material into policy; the advocate needs to be able to accurately reflect policy and hence close to the makers of foreign policy; the cultural diplomat needs to be credibly connected to the source of culture rather than policy and is helped by distance from the makers of foreign policy; the exchange diplomat's credibility rests on the perception of reciprocity within his or her work; the international broadcaster is judged by their compliance with the norms of their craft and hurt by being too close to the makers of foreign policy. This diversity in the sources of credibility means that any single structure of public diplomacy runs the risk of harming some or all of its components. The structure of public diplomacy can easily become the enemy of the practice of public diplomacy. All elements of public diplomacy are harmed by a perceived breach in the firewall between covert psychological operation and public diplomacy.

It is possible to imagine a state in which each element of public diplomacy can flourish in its own terms because it has its own home agency. The structure developed by Britain comes close to this. The advocacy function rests within the Foreign and Commonwealth Office where there is a division of public diplomacy. Cultural and exchange diplomacy are the responsibility of the British Council. Britain's international broadcasting function rests with the editorially independent World Service of the British Broadcasting Corporation. All elements of British public diplomacy include a listening function. Perhaps the best known is the radio monitoring service of the BBC at Caversham Park. In recent years the whole operation has been loosely coordinated by a Public Diplomacy Board, chaired by the Foreign Office Director of Communications and including two private members (both experts on aspects of communication). The minister for public diplomacy (as of October 2008, Caroline Flint) is a junior foreign office minister who is also minister for Europe. The advantage of the British system has been able to develop its own credibility and practice with minimal friction. This experience stands in stark contrast to that of the United States.

The Prehistory of U.S. Public Diplomacy

American public diplomacy is as old as the Republic. The first act of the American Revolution—writing the Declaration of Independence—was an exercise in public diplomacy, shaping a document to be read by the world that would explain the new nation. The founding fathers paid attention to international opinion, especially that of France, and the diplomatic missions undertaken by Franklin and then Jefferson both reflected a strong public diplomacy component. This was not preserved in the early Federal period and beyond. When the Civil War came, President Lincoln had to create his own network to get word of the Northern cause to the world. He achieved much through his own eloquence, but was not above bribing the odd journalist or covertly funding newspapers to advance the cause. The later years of the nineteenth and early twentieth century saw multiple private initiatives in the field of international culture. Commercial forces carried the American culture of Mark Twain, Stephen Foster, and Buffalo Bill Cody around the world, missionaries reached out to spread an Americanized religion and the philanthropic foundations of the Progressive era led by the Rockefeller Foundation spearheaded academic exchanges and "the diplomacy of the deed" in the form of international public health projects. President Theodore Roosevelt understood that a nation's power rested not only on its ability to project force but also on its perceived moral character. His initiatives included scholarships for China paid for from the Boxer Rebellion indemnity.

The Great War saw the coming of age of American public diplomacy. At the very moment that Hollywood overtook the war-paralyzed film studios of Europe to become story teller to the world, President Woodrow Wilson created a structure to tell the world exactly what the United States stood for. That structure—the Committee on Public Information (CPI)—managed the domestic war of words, but also included a network of bureaus, a news agency, film distribution, and even cultural centers to address foreign publics. The CPI succeeded in persuading the world of the viability of Wilson's vision of a world made safe for democracy by a collective security organization. His own countrymen were more skeptical. Congress saw the CPI as too powerful to survive the war, and the American public rejected the notion of joining the League of Nations.

During the interwar period America's private sector continued to take the lead in public diplomacy. Hollywood flourished blissfully unaware of its ideological contribution to America's place in the world. Private groups like the Institute for International Education advanced the cause of student exchanges. Expatriate communities partnered with host communities to create "Bi-national centers" to teach English and facilitate local understanding of American culture. The U.S. government was slow to become part of the mix. Early steps included the launch of a "wireless file": a regular cable of articles and key speeches from America sent by the State Department to all posts for circulation to the foreign media. But the challenge of Fascist propaganda in the western hemisphere demanded more. In 1938, as part of its policy of hemisphere defense, the State Department inaugurated a Division of Cultural Relations with programs aimed toward Latin America. As Europe tumbled into World War II, the United States intensified its activities in Latin America. The year 1940 brought a new Office of the Coordinator of Inter-American Affairs under Nelson Rockefeller, which was essential of regional propaganda bureau. The year 1941 saw steps taken by members of the intelligence community toward developing a shortwave radio capacity for the United States. Their work led to the creation of Voice of America (VOA) within weeks of America's formal entry into the war.

The World War II saw a rapid expansion of American information overseas. The White House led the way with an emphasis on a war of ideas. The Office of War Information (OWI), created in the summer of 1942, incorporated a range of international activities (including VOA).

The Department of State expanded its cultural programs, developing exchanges and appointing its first "cultural attaches" to key posts. The military occupation teams who moved into liberated territories deployed a host of media and educational operations to rebuild these areas in America's image. The structure was not perfect. Propaganda toward Latin America remained outside the fold because Nelson Rockefeller was a friend of the president and could make a personal case for autonomy. The operation of the information war was not without controversy. OWI and especially VOA seemed to have their own foreign policy, and Roosevelt was obliged to purge his propaganda structure in mid-conflict, bringing in commercial communicators in place of the new deal politicos. While a report conducted in the final weeks of the conflict stressed the need to preserve the apparatus of the information war into peacetime Congress had other ideas. The year 1945 would find American public diplomacy fighting for its postwar life.[1]

The First Reorganization: 1947–1948

There are a number of candidates for the title of founder of postwar American public diplomacy: Assistant Secretary of State for Public Affairs William Benton worked tirelessly from 1945 to 1947 to coordinate and maintain the State Department information program, VOA, and the information elements of the occupations of Germany, Austria, and Japan; Senator J. William Fulbright moved programs to a new level by diverting funds from the sale of war surplice into a program of international exchange, but the real founder of American postwar public diplomacy was Josef Stalin. Stalin succeeded where Benton and Fulbright failed. The scale of the international propaganda effort emanating from his Kremlin forced the even most isolationist American officials to accept that something had to be done to give America a voice to respond.

The first attempt to prepare the United States for the cold war was the cluster of activity surrounding the National Security Act of 1947. The act created a single Defense Department, the Central Intelligence Agency (CIA), National Resources Board, and coordinating structures of the National Security Council (NSC), but did not include any mechanism for coordination of their information work or representation from the information elements of state.[2] As the senior official concerned with public diplomacy was still only an assistant secretary of state, they had no seat at the NSC. Information work was not seen as needing special interagency coordination. The parallel case of coordinating covert propaganda work is instructive. That fall, the NSC approved NSC 4-A authorizing the CIA to conduct "covert psychological operations designed to counteract Soviet and Soviet-inspired activities." Secretary of State George C. Marshall made no request for State Department input but Benton's successor as Assistant Secretary George V. Allen argued that the State Department should retain authority over such work in peacetime. The compromise came in June 1948 when NSC 10/2 created an Office of Special Projects (later the Office of Policy Coordination or OPC) within the CIA. The secretary of state was belatedly given authority to nominate its director.[3]

The legislative authority for overt information work—the Smith-Mundt Act—passed into law in January 1948. The act provided a budget line for information and exchange work, but it was eventually read as prohibiting the domestic distribution of any of that information material.[4] Coordination with other elements of U.S foreign policy was limited, and one obvious problem with the Smith-Mundt was that its channels were conceived merely to apply policy. There was no sense that the information specialists funded under the act might be America's ears, usefully have input into forming policy in the first place. The Truman administration was never happy with its structure of international information. VOA and the information/exchange apparatus both sat awkwardly within the Department of State. The information program remained a perennial target for Republican attacks, which is probably why Truman appointed a Republican—Edward W. Barrett—to be assistant secretary of state for public affairs.

The later months of 1948 saw a major investigation of the entire executive branch chaired by ex-president Herbert Hoover. In November 1948, a two-man Task Force on Foreign Affairs, comprised of two Hoover-era assistant secretaries of state, James Grafton Rogers and Harvey H. Bundy, recommended that the entire information program be transferred to a new government corporation, merely steered by

State Department policy guidance.[5] The full Hoover Report did not support this idea and merely recommended a new post of "General Manager" with operational authority to coordinate all information activities and to execute policy. The State Department followed this recommendation, appointing Charles M. Hulten to the post of General Manager,[6] but the idea of an independent information agency did not go away.

Early in 1951, Truman moved to resolve the deadlock between state and the rest of the bureaucracy over the direction of psychological warfare.[7] On April 4, 1951, Truman created the Psychological Strategy Board (PSB) made up of the deputy secretary of defense, director of the CIA, and the under secretary of state: "for the formulation and promulgation, as guidance to the departments and agencies responsible for psychological operations, of over-all national psychological objectives, policies and programs, and for the coordination and evaluation of the national psychological effort." The board had a staff of seventy-five or so and an office just a block and a half from the White House.[8] In June Truman named a director for the PSB: former Secretary of the Army, Gordon Gray. The board never really worked properly. It was divided by turf wars and lacked political clout and did little more than agree the broadest interdepartmental priorities, but it was a start.[9] Examples of NSC use of the PSB include a move in February 1952 to clear up confusion over the discussion of the new and more powerful atomic weapons. The problem was that the official statements on U.S. strength necessary to deter Moscow created complacency at home and an image of U.S. bullying elsewhere in the world. PSB guidelines suggested that all U.S. officials issuing statements on nuclear weapons ask: "Will this statement create a fear that the U.S. may act recklessly in the use of these weapons."[10]

The Second Reorganization: 1953

Dwight D. Eisenhower's campaign for the presidency included a pledge to reinvigorate America's informational outreach to the world. As president, he promptly launched two inquiries into U.S. information overseas: the president's Committee on International Information Activities, chaired by William H. Jackson,[11] and the president's Advisory Committee on Government Organization, chaired by Nelson Rockefeller.[12] Meanwhile, the Senate Foreign Relations Committee continued an investigation of information formerly chaired by William Fulbright under the new chairmanship of Bourke Hickenlooper (R-IA).[13] While the net result of these three committees would be the creation of the United States Information Agency (USIA) as a single home for U.S information work, including VOA and elements from the occupation and Marshall Plan, in August 1953, the waters were muddied by political machinations. Senator Fulbright was unprepared to see the cultural and exchange program (which included "his" exchanges) taken out of the State Department and agreed only that USIA should be able to administer them in the field. American public diplomacy remained a "house divided."

Eisenhower wound up Truman's PSB and in its place created a miniature NSC for information matters—the Operations Coordination Board (OCB)—within the White House. The key to the success of this structure was the parallel appointment of a special assistant to the president for psychological warfare, C. D. Jackson, whose duties included chairing the OCB. Charismatic, driven and a friend of the president, Jackson had the political clout to broker interdepartment agreement on informational issues and for a season there was real coordination between the State Department, USIA, CIA, and other agencies with a stake in America's international information work. The major structural problem was the underlying hostility of the secretary of state, John Foster Dulles, to such a challenge to his sovereignty in matters of foreign affairs. During the course of 1954, he resisted Jackson and following Jackson's return to the private sector at the end of that year gave a really hard time to his successors, Nelson Rockefeller (who served in 1955 and 1956) and William H. Jackson (who served for the remainder of 1956 and 1957). Eventually, recognizing the intractability of State Department ire, Eisenhower "thought it best to abolish the office" and create a new position called special assistant to the president for security operations coordination, who would also be vice-chairman of OCB.[14]

Eisenhower believed passionately in the value of information in world affairs, or as he called it "the P factor" ("P" for psychology). He understood the need for both overt and covert elements in the overall American effort, and both VOA and Radio Free Europe (RFE) (and its sister Radio Liberty [RL]) flourished as a result. VOA developed an increasing emphasis on journalism and Eisenhower was content to allow RFE and RL to do the "hard ball" propaganda. In 1960, he approved the VOA's charter requiring it to be a source of balanced news. USIA also functioned well in the Eisenhower years, but the period ended with uncertainty. In the Senate, Lyndon Johnson and Mike Mansfield proposed returning all information work to the State Department and

Under Secretary of State Christian Herter carried the idea forward. The end of USIA loomed large in the deliberations of the president's Advisory Committee on Government Organization, now chaired by Arthur S. Flemming, and in August 1959 the White House drafted a bill to fold USIA back into state.[15] Protective of his baby, Eisenhower won a stay of execution by commissioning a new interagency committee chaired by Mansfield D. Sprague to "review the findings and recommendations" of the Jackson Committee of 1953 in the light of "changes in the international situation." The Sprague Committee, which reported in December 1960, upheld the existing structure but called for expanded work in the developing world to combat the rising challenge of Communism there. It helped set the agenda for the Kennedy years.[16]

USIA in the 1960s

The Kennedy administration was swift to demolish Eisenhower's OCB structure and, reinforced, the NSC and National Security Advisor now played a much more prominent role in foreign policy. Although Kennedy wooed his chosen director of USIA—Edward R. Murrow— with assurances of a role in policy making, Murrow found himself in the dark over key events like the plan for the Bay of Pigs invasion. It was the humiliation of learning of this impending event only when his deputy had breakfast with a *New York Times* journalist that prompted Murrow to demand that USIA be "in on the take-offs of policy" as well as the "crash landings." USIA's finest hour in this period was probably the special coverage of the Kennedy assassination, though the agency also shone in presenting the civil rights story to world. Both stories showed the American political system working to resolve problems that would have derailed many other states. Lyndon Johnson's stewardship of the Vietnam War brought an all-time peak in USIA's appropriations; it saw the coining of the term "Public Diplomacy" and immense efforts to sell the South Vietnamese regime to its own people, and the war to the world. This merely underlined that the best public diplomacy in the world could not sell a flawed policy. Kennedy was a keen customer for USIA's reports on world opinion, but seldom allowed Murrow's advice to impinge on a decision. Johnson had less tolerance for USIA's studying world opinion, largely because the opinion revealed was so negative. Both presidents followed Eisenhower's practice on including the USIA director on the NSC, though as a guest not a mandated member.

One issue of concern was the mixing of agency responsibilities within Vietnam. As lead agency in the Joint United States Public Affairs Office (JUSPAO) in Vietnam, USIA was involved in psychological warfare work. The agency complained about the continued jurisdiction of the State Department over cultural diplomacy and outside observers began to worry once again about the fitness of the 1953 structure for its purpose. In 1968 the president's Advisory Commission on Information, chaired by Frank Stanton of CBS, called for a major "in depth critique" of U.S. public diplomacy, Senate hearings concurred, placing public diplomacy on the agenda for the Nixon administration.[17]

The Third Reorganization: 1974–1978

Nixon and Kissinger had little tolerance for any role of public diplomacy in the foreign policy process. Kissinger sidelined the USIA director to an obscure NSC subcommittee.[18] It did not help that the director of the era, Frank Shakespeare, was passionately anti-Communist and regarded the notion of détente as morally wrong. The idea of a major review of U.S. public diplomacy bubbled under throughout the Nixon administration. In May 1973, the Senate Foreign Relations committee endorsed this idea and even proposed opening the sensitive question of the division of labor between the USIA and the State Department Bureau of Educational and Cultural Affairs. In July 1973, the State Department's cultural advisory body, the U.S. Advisory Commission on International Education and Cultural Affairs also proposed a major review. The two commissions resolved on a joint enquiry and, thanks to David M. Abshire, secured Georgetown University's Center for Strategic and International Studies as a home. Frank Stanton served as chair and the former associate director of USIA—Walter R. Roberts— acted as his project director. Roberts provided the core vision for the enquiry. Roberts was an admirer of the British model of public diplomacy and saw great advantages in the three-way division of labor between the BBC World Service, British Council, and British Information Service at the Foreign Office. The story of the Stanton panel was the story of Stanton's conversion to this approach.[19] A subsequent investigation of Stanton's conclusions by the Government Accounting Office, observed that the panel actively considered recommending a British Council model for U.S. cultural work "and was dissuaded from it only by the judgment that it might not be approved by the Congress." Stanton reported in 1975 and his recommendation that

VOA be made independent grabbed the headlines. His recommendations spurred a counterattack by USIA to hold onto the jewel in their crown and while the battle at least saw VOA's charter given the status of law, the fight was unresolved when the Ford administration left office in January 1977.

President Jimmy Carter demonstrated himself open to blue sky thinking in public diplomacy. He accepted the need to take culture and exchange out of the State Department and place it inside USIA, but his administration felt that a new agency should be created as a result. Officials settled on the imperfect name "U.S. International Communications Agency" or USICA (pronounced You-Seeker)— foreign observers were swift to note the anagram of CIA. The chief innovation in the Carter-era conception of U.S. public diplomacy was the notion of a "second mandate" or an obligation for U.S. public diplomacy to bring information into the United States.[20] This was a radical departure from previous approaches but unfortunately the initiative had no funds and very few "second mandate" events ever took place. By the end of the Carter administration, the deterioration of relations with the Soviet Union placed U.S. information high on the agenda once again.[21]

The Fourth Reorganization: 1983

Ronald Reagan campaigned for office pledging to reinvigorate VOA and America's other cold war voices. He was true to his word, placing USIA under the directorship of his dynamic friend Charles Z. Wick and backing Wick with the funds necessary to meet Soviet propaganda head on. Wick restored the USIA name and moved the agency in larger quarters. His relationship with the president gave him the necessary access to the NSC, and in some matters Reagan proved willing to overrule the rest of that body to go with an initiative he and Wick thought necessary, such as the launch of Radio Martí for Cuba.

As Reagan's showdown with the Soviet Union took shape, the administration looked to strengthen the infrastructure for U.S. information work. On January 15, 1983, President Reagan signed National Security Decision Directive (NSDD) 77 to strengthen public diplomacy. The directive built USIA into the core of decision making. It established a Special Planning Group (SPG) at NSC to oversee the planning and implementation of all public diplomacy, chaired by the National Security Advisor and including the secretaries of State and Defense, directors of USIA and AID, and the White House communications assistant. Four standing subcommittees reported to the SPG including, a public affairs committee co-chaired by NSC and the White House communications staff to coordinate foreign policy speeches at home; an International Information Committee, chaired by USIA to take over responsibility for Project Truth. NSDD 77 also set up an International Broadcasting Committee, chaired at NSC, to coordinate planning, antijamming, and transmitter modernization. The task of implementing the great democratization initiative, announced by Reagan in his Westminster speech and now known as Project Democracy, lay with an International Political Committee chaired by State.[22] For all its promise the new structure could not stand up to the habits of beltway bureaucracy. The SPG met increasingly rarely. In the final days of the administration, Wick noted that integrated committee structure envisioned by NSDD 77 no longer operated and proposed recreating it. Frank Carlucci declined any substantial revision preferring that NSC continue "coordinating, advising, and being ready to bring together interagency groups as the situation warrants."[23]

USIA and the Early 1990s

The political changes of 1989 were hailed by many as a vindication of U.S. public diplomacy; ironically this did not help USIA. In the Senate, those seeking a peace dividend increasingly looked on USIA as an agency whose time had passed, while the kudos accumulated by VOA's role in both the revolutions of Eastern Europe and the Tiananmen Square crisis in China renewed the centrifugal forces pulling for VOA independence and bogged the agency down in wasteful feuding. Despairing, President Bush was obliged to move both the sitting USIA and VOA directors to ambassadorships in Belgium and the Seychelles respectively. There was an example of what well-organized public diplomacy could achieve: the public diplomacy around the First Gulf War. In retrospect the First Gulf War now seems like a miracle of wise management: its limited goals; its attention to international law; its keen eye for alliance politics. U.S. public diplomacy was an important part of this. USIA experts were on hand to counsel the president in his decision making and to fight enemy narratives in the field. The smooth operation of the alliance owed much to their efforts, but such an achievement could not counter a growing sense in key quarters that the era of state-funded public diplomacy had passed. The true victors of the First Gulf War were Ted Turner and CNN, and USIA's paymasters on Capitol Hill now wondered why they needed to provide a parallel service.

The Fifth Reorganization: 1997–1999

The Clinton years brought the death-blow to USIA. The agency was caught in a pincer movement between an impulse from the Senate—led by Jesse Helms (R-SC)—to cut back across the entire range of the government's foreign operations and especially USIA, the Arms Control and Disarmament Agency (ACDA) and USAID, and the desire of certain people in the Clinton administration to win efficiencies at any price. Chief architect on the Clinton side was Assistant Secretary of State for Public Affairs James P. Rubin, who laid out his vision in a memo of March 27, 1997:

> The administration has a historic opportunity to adapt Cold War policy structures to a post-Cold War policy agenda. Toward that end, we should integrate ACDA, USIA, AID and a reinvented State Department in a carefully phased process. Within two years, the result would be a new streamlined structure, drawing on the best people and practices of the old agencies and fully capable of meeting the new challenges of the twenty-first century.[24]

Secretary of State Madeline Albright saw no reason to doubt Rubin's prophesy.

The final urgency was political. In the spring of 1997, President Clinton needed Senator Helms to agree to allow a Senate vote on U.S. adherence to the Chemical Weapons Convention and had to offer something in exchange. The junior foreign affairs agencies seemed an obvious concession. Albright brokered a simple quid pro quo conceding USIA and the Arms Control Agency in return for Helms's agreement not to block the Chemical Weapons Convention. On April 18, the president unveiled the new proposal. USIA would rejoin the State Department as of October 1, 1999, with public diplomacy falling under a new under secretary of state. The ACDA would also be consolidated, and AID would retain operational but not budgetary independence. VOA would be free from the whole structure under the Broadcasting Board of Governors (BBG). Despite the quid pro quo with Helms, Clinton assured the press that while he certainly hoped that the Chemical Weapons Convention might now pass, "there was no linkage."[25]

An accompanying "Fact Sheet" set out what amounted to the Rubin plan. It trumpeted the new arrangement as a great breakthrough that prepared the United States for the complex needs of the twenty-first century, and quoted the president: "the era of big government is over." The fine print for the fate of USIA followed Rubin's plan: "The United States Information Agency and the State Department will be integrated over a two-year period. During that process, the Director of USIA will be double-hatted as the new Under Secretary of State for Public Diplomacy. This process will likely begin with an integration of related functions, such as legislative and public affairs; after that, the integration process will turn toward USIA's overseas press expertise and State's press offices. The distinctiveness and editorial integrity of VOA and the broadcast agencies will be respected. A new bureau will be created within the State Department to handle cultural and exchange issues."[26]

The new broadcasting structure—the BBG—created at the end of the first Clinton administration seemed like a massive advance for VOA. Policy input into their broadcasts would be limited to the ex-officio membership of the board given to the secretary of state under the new structure (and USIA director under the old). What the VOA did not detect was that rather than locking out political influence, the new structure had the potential to lock it in. The BBG could easily become an echo chamber amplifying the ideas of the political appointees on the board and riding roughshod over the traditional practices and views of constituent stations—VOA, WORLDNET TV, RFE/RL, Radio, and TV Marti and the newcomer, Radio Free Asia.

USIA director Joseph Duffey had been ignored at every point in the reorganization and had no desire to take the position of under secretary. He left USIA for a post in the private sector at the start of the agency's final year. The first to occupy the role of under secretary would be former deputy White House chief of staff and VOA director Evelyn Lieberman. Lieberman approached her new role as Under Secretary of State for Public Diplomacy and Public Affairs with a keen understanding of both the noble aims of the merger—bringing the idea of public diplomacy out of the backwater of USIA into the mainstream of U.S. foreign relations—and the dangers that the old culture of the State Department could overwhelm the distinctive approach of the information agency. She was all too aware of the State Department's age-old superiority complex and the equally obvious inferiority complex at

USIA. Her priority in the limited amount of time available to her was to get workable administrative procedures in place for the next administration and "re-empower folks to do what they'd always done." She spent much of her energy in office visiting old USIA posts listening to grievances and reassuring PAOs that all would be well under the new system. While sympathetic to the old USIA staff Lieberman was not blind to their failings. She was aware that a certain promotion fever had set in as the merger with state neared and that some USIA staff had been over promoted. She was obliged to insist that staff accepted drug testing along with their new home at state. But in public she stood by her colleagues.[27] In an op-ed piece for the *Washington Times* she argued, "An effective public diplomacy operation will help advance American interests, modernize our operations overseas and make clear the values that form the basis for our leadership of the world."[28] Unfortunately the new structure made this task all but impossible to achieve.

The functions of USIA were now divided between two offices equivalent to the old "E" bureau and the "I" bureaus of USIA: the Bureau of Educational and Cultural Affairs and the Bureau of International Information Programs. USIA's television operation WORLDNET was split in two so that its news programs remained under the BBG but its interactive work, which allowed American policy makers to connect directly with gatherers of press in foreign countries and USIA's three foreign press centers, into the State Department's press machinery as a new Bureau of Public Affairs. USIA's Office of Media Research and Media Reaction became a part of the Bureau of Intelligence and Research. The structure had some elegance on paper, but it was subject to the human factor of institutional pride on one side and humiliation on the other. Everyone at USIA knew that the State Department colleagues called USIA "useless"—and the State Department saw the incomers as people whose historical function had ended with the close of the cold war rather than harbingers of a new era.

Lieberman was concerned that the public diplomacy function should be fully integrated into the State Department and that there should be no shadow USIA remaining like an agency within an agency. Though she was able to promote and manage public diplomacy specialists, all of the agency's field staff were merged into regional bureaus and hence became subject to the intermediate authority of the relevant assistant secretary of state. Under this design the under secretary would lead and intervene when necessary.[29] While the logic was sound, the system was vulnerable in its early years to the relative strengths of individual under secretaries. A prolonged vacancy or an under secretary who paid limited attention to management duties could allow the balance of power to shift toward the assistant secretaries. Both would characterize public diplomacy in the early years of the George W. Bush administration.

The Path Not Taken: Jamie Metzl and PDD 68

In the midst of the reorganization, there was a remarkable bureaucratic end-run by a relatively young White House staffer who, as he put it, was not used to hearing the word "No." His name was Jamie Metzl. At a time when budgets for public diplomacy were shrinking, Metzl argued for both the rejuvenation of the activity and its coordination.

Metzl joined the NSC as a White House Fellow in September 1997, around the same time that he published articles in *Foreign Affairs* and the *American Journal of International Law* arguing that in cases like Rwanda, where local media were inciting genocide, there was an overwhelming moral case for an outside power to mount jamming. Metzl not only saw a need in extreme cases for the United States to block messages of opponents but also to coordinate day-to-day foreign policy information work across the executive branch. He looked for a mechanism to accomplish this, found it lacking, and set about creating it. His boss, NSC intelligence and counterterrorism chief Richard Clarke, endorsed the plan and allowed Metzl to lead an interagency International Information Working Group to take the matter further. The group convened in early 1998 and by the middle of the year had created a draft structure.[30]

The working group concluded that the United States indeed needed a strategic authority to coordinate the country's international information, and more specifically to influence and mitigate conflict around the world. The group imagined a range of policy options for the U.S. government but placed particular emphasis on enabling local media. They called their proposed structure the International Public Information Group (IPI) and planned that its operation, as its title implied, would be transparent. The IPI structure began to operate and moreover proved its value that autumn as the United States moved into a crisis with Iraq. Metzl followed up by pushing for the IPI to become a formal part of the U.S. foreign policy machinery and drafted what would become Presidential Decision Document (PDD) 68. But one key detail changed. Metzl had hoped that the IPI would be located in the NSC but faced the difficulty of the president's commitment not to expand the White House bureaucracy. Meanwhile the State Department saw the group as a necessary part of its new consolidated structure of public diplomacy and agitated to have the unit relocated from the NSC to Foggy Bottom. In February 1999, Metzl moved into an office on the sixth floor of the State Department as Senior Coordinator for Public Information. Power remained on the floor above with Madeleine Albright and Assistant Secretary of State Rubin, but Metzl still had a chance to take advantage of the vacuum to be left by the demise of USIA and create a revolutionary structure in its place.

The principal task facing Metzl and IPI group in 1999 was to coordinate the information response to the Kosovo Crisis. During the run up to the war, IPI created an interactive television program for Albanian television called *Agreement for Peace,* which allowed Madeleine Albright, Senator Bob Dole, and other senior Americans to present the peace plan to Albanian and Kosovo-Albanian journalists. IPI estimated that 70 percent of the population of Kosovo saw the program. In the following months, IPI coordinated 140 further television programs for Albania, Macedonia, Bosnia, and elsewhere in the region.[31] Its other activities included the creation of an alliance of international broadcasters to combat Serb propaganda known as the "Ring around Serbia." IPI estimated the audience for the combined broadcasts at 40 percent of the Serb population during the bombing and around 12 percent thereafter.[32]

The whole Kosovo crisis played into Metzl's argument that the United States needed a permanent structure to coordinate its international information and on April 30, President Clinton signed PDD 68, the necessary order to establish the IPI. The document, drafted largely by Metzl, began:

The United States will improve its use of public information communicated to foreign audiences. Our objectives are to improve our ability to prevent and mitigate foreign crises, and to promote understanding and support for US foreign policy initiatives around the world.

PDD 68 acknowledged that "dramatic changes in the global information environment" required "a more deliberate and well-developed international public information strategy" for "promoting" United States' "values and interests." It made specific reference to the damage

wrought by "malicious and inaccurate information" in Bosnia and
Rwanda. It continued:

> Effective use of our nation's highly-developed communications
> and information capabilities to address misinformation and incite-
> ment, mitigate inter-ethnic conflict, promote independent media
> organizations and the free flow of information, and support dem-
> ocratic participation will advance our interests and is a critical
> foreign policy objective.

To this end PDD 68 set out a structure to monitor world opinion and
coordinate U.S. government information activity.

The core of the IPI structure would be the interagency IPI core
group (ICG), to be chaired after the merger of USIA into state by
the under secretary of state for public diplomacy and public affairs
or his designee. Members would include state, defense, AID, and the
National Intelligence Council. ICG would maintain its own secretar-
iat, including staff on detail from the Pentagon. It would "establish sub
groups on regional, functional, and translational issues as appropriate."
It would initiate a major program of training in international public information planning and delivery for civilian and military staff,
with interagency personnel exchanges and annual exercises organized
with the National Defense University, Army War College, National
Foreign Affairs Training Center, and others. PDD 68 also emphasized
the need to cultivate links with private sector and NGO partners working for the "development of civil society and the free exchange of ideas
and information," and to "place the highest priority on supporting the
development of global and indigenous media outlets which promote
these objectives." The document set a deadline of ninety days to define
the ICG's "policies, programs and scope of work," and of ten months
to present a national strategy and full reports on implementation and
funding.[33]

PDD 68 had real vision. It held the potential to create the sort
of cohesive approach to international information issues not seen
in the United States since the 1950s. Unfortunately, even with the
president's signature, traditional closed approaches to information,
the world of overlapping vested interests, bureaucratic rivalries, and
conflicting agendas between and within federal foreign agencies
still posed formidable obstacles for Jamie Metzl's baby. IPI alarmed
certain traditionalists within the administration and they prepared a
counterattack.

On July 28, the very day on which the full IPI Core Group held its inaugural meeting under the chairmanship of State's new head of planning, Morton Halperin, *Washington Times* ran a front-page story about the office, quoting at length from its charter. *Washington Times* journalist Ben Barber pointed to a caveat in the document, which suggested that domestic news could be "synchronized" and "deconflicted" to avoid sending a mixed message. This raised the specter of a government overseas propaganda unit, which Barber claimed would include CIA input, shaping domestic news. In fact CIA's role would be marginal and Metzl had a clear understanding of the need for firewalls between information and covert operations, but the story stuck. It was the nightmare the Smith-Mundt Act was supposed to prevent. "Numerous clauses in the document," Barber observed, "have an Orwellian ring that gives the impression of a vast, coordinated propaganda operation."[34] In following days the *Washington Times* milked the story for all it was worth, running alarmed comment from both the right and the left. The domestic propaganda charge hurt. The White House scrambled to put the genii back in the bottle.[35]

The merger of USIA into state in October 1999 robbed public diplomacy of leadership at agency director level. A need for the interagency coordination of public diplomacy remained—and as never before agencies like USAID, defense, and justice were main players in the field—but the remit of the unit with the potential to bring the necessary interagency cohesion—the IPI group—had still to be defined. In the summer, its director Jamie Metzl published a thoughtful piece in the *Washington Quarterly* stressing the need for the United States to embrace international information as not just a valuable tool but a substitute for armed intervention. He bemoaned the poor handling of public diplomacy around the United States refusal to sign a landmine treaty or the bombing of the Sudanese pharmaceutical plant in August 1998, but looked to the opportunities available in a wired world. "In foreign affairs," he concluded, "just as in economics, success will belong to those who internalize the lessons of an increasingly open global political system."[36] Others in the State Department had no desire to "internalize lessons" of openness or anything else.

Traditionalist elements at the State Department were worried that IPI would be overly influential and resented Metzl's brash style. They scented the potential for an inflated structure with a representative in every functional and geographical bureau across State, CIA, and the Defense Department. The final form of the unit, unveiled in October 1999 after the merger of USIA into state, was significantly less ambitious. The *Washington Times* reported that Metzl's "wings" had been clipped. Metzl had not inherited legions of USIA personnel following consolidation. Evelyn Lieberman herself explained pointedly that Metzl worked under her supervision. She stressed that IPI was for foreign audiences only and underlined that the old firewall between the CIA and USIA would be maintained in the present structure. A State Department spokesman noted that the IPI was now busy building support for UN peacekeeping in East Timor.[37] The ideas behind IPI remained in circulation. The White House National Security Strategy for a New Century, of December 1999 endorsed PDD 68, the IPI structure, and the notion of an "obligation" to "counter misinformation and incitement, mitigate inter-ethnic conflict, promote independent media organizations and the free flow of information, and support democratic participation helps advance U.S. interests abroad."[38]

The IPI structure soon bogged down in the morass that was post-USIA American public diplomacy and an opportunity to rebuild the sort of coordinated structure of the era of Eisenhower and C. D. Jackson was lost. Metzl left the State Department in the course of 2000 with growing worries for the future of U.S. public diplomacy.[39]

Conclusion: 9/11 and Beyond

In the wake of the attacks of September 11, 2001, Washington bristled with reports on the deficiencies of American public diplomacy and prescriptions for remedies. The wisest analysts noted that the heart of America's problem was not the presentation of its policy but the policy itself.[40] Of course the best public diplomacy is more than a matter of presentation; it is a dynamic two-way process of engagement with foreign publics that produces better policy. On July 30, 2002, the same day as a Task Force of the Council on Foreign Relations released a report on the failings of American public diplomacy, the press carried a White House announcement of the creation of a new Office of Global Communications (OGC) to coordinate the administration's response to the anti-American currents in world public opinion. In his associated statement, White House spokesman Ari Fleischer explained that the president believed it was important to "listen to other countries" but this did not seem a high priority of the OGC structure.[41] The initiative proved to be preparation for that autumn's campaign to justify an invasion of Iraq in the following spring. Moves to improve the coordination of U.S. public diplomacy proceeded apace. On September 10, 2002, National Security Advisor Condoleezza Rice created a Strategic Communication Policy Coordination Committee drawing together staff from the NSC, OGC, and relevant agencies at the assistant secretary level. It was a step in the right direction in theory, but in operation was not a success. The Department of Defense held disproportionate sway and the entire public diplomacy operation was absurdly underfunded.[42] One major problem for American public diplomacy lay in the field of leadership. Bush's first under secretary of state for Public Diplomacy, Charlotte Beers, brought little clout to the interagency process, and her successor, Margaret Tutwiler, was not in the post long enough to make a difference. Following his reelection, and with criticism of the Iraq war mounting, President Bush successfully prevailed on his trusted communication aide Karen Hughes to take the job. Hughes could do little to stem the flood-tide of criticism of the United States but she did bring bigger budgets and strengthened the position of the State Department and Public Diplomacy in the interagency tussles with the Pentagon. In the end even "Hurricane Karen," as the president called her, knew when she was beaten and returned to private life in Texas, leaving public diplomacy in the hands of former pundit James Glassman.[43]

As the election of 2008 approached, reports on the restructuring of American public diplomacy proliferated. Some contained wisdom—expanded funding—empowering an official to speak for public diplomacy in the inner circle of the White House, investing in independent agencies for cultural work or even listening—but others looked to a crudely militarized model whereby all American public diplomacy was channeled under the rubric of Strategic Communication.[44]

In all the frenzy of reports and counter proposals, it is to be hoped that the experience of other countries might be considered, and especially the benefits that have accrued to Britain, Germany, France, Italy, Spain, and many others from fire-walling cultural diplomacy in its own agency. In the struggle for a new structure for American public diplomacy vested interests will clash and turf battles will be fought. One can only hope that the White House will be able to provide sufficient vision to draw out the best public diplomacy structure for the United States rather than merely balance the gripes of its constituent players, and create a structure that is truly fit for purpose. If they accomplish this task, it will be a first in the history of American public diplomacy.

Notes

1. These paragraphs are a condensing of the prologue to Nicholas J. Cull, *The Cold War and the USIA: American Public Diplomacy and Propaganda, 1945–1989* (Cambridge: Cambridge University Press, 2008). For further detail and notes, consult that volume.
2. On the National Security Act see Charles E. Nue, "The Rise of the National Security Bureaucracy," in *The New American State: Bureaucracies and Policies since World War Two,* ed. Louis Galambos (Baltimore: Johns Hopkins University Press, 1987) and Melvyn P. Leffler, *A Preponderance of Power: National Security, the Truman Administration and the Cold War* (Palo Alto: Stanford University Press, 1992).
3. *Foreign Relations of the United States* (hereafter FRUS) 1945–1950, *The Emergence of the Intelligence Establishment.* docs 241, 250, 252, 253, 257, 264, 291–93, 306. For discussion see W. Scott Lucas, *Freedom's War: The American Crusade against the Soviet Union* (Manchester: Manchester University Press, 1999), 61 et seq. and Peter Grose, *Operation Rollback: America's Secret War behind the Iron Curtain* (Boston and New York: Houghton Mifflin, 2000).
4. Smith-Mundt is PL 80–402; The restrictive section is 501. For an analysis of the evolution of the law see Allen W. Palmer and Edward L. Carter, "The Smith-Mundt Act's Ban on Domestic Propaganda: An Analysis of the Cold War Statute Limiting Access to Public Diplomacy," *Communication, Law and Policy* 11 (2006): 1–34.
5. *Subcommittee on Overseas Information Programs of the United States, Staff Study No. 4, Organization of United States Overseas Information Functions,* p. 5 also Acheson to Benton, January 24, 1951, FRUS 1951, vol. 1, p. 909. "Report on the Organization of the Government for the Conduct of Foreign Affairs" for Foreign Affairs Task Force of the Commission on Organization of the Executive Branch of the Government. Nelson Rockefeller had floated the same idea of an independent information agency in the autumn of 1945 see NA RG59, Assistant Secretary of State for Public Affairs 1945–1950, box 13, correspondence, 1945–1950, file "Information—Overseas Program," esp. Ferdinand Kuhn to Benton, October 8, 1945.
6. Hulten had proved himself as assistant director for management for the wartime OWI and more recently as a deputy assistant secretary of state, first for public affairs and then for administration.
7. On January 4, he referred the deadlock for adjudication by the Bureau of the Budget and a "special consultant" Admiral Sidney Souers, who was the former Director of Central Intelligence and the first executive secretary of the NSC. On January 18, Souers delivered his recommendation proposing a board "under the NSC" with a chairman appointed by the president. Harry S. Truman Presidential Library (hereafter HSTL) SMOF PSB files, box 9, PSB 091.412, W. K. Scott to USoS (Webb), February 20, 1951.
8. FRUS 1951, vol. 1, Truman, directive, April 4, 1951, p. 58 and note p. 921; FRUS 1951, Vol. IV, pp. 58–60; also HSTL SMOF, box 25, PSB, file 334–1, Webb to Marshall, May 2, 1951 and for dissent from the new structure memo by Frank Wisner for Assistant Dir. CIA, May 28, 1951.
9. HSTL OF, box 1656, 1290-D, Barrett to Short (White House), June 25, 1951 with press release June 20 attached.
10. FRUS 1952–1954, vol. II, pt. 2, Lay (NSC) to Raymond Allen (PSB), February 27, 1952.
11. *Public Papers of the Presidents: Dwight D. Eisenhower,* vol. 1. 1953, p. 8, noting that the decision was taken at cabinet on January 23, 1953. For advanced news of the Jackson Committee see James Reston, "Eisenhower Plans Key Staff to Guide 'Cold War' Policy," *New York Times,* January 11, 1953, quoting heavily from Eisenhower's San Francisco speech of October 8, 1952.
12. Cary Reich, *The Life of Nelson Rockefeller: Worlds to Conquer, 1908–1958* (New York: Doubleday, 1996), 500–505. The Rockefeller committee promised to pick up where the

Truman-era Hoover Commission had left off. Although not restricted to information, this was a major element in its brief. Its three members were Nelson Rockefeller (the chairman), Milton Eisenhower (youngest brother of the president), and Arthur S. Flemming. Milton Eisenhower—like Rockefeller—had worked in wartime propaganda.

13. The Senate subcommittee's agenda included the possible removal of information activities from the State Department. Dwight D. Eisenhower Presidential Library (hereafter DDEL) Jackson Committee, box 1, "congress," Overseas information programs of the United States, Interim report of the committee on foreign relations pursuant to the provisions of S. Res. 74, 82nd Congress, 2nd session. Also box 11, "Hickenlooper subcommittee." Marcy (Subcommittee staff) to Washburn, April 10, 1953; also *FRUS* 1952–1954, vol. II, pt. 2, p. 1627.

14. DDEL OSANA—OCB/subject, box 1, Coordination of information and public opinion aspects of National Security Policies, esp. president to secretary of state, July 21, 1959.

15. DDEL PACGO box 17, [#124 (2)], Meeting... with the President to discuss the reorganization of the Department of State, June 12, 1959.

16. DDEL WHCF OF 133-M-1, box 673, Eisenhower to Sprague, December 2, 1959; The details of the committee are from DDEL DDE Papers as president (Ann Whitman file), administrative series, box 37, Sprague Committee file 2.

17. The previous two paragraphs are a condensation of Cull, *The Cold War and the USIA*, Chapters 4–6.

18. Association for Diplomatic Studies and Training Oral History, online at Library of Congress (hereafter ADST): Monsen. For correspondence see Richard Nixon Presidential Materials, WHCF, FG6–6 (NSC) box 1, Exec., Stanton to Kissinger, January 10, 1969; FG230 (USIA) box 1, Exec., Advisory Commission to president, February 3, 1969; president to Stanton, February 20, 1969.

19. Interviews: Walter Roberts, November 10, 2001, Frank Stanton, July 28, 2002, Leonard Marks, May 15, 2003 and ADST oral history, Olom. Government Accounting Office, *Public Diplomacy in the Years Ahead—An Assessment of Proposals for Reorganization*. May 5, 1977, p. 21.

20. For the text of the reorganization see Executive Order 12048, March 27, 1978, *Public Papers of the Presidents: Jimmy Carter,* 1978, vol. 1, pp. 606–607.

21. This assessment is a condensation of Cull, *The Cold War and the USIA*, Chapter 9.

22. Interviews: Walter Raymond December 12, 1995 and Michael Schneider, December 5, 1995. For USIA background on Project Democracy from early 1983 see National Archives (hereafter NA) RG 306 A1 (1066), USIA historical collection, box 207, subject files, "Project Democracy, 1981–82" and "...1983." For online copy of NSDD 77 see http://www.fas.org/irp/offdocs/nsdd/nsdd-077.htm accessed October 27, 2008. The document defined public diplomacy as "those actions of the U.S. government designed to generate support for our national security objectives." For early meetings of the International Broadcasting Committee see Ronald Reagan Library (hereafter RRL) WHORM sf FG 298–01, 150814, Tomlinson (VOA) to McFarlane, May 20, 1983. The system included a Senior Planning Group, chaired at NSC by Raymond with Schneider representing USIA, Craig Alderman (Deputy Under Secretary of State for Defense) from the Pentagon, Gerald Helman from the State Department and a representative from USAID.

23. RRL Executive Secretary, NSC filing system, file 8708249, Dean to Carlucci, "Items for consideration from SPG meeting on public diplomacy, November 5, 1988" November 9, 1988.

24. Joseph D. Duffey papers (private hands), memo by James Rubin, "Reinventing and integrating the foreign affairs agencies," March 27, 1997.

25. Bill Clinton, *My Life* (Hutchinson: London, 2004), 753 and *Public Papers of the Presidents: William Jefferson Clinton,* 1997 vol. 1, pp. 454–456. As the president hoped, on April 24, 1997 the senate approved the chemical weapons convention.

26. White House Fact Sheet on Foreign Policy Agencies, April 18, 1997, online at http://www. clintonfoundation.org/legacy/041897-fact-sheet-on-foreign-policy-agencies.htm

27. Interview: Evelyn Lieberman, February 7, 2006.

28. Evelyn Lieberman, "Diplomacy Redefined, Closing the Public Information Gap," *Washington Times,* October 5, 1999, p. A21.

29. Interview: Lieberman.

30. Interview (telephone): Jamie Metzl, July 6, 2005. See also Mark Thompson, "Defining Information Intervention: An Interview with Jamie Metzl," in *Forging Peace: Intervention, Human Rights and the Management of Media Space,* ed. Monroe E. Price and Mark Thompson (Edinburgh: Edinburgh University Press, 2002), 53–55.

31. Thompson, "Defining Information Intervention," 53–55.

32. Interview: Metzl; Thompson, "Defining Information Intervention," 53–55; Monroe Price, *Media and Sovereignty: The Global Information Revolution and the Challenge to State Power* (Boston: MIT Press, 2002), 175, 218.

33. Interview: Metzl; PDD 68, "International Public Information," April 30, 1999. For comment see Price, *Media and Sovereignty,* 172–177.

34. Interview: Metzl. Ben Barber, "Group Will Battle Propaganda Abroad," *Washington Times,* July 28, 1999, p. A1.

35. Ben Barber, "Information Control Plan Aimed at US—Insider Says; International Agency to Be Used for 'Spinning the News' " *Washington Times,* July 29, 1999, p. A1; "White House Says Information System Not Aimed at US," *Washington Times,* July 30, 1999, p. A1. See also Helle Bering, "Professor Albright Goes Live," *Washington Times,* August 4, 1999, p. A17. Anne Gearan, "Administration Creating New Council to Combat Overseas Propaganda," *Associated Press,* August 9, 1999, source for "US Creates News Agency," *Washington Post,* August 13, 1999, p. A23. As precedent for this story, Barber's source also claimed that the White House Strategic Planning Directorate (created in July 1996) had worked through State and USIA to apply pressure on U.S. editors and foreign correspondents for supportive coverage of troop deployments in Bosnia. Readers might have been reassured that had this pressure been inappropriate it would have been raised before this date by any one of the distinguished journalists targeted rather than by a former staffer.

36. Jamie F. Metzl, "The International Politics of Openness," *Washington Quarterly,* vol. 22, issue 3, Summer 1999, pp. 11–16, for comment see Joel Bleifuss, "Ready, Aim, Inform," *In These Times,* March 20, 2000, p. 2.

37. Ben Barber, "IPI Chief's Wings 'Clipped' by State," *Washington Times,* October 7, 1999, p. A15. For concerns over USIA and CIA see Kathleen Koch, "State Department's Absorption of USIA Raised Concerns," CNN Worldview, tx 18:08 ET, October 9, 1999 transcript accessed via LexisNexis, also Ben Barber, "Envoys Fear Lift of Ban on CIA," *Washington Times,* January 11, 1999, p. A1 which quotes two former CIA directors affirming the value of the firewall and Ben Barber, "CIA Spies Won't Be Cultural Attaches," *Washington Times,* January 12, 1999.

38. 'National Security Strategy for a New Century, December 1999 released January 5, 2000: http://www.clintonfoundation.org/legacy/010500-report-on-national-security-strategy. htm

39. Interview: Metzl.

40. For an aggregation of the first wave of these reports see the appendix to the Defense Science Board Task Force on Strategic Communication, September 2004, online at http://www. acq.osd.mil/dsb/reports/2004–09-Strategic_Communication.pdf

41. Karen De Young, "Bush to Create Formal Office to Shape US Image," *Washington Post,* July 30, 2002, p. A1.

42. Defense Science Board Task Force on Strategic Communication, p. 25.

43. For comment on U.S. public diplomacy since 9/11 see William Rugh, *American Encounters with Arabs: The "Soft Power" of American Diplomacy in the Middle East* (New York: Praeger, 2005);

Nancy Snow, *The Arrogance of American Power: What U.S. leaders Are Doing Wrong and Why Its Our Duty to Dissent* (Lanham, MD: Rowman and Littlefield, 2006); Carnes Lord, *Losing Hearts and Minds? Public Diplomacy and Strategic Influence in the Age of Terror* (New York: Praeger, 2006).

44. Positive reports include the Brookings/Congressional report by Kristen Lord, the White Paper issues by Business for Diplomatic Action, and the book by Mike Medavoy and Nathan Gardils, *American Idol after Iraq*. The worrying hint of militarization could be detected in the legislation introduced by Senator Brownback in October 2008.

CHAPTER THREE

The Lessons of Al Hurra Television

SHAWN POWERS AND AHMED EL GODY

Throughout its four-year existence, Al Hurra, the U.S.-backed satellite channel available throughout the Middle East, has been embroiled in controversy. Launched soon after the invasion of Iraq, Al Hurra was tasked with the goal of accurately representing U.S. policies and opinions in the region in an effort to combat the rise of anti-American sentiment. Further, Al Hurra was supposed to provide high-quality journalism that would both result in a more informed and democratically engaged Arab citizenry and improve the quality of journalism throughout the region.

To date, Al Hurra has failed to achieve its goals, and this study argues that there are four primary lessons that can be taken away from Al Hurra's failure: (1) editorial independence is essential to having any say in informing Arab public opinion, and it must be achieved both in practice and in the eyes of audiences; (2) brands matter, and Al Hurra's name and mission are grounded in presumptions that trigger Arab impressions of America as an imperial power, the exact impressions that public diplomacy efforts should be trying to combat; (3) understanding and adapting to the Arab media environment are essential for a broadcaster's success; and (4) the traditional benchmarks used to measure the success or failure of international broadcasting ventures must change to reflect the long-term goals of the U.S. government's overall public diplomacy efforts.

The Rise of Al Hurra

Al Hurra—"The Free One"—is a U.S. government-funded broadcaster available throughout the Middle East. Established in February 2004,

Al Hurra TV, along with its FM radio counterpart, Radio Sawa (launched in 2002), represent America's largest commitment to public diplomacy in the region. From 2002 through 2008, the U.S. government has invested just less than $500 million dollars in the two broadcasters.

Overseen by the Broadcasting Board of Governors (BBG), an independent agency reporting directly to Congress, Al Hurra's mission is to promote freedom and democracy in the region through the accurate and objective representation of U.S. policies. One of the BBG's responsibilities is to serve "as a firewall to protect the professional independence and integrity of the broadcasters," including Al Hurra.[1] Broadcasting from Springfield, Virginia, the station's programming includes a mix of traditional newscasting, cultural programming, political talk shows, documentaries, as well as American entertainment programming dubbed into Arabic. Both Al Hurra and Radio Sawa operate under the umbrella of a nonprofit corporation, funded by Congress, called the Middle East Broadcasting Network (MBN).

Before Al Hurra, U.S. broadcasting consisted of a resource-strapped Voice of America (VOA) Arabic that was broadcasting just seven hours a day using "antiquated shortwave and minimal range medium wave transmitters."[2] Competing against a growing number of FM radio and satellite television stations, VOA Arabic programming had a very small audience. Moreover, the failure of the Camp David negotiations to produce a lasting peace in the region and the onset of the second Palestinian Intifada provided the required political urgency for a revamped broadcasting service to the Middle East. Many were openly concerned that a failure to combat hateful and extreme media in the region could result in a culture of violence and terrorism. The terrorist attacks on America on September 11, 2001 gave the final impetus for plans to overhaul U.S. broadcasting in the region.[3]

Al Hurra was the brainchild of BBG Board Member Norm Pattiz, founder of Westwood One, the nation's largest radio network. Pattiz had hoped to establish "one of the largest Arabic-language newsgathering operations in the world" that would look much "like a CNN or an MSNBC or Fox News, or an Al-Jazeera...only it will be much more visually appealing."[4]

Al Hurra has three different streams, though there is significant programming overlap between all three: (1) Al Hurra TV, focuses on the broader Arab public; (2) Al Hurra-Iraq, provides news specifically addressing issues in Iraq; and (3) Al Hurra-Europe, launched in August 2006, focuses on reaching Arabs in the UK, France, and Germany.

While Al Hurra TV and Al Hurra-Europe are currently only available via satellite, Al Hurra-Iraq uses a combination of satellite and terrestrial transmitters to increase its reach within Iraq.[5]

According to a 2006 Government Accountability Office (GAO) report, Al Hurra was also established to "increase the standards of other broadcasters in the region, and to offer distinctive and provocative programming unavailable on other stations." Testifying before the congressional subcommittee on the Middle East and South Asia, BBG Board Member Jeffrey Hirschberg said, "Al Hurra was created as an alternative to existing Arab-speaking media, which had in common a number of things, including hate-speak, disinformation, incitement to violence, government censorship and journalistic self-censorship."[6] In its 2009 budget request to Congress, the BBG argued "Alhurra is the only Arabic-language television service in the region that provides consistently balanced news coverage and current affairs programming that addresses important, controversial topics, including the rights of women, religious freedom, and human rights."[7] Thus, in the short-term, Al Hurra hopes to counter what it sees as "anti-American propaganda" that may contribute to misperceptions about American polices and culture. Beyond that, Al Hurra has two additional long-term goals: (1) to enhance the overall quality of news throughout the region by providing high-caliber news formats and journalism, and (2) introduce a range of taboo topics in the region, along with deliberative formats, to foster an engaged public in the region that could eventually push for further political reform.

Yet, both the Arab media environment and its audience have changed dramatically since Al Hurra's launch. Many have noted that Al Hurra faces a growing number of competitors in the region. The Pan Arab Research Center predicts that by end of 2008, Arab viewers will be able to access as many as 500 channels via satellite TV. Among this sea of channels are more than fifteen channels devoted to news, including popular Arab-based broadcasters as Al Jazeera and Al Arabiya.[8] Moreover, since Al Hurra's launch in 2004, Russia (Russia Today), France (France 24), the United Kingdom (BBC Arabic TV), and Germany (Deutsche Welle) have each spent considerable resources creating and improving similarly styled news-oriented satellite stations that Al Hurra must also compete against. And, as Arab media scholar Marc Lynch notes, these "other countries won't face the distinctive problem of anti-Americanism."[9]

The Arab mediascape is now best described as a "paradox of plenty," where citizens have quickly adapted from an information-poor media environment, dominated by government censorship and propaganda, to an information marketplace that offers something for everyone. Although Al Hurra is grounded in a counterpropaganda model of broadcasting that was successful during the cold war and its immediate aftermath, "the communication environment in the Arab world is vastly more complex and competitive than the post-Soviet media scene."[10] Al Hurra is now competing with an increasingly sophisticated and competitive satellite market. The challenge of designing programming that effectively reaches a significant audience has changed. Not only have the number of quality news channels in the region grown, but also the scope and caliber of entertainment programming. In terms of providing distinctive content capable of attracting significant audience attention, the bar has certainly been raised. Thus, questions of credibility, style, and cultural fit have taken on a new level of importance in assessing Al Hurra's efforts at successfully competing in today's Arab media market.

Controversies and Criticisms

When Al Hurra was launched in 2004, it received little praise from Arab viewers. In its first weekend of airtime, Al Hurra featured and repeated an exclusive interview with President Bush, drawing attention to Al Hurra's ties to the American government and setting a strong propagandistic tone for the few viewers who had tuned in. According to one viewer in Cairo, "Why would I watch Bush on television when every day I can read what he says... We know what the American policies are, and we still don't like them."[11] Contrary to Pattiz's hope of establishing a more advanced and appealing version of existing Arab news networks, "[w]hen Al Hurra began, Arab viewers... were deeply disappointed because the quality of the programs was poorer than the quality of Arab satellite TV."[12] Marwan Kraidy cites the Middle East's history of being "bombarded by international propaganda broadcasts from other Arab nations, Nazi Germany, France, the United States, Great Britain, and the Soviet Union" as an additional factor limiting the possibility for success of a broadcaster so closely tied to an unpopular government like the United States.[13]

In 2006, the United States GAO issued a report documenting the many challenges facing Al Hurra and Radio Sawa, notably poor management and weak performance. Moreover, the GAO found that Al Hurra "lacks regular editorial training and has not fully implemented a comprehensive, regular program review process to determine whether its programming complies with those standards or with MBN's mission."[14] As it turns out, the GAO's concern over the lack of training for journalists and editors and quality-control measures was quite justified. In the following months, these failures resulted in several examples that would be used to argue that Al Hurra was not living up to its mission of providing a high-quality news product that worked to combat myths and stereotypes about the United States.

In March 2007, Al Hurra gained significant media and public attention when Joel Mowbray, a conservative syndicated columnist for Knight-Ridder and a frequent contributor to the National Review, published a series of articles in the *Wall Street Journal* accusing the channel of providing "platforms to Holocaust deniers and Islamic terrorists."[15] In these articles, Mowbray revealed that Al Hurra had aired the entirety of Hezbollah leader Hassan Nasrallah's December 7, 2006 speech, a violation of Al Hurra's Journalistic Code of Ethics and its congressional mandate, and that they provided extensive and deferential coverage of a Holocaust denial conference held in Tehran in December 2006. In May 2007, Congress held hearings to further examine the accusations. In a statement before Congress, BBG member Joaquin F. Blaya acknowledged the channel's mistakes and assured Congress that corrective measures had been taken and that terrorists and Holocaust deniers would never again use the channel as a platform.[16]

The congressional hearings drew attention to a challenge that Al Hurra was facing: whether its mission was to provide objective news or to promote U.S. policy in the region. Al Hurra's Journalistic Code of Ethics advises Al Hurra's reporters to provide information in: "[a] factual, objective context that enhances understanding of the events and issues and provides clarity without distortion or bias. Objective language shall be used to reflect events and issues accurately and dispassionately. Broadcasters shall present opposing or differing views accurately and in a balanced manner on all issues."[17] Yet, in response to Blaya's admission that mistakes had been made, members of Congress blasted Al Hurra for failing to live up to what they saw as its mission: to promote an American framing of news in the Middle East. For example, the subcommittee chairman, Congressman Gary Ackerman, argued: "You are part of the government. You have something to sell, and you have a good product to sell: That is America, and that is the truth," adding, "[Al Hurra] was not created just so that we could present both sides of the issue. We are the other side of the issue."[18] Congressman Mike Pence further confused Al Hurra's public diplomacy role, arguing that

Al Hurra is "a diplomatic mission of the United States of America . . . this is not a 'we report, you decide' television station. We are about promoting the truth about the free world and the United States of America in this region." Such explicit congressional pressure not only highlights the difficulty in Al Hurra's ability to provide news "without distortion or bias" while avoiding congressional ire, but also begs the question of the effectiveness of the alleged "firewall" that the BBG is supposed to play between the official foreign policy objectives of the United States and Al Hurra's ability to practice journalism in ways that "serve as a model of the free marketplace of ideas and a free press in the American tradition."[19]

Beyond Congress, Al Hurra has also faced criticism with regard to the overall quality of its product. Arab journalists and academics trained in media and journalism have noted that Al Hurra's technological operations are far less advanced when compared to other Arab broadcasters. Graphics are also described as "simple" and similar to what you would see on a "university television channel," and transitions between commentators, journalists, and anchors are often awkward and poorly timed. Moreover, Al Hurra relied on "on the ground," investigative journalism less than its Arab competitors. There was a significant lack of images coming from events that were taking place. Critics argued that even the quality of the Arabic spoken on Al Hurra was exceptionally poor and showed a lack of journalistic experience in the Arab media environment.[20] Adding to the perception of Al Hurra's "simple" journalism is the fact that a large part of its news is "outsourced" to Associated Press Television News (APTN), "the primary source of foreign news and technical support for . . . Al Hurra."[21]

In June 2008, Al Hurra was once again embroiled in controversy after two scathing media reports—one produced by the media watchdog ProPublica that was aired on CBS's *60 Minutes,* the other by the *Washington Post*'s Craig Whitlock—echoed many of the previous criticisms and added evidence to several new ones. ProPublica's critique was that Al Hurra was far from pro-United States in its broadcasts that, along with interviews with senior U.S. officials, habitually aired adversarial views from all other sides—ranging from the Sunni Iraqi insurgency, through the Popular Front for the Liberation of Palestine, Hamas, and Islamic Jihad, to pro-Hezbollah and pro-Iranian leaders and radical Shiite Islamists. In addition to the anti-American inflammatory rhetoric, ProPublica decried Al Hurra's managerial inefficiency, favoritism in hiring, and lack of proper editorial and financial oversight as misuse of taxpayers' money. It further drew attention to a gaping linguistic and cultural disconnect between the network's senior management on one hand, and its executive producers, reporters, and newscast content on the other.[22]

Just a month later, ProPublica reported that Al Hurra's Baghdad bureau had been airing stories with a consistent and strong pro-Iranian tilt and that "State Department officials and U.S. diplomats in Baghdad have privately complained for years that Alhurra's Iraq broadcasts seem more interested in promoting the policies of the radical Shiite regime in Iran rather than those of the United States government." Along these lines, in the midst of Iraq's first elections, U.S. Ambassador to Iraq Christopher Ross wrote to his colleagues at the State Department that too many Iraqis did not understand the electoral process and that Al Hurra was not helping. As a result, "[w]hen the election season ended, candidates who ran with the support of the White House had done poorly. American fingers that had pointed at Al Jazeera were now aiming at Al Hurra." Ross's account of the events was confirmed when Alberto Fernandez, director of public diplomacy in the Middle East, e-mailed then Undersecretary of State for Public Diplomacy Karen Hughes to report that the Baghdad bureau was controlled by "radical Shiite Islamists who favored their political brethren and discriminated against and intimidated members of other parties...especially during the Iraqi electoral season of December 2004 to December 2005."[23]

Moreover, fueling criticism that the Baghdad bureau was violating Al Hurra's journalistic code of ethics, the investigation revealed that the bureau had recently interviewed Mishan Jabouri, a fugitive on the run from Interpol, the U.S. military, and Iraqi security police.[24] During the interview, Jabouri commented, "[I] was disappointed that a truck bomb had recently passed by a U.S. military checkpoint only to attack Iraqi security forces nearby," indicating his support for insurgent attacks against U.S. troops. Finally, the investigation found that there had been almost no oversight of the bureau's operations or financial records, and that "ghost" employees were often on payroll despite having never worked at the bureau, an allegation confirmed by former Al Hurra news director Larry Register.[25]

The criticisms leveled generated a wave of media coverage and an intense exchange between the channel's critics at ProPublica and its supporters at the BBG. While important points were raised on both fronts—addressing the station's failures to project a fair image of the United States on the one side, and defending its mission of providing credible programming of high journalistic standards on the other—little agreement emerged in the way of envisioning what would constitute a truly effective U.S. public diplomacy strategy for engaging the Arab world. Finally, as a result of the recent controversies, the ranking member of the House Foreign Relations Committee that oversees Al Hurra, Rep. Ileana Ros-Lehtinen, called on Chairman Berman to "hold immediate oversight hearings and initiate an investigation into reports detailing significant managerial weaknesses at Al Hurra Television."[26]

Are People Watching?

In addition to the intense political scrutiny Al Hurra has received in the United States, it has also been criticized for being unimportant among Arab audiences. Shibley Telhami, in collaboration with Zogby International, has conducted public opinion and media consumption research in Arab countries since 2003. In 2008, Telhami found that among 4,046 participants from Egypt, Jordan, Lebanon, Morocco, Saudi Arabia (KSA), and the UAE, a mere 2 percent of participants responded that Al Hurra was the "network's news broadcasts [they] watch most often," compared to 53 percent of participants who listed Al Jazeera as the news broadcaster they watch most often. While the 2 percent figure is an increase from Al Hurra's audience share in 2006 (when Telhami found that only 1 percent of respondents watched Al Hurra most often), it is a very small audience share when compared to its competitors. Moreover, only 9 percent of respondents said they tuned into Al Hurra "5 or 6 times a week," compared to 60 percent of participants who responded that they tuned into Al Jazeera as often.[27] Combined, these figures are especially enlightening because they show that while 9 percent of the respondents are watching Al Hurra almost daily, only 2 percent found its news product to be compelling enough to describe it their primary source of broadcast news. This poll seems to provide clear evidence that Al Hurra is failing to provide a news service that stands as a compelling alternative to its competitors in the region.[28]

The BBG, however, disagrees and argues that Al Hurra's viewership is increasing, particularly in Syria and Iraq: "Independent research indicates that Alhurra has the largest weekly audience of any non-Arab broadcaster in the Middle East, up from 21 million in 2006 to 26 million today. In the strategically critical countries of Iraq and Syria, Alhurra's weekly reach rates are 56 percent and 55 percent, respectively."[29] Yet, as William Rugh points out, the BBG's presentation of their opinion data has often been misleading: "Arab viewers and listeners asked if they have watched Al Hurra or listened to Radio Sawa this week will probably answer yes even if have only watched or listened for one minute, while devoting most of their time to other channels. A much better test of audience penetration would be to ask which channel the audience prefers."[30] Indeed, Telhami's survey research provides evidence for exactly this point: while many viewers may tune into Al Hurra on occasion, it is rarely identified as the news broadcaster of choice.

Moreover, the BBG's audience research fails to differentiate those viewers that tune into Al Hurra for news from viewers who tune in for entertainment or other nonpolitical cultural programming, a distinction that is important to understanding what type of influence Al Hurra may have when it comes to Arab opinion of U.S. policies in the region. Finally, the GAO has challenged the BBG's conclusions as well, arguing: "Documentation we reviewed indicated that the BBG extensively uses nonprobability audience survey results that cannot be reliably projected to represent a broader population in the region."[31] In other words, the BBG's survey focused on participants who were statistically unlikely to reflect the average viewer of Arab news media, thus calling into question whether the survey results accurately reflected viewing habits of an average audience.

Moving Forward: Lessons Learned

In a 2008 interview, Daniel Nassif, the newly appointed news director for Al Hurra, describes the organization's mission as providing "accurate and objective news to the region," adding "Alhurra's role is to report US policy accurately to an audience that has often not received accurate and objective reports." It is hard to reconcile how the newly appointed news director's vision will work with stern congressional demands for Al Hurra to "promote the American story." Nassif argues that Al Hurra has "a distinct advantage because we are free to discuss any topic while other networks in the region are limited by concerns about offending their backers," an assertion that hardly seems to accurately describe the current level of Al Hurra's political support.[32] Indeed, Nassif could just as easily be referring to Al Jazeera, the Qatari-based satellite news giant that has staked its organizational reputation on continuing to initiate debates on socially taboo topics at the expense of its backer's—the government of Qatar—diplomatic capital.

It is precisely this "identity crisis" that has plagued Al Hurra's operations since its launch and will likely continue to hinder the broadcaster's ability to gain any significant influence in the region. Along these lines, Marc Lynch argues that Al Hurra's problems boil down to the impossible balance required to appease its congressional critics while also providing coverage that resonates with an opinionated Arab audience. Al Hurra's repeated (rhetorical) acquiescence to congressional pressure by promising that its content best represented U.S. policy quickly cost Al Hurra credibility among an Arab audience already critical toward much of America's current foreign policies.[33] William Rugh describes the Al Hurra's predicament as an "existential dilemma," where its dependence on congressional support makes it difficult for the broadcaster to distance itself far enough from U.S. foreign policy in the region to garner any significant audience share.[34] When asked about Al Hurra, Arab viewers often associate its coverage of Middle East politics and U.S. foreign policy with the propaganda offered by the Arab government-run broadcasters that dominated their televisions before the era of satellite news. Contrasting the success of Al Jazeera, which has in the past been perceived as operating independent of the larger geopolitical centers in the region, to the widespread disappointment of Al Hurra, which is seen as a direct extension of the U.S. government, provides the first important lesson for U.S. broadcasting in the region: the perception and practice of editorial independence is essential for any broadcaster to sustain audiences and gain influence in the Middle East.

An example of how Al Hurra's lack of editorial independence has hurt its ability to achieve its goals is the inconsistent handling of news of human rights violations and political repression, particularly in countries whose governments are considered allies or otherwise helpful for U.S. policy in the region. For instance, Al Hurra's failure to consistently cover Egyptian President Mubarak's government, particularly with regard to its treatment of public protesters and journalists who have been critical of the Egyptian government, is a telling example of Al Hurra's prioritization of short-term success (cooperation with governments in the region) that comes at the expense of achieving its long-term goals (democratic governance).[35] Similarly, Naomi Sakr recalls when Al Hurra interviewed Tunisian Foreign Minister Abdelwahab Abdallah shortly after U.S. Secretary of State Colin Powell had criticized Tunisia for its repressive political system and allegations of torture, the interviewer failed to even raise either issue, despite having the political cover of Secretary Powell's remarks.[36]

Moreover, Al Hurra's failure to compete effectively with its regional rivals underscores both the importance and difficulty of establishing a brand that will attract audiences. In today's hypercompetitive media environment, creating a brand is an essential means by which viewers choose what to pay attention to. "The communication of a brand name plays a much more prominent role in global media, almost to the extent that the presentation of a brand name is equally important as relying on the brand name itself."[37] For a broadcaster, a brand is determined primarily by two conditions: (1) presenting a likeable product and image, and (2) consistency. Unfortunately, Al Hurra has failed on both fronts.

From the outset, Al Hurra's promoters marketed the broadcaster as being "Made in America," arguing that Al Hurra's mission is to deliver "America's message to the world passionately and relentlessly."[38] Such an approach pegs Al Hurra's identity to that of a widely unpopular government and a set of policies that are perceived by many as undercutting the American values and principles that have traditionally been effective at branding other U.S. government-backed broadcasting efforts, such as VOA. Rather than being identified with principles that are widely supported among Arab publics—freedom of the press, democratic and transparent governance, and human rights—Al Hurra has been framed as an extension of the Bush administration's War on Terror, a reality that has plagued the channel's efforts to garner much influence. Moreover, most Arabs see Al Hurra's content as propagandistic, particularly when covering the Arab-Israeli conflict and Iraq. It is significant that among all Al Hurra's viewers, Iraqis more than any others find the channel untrustworthy, and by a very substantial margin.[39] It is likely that the stories and images of Iraq that are seen on Al Hurra simply do not match the conditions on the ground for the Iraqi's that tune in. Along these lines, as a former producer for Al Hurra describes it, "Al Hurra reporters covering Iraq focus on more human interest and positive stories. For instance, 'electricity has arrived in this neighborhood,' not 'this neighborhood still doesn't have electricity.' "[40]

Indeed, Al Hurra's approach to branding its news as a superior, American version of journalism may have further strengthened perceptions of the United States as an arrogant, disrespectful and bullying nation, perceptions that have hindered other American public diplomacy efforts in the region. Al Hurra's mission presumes that Arab citizens need the United States to provide them with the correct and most accurate information, a presumption that most Arabs reject. Al Hurra's name itself—"the free one"—implies that news outlets indigenous to the Arab world lack the same freedoms or talents of Western news organizations, another presumption that many Arabs reject. Along these lines, a Cairo-based magazine writer, Amy Moufai, said that she was "very surprised they would choose a name like that which highlights the fact they don't know what they are doing in the Middle East. It reeks of the whole notion of a white man's [burden]. 'Let us teach you our free ways.' "[41] Marwan Kraidy adds to this point, noting that Al Hurra's attempt to compete with Arab news media is also likely to be received poorly given the increasingly important role that media organizations are having on local economies throughout the region: "Arab media institutions play a growing socioeconomic role. As a result, people feel protective of these socially embedded institutions, and harsh criticism of Arab media from Washington adds to negative opinions of the United States."[42]

This mentality is not only reflected in Al Hurra's brand or image, but also in its content. A group of journalists and academics in Cairo noted that Al Hurra's news narrative continually reflected a story of how the political and social failings that many throughout the Arab world faced were framed as the fault of Arab governments and people. The group noted that while other news outlets would explore the role of political actors outside of the Arab world's involvement in Arab conflicts (e.g., the United States, Israel, and the United Nations), Al Hurra repeatedly focused on the failures of Arab political and opinion leaders. Thus, even when Al Hurra was appropriately critical of Arab governments and polices, it often came across as American condescension, further alienating its Arab audiences.[43]

Given this, it should not come as a surprise that in his study of audiences in five Arab countries (Kuwait, the UAE, Jordan, Palestine, and Morocco), Mohammed el-Nawawy found that "attitudes toward US foreign policy have worsened slightly since their exposure to Radio Sawa and Television Alhurra. In their answers to an open-ended question about what they liked or disliked about Sawa and Alhurra, most respondents noted that the US administration was trying to manipulate Arab opinion through networks like Sawa and Alhurra."[44] In Cairo, viewers pointed to Al Hurra's one-sided coverage of Iraq, the Arab-Israeli conflict, and human rights issues (e.g., being critical of Arab governments' human rights policies while offering defenses of abuses at Abu Ghraib and Guantanamo Bay) as evidence of the U.S. government's hypocrisy, another critical factor that feeds into anti-American sentiment in the region.[45] Thus, Al Hurra's brand, pinned to a perception of American arrogance, will likely limit its influence in the region for some time, regardless of the quality of its news product.

A third lesson learned from Al Hurra's experience is the necessity of examining and adapting to specific media environments. Al Hurra's difficulty in creating an institutional identity that resonates with Arab viewers may stem from a deeper misunderstanding of today's Arab media environment. From the outset, Al Hurra's mission has centered on rectifying what the U.S. government felt was a deficit of accurate information about U.S. policies and culture. Nancy Snow describes the mentality as, "If we can just get our message out there, make it louder, make it stronger, make it bolder, then we'll be well on our way to repairing miscommunication problems."[46] Yet, this way of thinking misunderstands the nature of America's public diplomacy troubles. Arab anti-American sentiment and opposition to U.S. policies in the region stem from a number of historical factors, including the legacies of European colonialism, as well as some important substantive disagreements about the purpose and effect of U.S. policy, not a lack of access to information.

According to Marwan Kraidy, "the most popular Arab television programs have been those with the following features: (1) historical or political resonance, (2) narratives of social mobility, (3) and interactive features."[47] The perception of Al Hurra as being similar to Arab government propaganda of the past (history), as well as its being tethered to the U.S. government for resources (political) means that it resonates among Arab viewers in precisely the wrong ways. Moreover, given the congressional hostility toward airing views that are unflattering of U.S. policies, Al Hurra is restricted in its ability to provide many interactive features. Interactivity, at its core, requires inviting viewers to contribute content in real-time, a condition that is not conducive to Al Hurra's need to consistently control its message. Today, programming that effectively reaches large Arab audiences requires a certain level of interactivity. Interactive features provide Arab audiences with a means of openly expressing their opinions and hope that those opinions may actually be listened to and have an impact on what is said or done. A good example of the integration of interactive features into satellite TV is *Star Academy*, an Arab reality show similar in theme to *American Idol*, where viewers use their cell phones' short-message-service (SMS) function to both "vote their favorites on the show and also carry on conversations that ran across the bottom of the screen, making television an interactive medium."[48] Al Jazeera also makes use of its Web site in this way, something that Al Hurra has not sufficiently pursued.

Al Jazeera's success is partially tied to its ability to integrate viewers' SMS messages and phone calls into real-time interviews. Moreover, its web content is highly interactive, encouraging visitors to contribute comments on stories, as well as take polls regarding their opinions on current events.[49] Not only does interactivity pull viewers in and amplify Al Jazeera's image of representing the interests of its viewers, it also provides Al Jazeera with free access to the opinions of a large number of its viewers, information that most broadcasters have to pay money for. If a U.S. broadcaster integrated this level of interactivity into its programming, it would not only attract audiences, but it would also provide the U.S. government with an additional means of measuring opinions of the "Arab street." Web sites are ideal for use as discussion forums, which is something else that Al Hurra has not adequately done with its site.

Al Hurra's ongoing battle with Congress provides an additional lesson: today's news broadcasters need to adjust the benchmarks that have traditionally been used to measure their success or failure. Both Al Hurra and Radio Sawa have relied on two critical measures when they have surveyed Arab audiences to gauge their influence in the region: (1) have you watched Al Hurra in the past seven days? and (2) do you find Al Hurra's content to be trustworthy? The BBG asks these questions to end up with a relatively large number of viewers who have tuned in, a tactic to impress Congress. For example, Congressman Howard Berman, upon hearing BBG reports of gains in Al Hurra's weekly viewership, said: "more than 20 million people in the Middle East are watching Alhurra. That is an impressive number."[50]

Yet, these numbers become more inflated and meaningless as Arab viewers adjust to today's information-rich media environment. Both Congressman Berman and the BBG assume that simply because someone has tuned in to a program, no matter for how long, that they will be influenced by its content. Although this may have been the case during the cold war, where there was a dearth of credible information, it simply no longer holds true. Audiences today have access to information through multiple mediums, and consumers often tune in the most to broadcasters that provide news that supports their preexisting opinions. Indeed, news that is contrary is often disregarded.[51] Thus, the real questions are: what channels viewers are watching the most, for how long and why? Al Hurra's reports, prepared at the behest of a Congress eager to hear that its resources have not gone to waste simply do not provide an accurate measure of Al Hurra's influence on Arab public opinion.

Moreover, the focus on ratings offers an example of how Al Hurra's emphasis on short-term "success" has come at the expense of achieving its long-term goals of improving the quality of journalism and governance in the region. In 2006, the GAO found that Al Hurra had "not yet established a formal long-term strategic plan," a fact that reflects poorly on its ability to achieve its rather ambitious long-term goals.

Rather than work as a surrogate for the policies of the United States, Al Hurra should be better integrated with other, long-term public diplomacy and development goals in the region. Improving the quality of journalism and governance is not simply about spreading information, but requires training, support for exchange programs, and direct engagement with critical public opinion makers. Working with other Arab journalists, for example, could be one way to improve the image of Al Hurra as well as the journalistic practices of other Arab media.

Conclusion

Successful public diplomacy, at its core, must be grounded in mutual understanding and respect. This is especially true for U.S. public diplomacy in the Middle East, where many feel that the United States has a tendency to behave arrogantly toward the Arab citizenry. U.S. public diplomacy practitioners have come around to this reality, and they have begun to integrate listening and engagement into public diplomacy strategies around the world. Unfortunately, Al Hurra has been slow to adopt the new pillars of public diplomacy into its mission or organizational identity. As Al Hurra's news director explains, "So rarely does a show go on Alhurra without having somebody from the State Department or from Washington think tanks refuting what stations like Al-Jazeera are saying."[52] It is precisely this mentality—aggressive, U.S.-centric, unidirectional—that is at the heart of Al Hurra's inability to gain an audience or influence in the Middle East.

U.S. public diplomacy needs to be based on a dialogue with citizens of the Arab world rather than monolithic sending of messages. Arabs were bombarded with state-sponsored news throughout the second half of the twentieth century and have collectively learned how to disregard information that they suspect to be propagandistic in nature. Moreover, in today's media environment, unidirectional broadcasting is not likely to even get the attention of the Arab youth, not to mention be able to inform their opinions. Al Hurra today stands as a symbol of the past, a relic that continues to embody the arrogant and disrespecting public diplomacy strategies that have furthered Arab resentment of American policies and culture, not reduce it.

There are four broad lessons that must be learned from the first four years of the Al Hurra experiment. First, editorial independence is essential if the channel is to have any say in influencing Arab public opinion, and it must be achieved both in practice and in the eyes of the audience. Al Hurra's identity crisis, stemming from the tension of maintaining editorial independence while appeasing its congressional critics who insist on a pro-U.S. spin on news, is at the heart Al Hurra's failure to affect Arab public opinion. For the most part, the struggle has resulted in a news product that is widely received as bland propaganda reminiscent of Arab government broadcasting from a previous era.

Second, brands matter, and Al Hurra's name and mission are grounded in presumptions that trigger Arab impressions of America as an arrogant, bullying country. For a U.S. broadcaster to become successful among Arab audiences, it will have to construct an image, based on its content and outlook, which does not conform to existing stereotypes of America.

Third, understanding the specificity of the Arab media environment is essential for a broadcaster's success. Al Hurra faces a fiercely competitive, oversaturated media environment that offers something for everyone. News today is a highly personal topic, particularly in the Arab world. Audiences are drawn to stories that are told in ways that connect the history of the region to current events. Al Hurra's "spin" on today's news is not only out of sync with the thinking of the Arab world, but it also fails to utilize new communications technologies that are giving Al Hurra's competitors superior means to engage with their audiences.

Finally, the traditional benchmarks used to measure the success or failure of international broadcasting efforts are no longer relevant. Focusing on short-term goals such as the number of viewers who have tuned in during the past week not only fails to provide a sense of how much influence a broadcaster has, but also serves to obfuscate the more important, long-term goals of improving the overall quality of journalism and governance in the region.

The Al Hurra experiment symbolizes the damaged state of American public diplomacy. It relies on outdated assumptions and wishful thinking and fails to recognize how technological advances of the past decade have changed the communications environment. The philosophy behind Al Hurra's approach is rooted firmly in the public diplomacy strategies of the cold war. They do not work anymore.

Notes

1. Al Hurra TV, "About Us," available online at: <http://www.alhurra.com/Sub.aspx?ID=266>
2. Myrna Whitworth, "America's Voice as It Could Have Been," *Arab Media & Society*, May 2007.
3. Alan L. Heil, "2007: A Fateful Year for America's Voices?" *Arab Media & Society*, February 2007.

4. Cited in: Alex Ben Block, "Al Hurra Gallops Into Mideast Media Mix," *Television Week*, March 2, 2004, available online at: < http://ics.leeds.ac.uk/papers/vp01.cfm?outfit=pmt& folder=1259&paper=1377>

5. United States Government Accountability Office, "US International Broadcasting: Management of Middle East Broadcasting Services Could be Improved," GAO-06–762 (2006).

6. D. Jeffrey Hirschberg, "Public Diplomacy in the Middle East and South Asia: Is the Message Getting Through," testimony before the House Subcommittee on the Middle East and South Asia of the Committee on Foreign Affairs, May 16, 2007.

7. Broadcasting Board of Governors, "Fiscal Year 2009 Budget Request," (2008), available online at: <http://www.bbg.gov/reports/budget/bbg_fy09_budget_request.pdf>

8. Pan Arab Research Center, "Harvest Y2006," Middle East Media Guide (2006).

9. Cited in: Alan L. Heil, "Rate of Arabic Language TV Start-Ups Shows No Sign of Abating," *Arab Media & Society*, May 2007, p. 2.

10. Marwan M. Kraidy, "Arab Media and US Policy: A Public Diplomacy Reset," *Stanley Foundation Policy Analysis Brief*, January 2008.

11. Quoted in: Matthew Craft, "US Arabic Channel a Turn-Off," *The Guardian*, February 16, 2004, available online at: < http://www.guardian.co.uk/media/2004/feb/16/broadcasting. usnews>

12. William A. Rugh, "Broadcasting and American Public Diplomacy," *Transnational Broadcasting Studies* 14 (Spring 2005), available online at: <http://www.tbsjournal.com/ rugh.html>

13. Kraidy, "Arab Media and US Policy."

14. United States Government Accountability Office. "US International Broadcasting."

15. Joel Mowbray, "Register's Last Hurrah?" *Wall Street Journal*, June 7, 2007.

16. Joaquin F. Blaya, "Public Diplomacy in the Middle East and South Asia: Is the Message Getting Through," testimony before the House Subcommittee on the Middle East and South Asia of the Committee on Foreign Affairs, May 16, 2007.

17. United States Department of State and the Broadcasting Board of Governors Office of Inspector General "Report of Inspection: Al Hurra's Programming Policies and Procedures." OIG Report No. ISP-IB-08–45 (2008).

18. Gary L. Ackerman, "Public Diplomacy in the Middle East and South Asia: Is the Message Getting Through," testimony before the House Subcommittee on the Middle East and South Asia of the Committee on Foreign Affairs, May 16, 2007.

19. United States Department of State, "Report of Inspection."

20. Focus group. Cairo, Egypt. March (2008).

21. Alvin Snyder, "The Great Alhurra Debate," *Worldcasting*, December 5, 2005, available online at: <http://uscpublicdiplomacy.com/index.php/newsroom/worldcast_ detail/051207_the_great_alhurra_debate>

22. Graham Messick, Michael Karzis, Dafna Linzer, and Michael Radutzky, "US-Funded Arab TV's Credibility Crisis," *CBS News & ProPublica*, June 22, 2008, available online at: <http://www.cbsnews.com/stories/2008/06/19/60minutes/main4196477.shtml>

23. Dafna Linzer, "Alhurra's Baghdad Bureau Mired in Controversy," *ProPublica*, July 8, 2008, available online at: <http://www.propublica.org/feature/alhurras-baghdad-bureau-mired-in-controversy-708/>

24. Ibid.

25. Ibid.

26. Ileana Ros-Lehtinen, "Letter to Howard L. Berman, Chairman, Committee on Foreign Affairs, US House of Representatives," June 23, 2008, available online at: <http:// s3.amazonaws.com/propublica/assets/alhurra/alhurra-investigation.pdf>

27. Shibley Telhami, "2008 Annual Arab Public Opinion Poll," *Survey of the Anwar Sadat Chair for Peace and Development at the University of Maryland with Zogby International* (2008).

28. For further detail, Telhami has posted the findings and raw data from his field work online at: <http://sadat.umd.edu/surveys/index.htm>
29. Broadcasting Board of Governors, "Broadcasting Board of Governors Corrects the CBS 60 Minutes Story about Alhurra Television," June 23, 2008, available online at: <http://www.bbg.gov/_bbg_news.cfm?articleID=243&mode=general>
30. Rugh, "Broadcasting and American Public Diplomacy."
31. United States Government Accountability Office, "US International Broadcasting," 4.
32. Daniel Nassif, "We Do Not Spread Propaganda for the United States," *Middle East Quarterly* XV, no. 2 (2008): 63–69.
33. Marc Lynch, "America and the Arab Media Environment," in *Engaging the Arab & Islamic Worlds Through Public Diplomacy*, ed. William A. Rugh (Washington, D.C.: Public Diplomacy Council, 2004), 90–108.
34. Rugh, "Broadcasting and American Public Diplomacy."
35. Focus group. Cairo, Egypt. March (2008).
36. Naomi Sakr, *Arab Television Today* (London: I.B. Tauris, 2007), 63.
37. Stig Hjarvard, "Mediated Encounters: An Essay on the Role of Communication Media in the Creation of Trust in the 'Global Metropolis,'" in *Global Encounters: Media and Cultural Transformation*, ed. Gitte Stald and Thomas Tufte (Luton, UK: University of Luton Press, 2002), 69–84, 80.
38. Kenneth Y. Tomlinson, "The Broadcasting Board of Governors: Finding the Right Media for the Message in the Middle East," testimony before the Senate Subcommittee on International Operations and Terrorism, April 29, 2004.
39. Broadcasting Board of Governors, "Radio Sawa and Alhurra TV: A Performance Update," June 20, 2008, available online at: < http://www.bbg.gov/reports/others/Alhurra-Sawa_Research_Data_June20–2%5B1%5D.ppt>
40. Cited in: Ellen McCarthy, "Va.-Based, US-Financed Arabic Channel Finds Its Voice," *Washington Post*, October 15, 2004, 01.
41. Cited in: Nancy Snow, "Al Hurra-Al Who?: Haven't Heard? We're Free, They're Not!" *Commondreams.org*, March 9, 2004, available online at: <http://www.commondreams.org/views04/0309–06.htm>
42. Kraidy, "Arab Media and US Policy," 5.
43. Focus group. Cairo, Egypt. March (2008).
44. Mohammed el-Nawawy, "US Public Diplomacy and the News Credibility of Radio Sawa and Television Al Hurra in the Arab World," in *New Media in the New Middle East*, ed. Philip Seib (New York: Palgrave Macmillan, 2007), 119–138.
45. Focus group. Cairo, Egypt. March (2008).
46. Snow, "Al Hurra-Al Who?"
47. Kraidy, "Arab Media and US Policy," 4.
48. Philip Seib, *The Al-Jazeera Effect* (Washington D.C.: Potomac Books, 2008), 52.
49. Marc Lynch, *Voices of the New Arab Public: Iraq, Al-Jazeera, and Middle East Politics Today* (New York: Columbia University Press, 2006).
50. Howard L. Berman, "Broadcasting Board of Governors and Alhurra Television," testimony, Hearing before the Subcommittee on Oversight and Investigations of the Committee on International Relations, November 10, 2005.
51. Kai Hafez, *The Myth of Media Globalization* (Cambridge, MA: Polity, 2007).
52. Nassif, "We Do Not Spread Propaganda," 66.

PART II
_____

From the Outside: Appraising American
Public Diplomacy

CHAPTER FOUR

The View from Russia

VICTORIA V. ORLOVA

American public diplomacy gained worldwide recognition during the cold war when the great battle for hearts and minds between the United States and the Soviet Union defined the epoch. The main agents of American public diplomacy, such as the United States Information Agency (USIA), Voice of America (VOA), and Radio Liberty, exported Western ideas to the Soviet people. Despite the Soviet propaganda of anti-Americanism and regular attempts to jam "enemy" radio broadcasting, Western ideas and beliefs penetrated the Iron Curtain. It was a double-edged informational weapon. U.S. radio gave the Soviets, who lived in an informational vacuum, a critical and truthful view of Soviet reality and kept their hopes alive, reporting about "another" life, promising great opportunities for everyone, freedom of expression, equal rights, and the free market.

Electronic Bridges

Articulating American values, the VOA promoted an appreciation of U.S. policies and culture and created a unique cross-cultural environment. Radio Liberty, focused on objective analysis of Soviet society, reported about the challenges of daily life in the Soviet Union. It served as an objective source of information, covered a wide range of issues (including dramatic events in Czechoslovakia in 1968 and in Helsinki in 1975), and acquainted the Soviet people with views of Soviet dissidents such as Andrei Sakharov and Alexander Solzhenitsyn and with literary works banned in USSR. During the period of glasnost, U.S. radio broadcasting remained a unique information source for the Soviet people. For instance, VOA's coverage of the Chernobyl disaster and its recommendations about avoiding radiation poisoning made the American voice vital and trustworthy for Russians, Ukrainians, and Eastern Europeans.

Another unique form of communication between the United States and the USSR was a live spacebridge, involving an interactive satellite TV link. It was people-to-people communication, public videoconferences like "interactive theatre," connecting American and Soviet publics in TV studios where participants discussed various themes. Spacebridges were launched in 1982, but became most significant in 1985–1986, when Vladimir Pozner, then a commentator on Gosteleradio, and Phil Donahue, a U.S. talk show host, held "Citizens' Summit" (Leningrad–Seattle) and "Citizens Summit-2: Women to Women" (Leningrad–Boston) in the context of glasnost in the Soviet Union. Public discussions involved controversial and provocative issues and quickly became enormously popular. The live communication deeply affected the Soviets and "transformed the Soviet public's image of itself."[1] Besides U.S. radio broadcasting, exchanges in culture, education, science, and technology between the United States and the Soviet Union were channels of influence and helped to promote American values among the Soviet people. Thus, soft power shaped social and psychological factors, accelerating changes inside Soviet society.

Analyzing a role of U.S. public diplomacy during the cold war, Carnes Lord and Helle C. Dale said, "There is every reason to conclude that American public diplomacy and psychological operations at the end of the Cold War measurably hastened the fall of the Soviet Union and the dissolution of the Communist world. In the end, ideas made a difference."[2] Not only ideas but also symbiosis of hard and soft power shaped the outcome of the determinative battle of the twentieth century.

President Ronald Reagan used public diplomacy while also deciding to end a détente-oriented decade and start a major military buildup.[3] The combination of U.S. soft power and effective political and military strategies inevitably led to political transformation in the Soviet Union. Also, Ronald Reagan and Mikhail Gorbachev achieved an incredible breakthrough, changing foreign policy priorities in ways that contributed to the end of the two nations' long-lasting confrontation. At the same time, Gorbachev's liberal ideas of glasnost, perestroika, and "new thinking" based on democratic values accelerated irreversible shifts in the Soviet Union. As Dimitri K. Simes, president of the Nixon Center, noted, Gorbachev's "dramatic reduction of Soviet subsidies for states in the Eastern bloc, his withdrawal of support for old-line Warsaw Pact regimes, and perestroika created totally new political dynamics in Eastern Europe and led to the largely peaceful disintegration of various communist regimes and the weakening of Moscow's influence in the region."[4]

The end of the cold war declared in 1989 at the Malta summit by Mikhail Gorbachev and George H. W. Bush evoked new hopes and high expectations. The world was further altered by the fast-paced processes of democratization in the Soviet Union that undermined the Soviet hierarchy and resulted in the collapse of the Communist system and the dissolution of the Soviet Union. That meant that the bipolar system was buried and world entered a new historical phase—a unipolar world under U.S. leadership.

It would seem that after the end of the ideological confrontation, former rival powers could come to mutual understanding, find common points of interests, and support collaboration in various spheres of life. These expectations came from the evolution of U.S.-Russian relations and a special attitude of the Russians toward the Americans.

America always evoked ambivalent feelings in the Soviet Union (and then in Russia). As the *Economist* wrote, "For much of the 20th century, the chief object of Russian admiration and revulsion has been the United States—the country that, with its combinations of fissiparous diversity and fierce patriotism, insularity and messianic sense of destiny, Russia arguably most resembles."[5] At the same time the basic differences between American and Soviet systems were so profound that neither elites nor publics had been able to find mediators to provide adequate communication linking the nations.[6] The long-term conflict between superpowers was based on polarization that increased competition and cultivated the image of "enemy." Unfortunately, this aspect of the U.S.-Russia relationship remains alive despite tectonic geopolitical and social shifts in the world.

Since the end of the cold war, relations between the United States and Russia have been awkward, unsteady, and have varied from strategic partnership to cold war-style antagonism. In recent years, they have deteriorated so much that they have evoked the specter of a new cold war. Stephen F. Cohen believes that U.S.-Russian relations "are worse today than they have been in twenty years,"[7] because the two nations face as many serious conflicts as they did during the cold war.

Collisions over NATO's eastward expansion, the antiballistic missile treaty, nuclear proliferation, engaging Iran, and issues involving Ukraine, Georgia, Belarus, and Venezuela led to a growing rift between the United States and Russia. A report on U.S.-Russian relations initiated in 2005 by the Carnegie Endowment for International Peace and the Moscow Polity Foundation revealed that "1) U.S.-Russian relations are no longer central to the international system, or even (albeit to a different degree) to either country; 2) Washington's ability to influence Russian domestic developments and Moscow's ability to influence U.S. foreign policy are very limited; 3) U.S.-Russian relations are essentially asymmetrical, not merely in the sense of the disparity in the roles the two countries are playing on the world stage, but even more so as far as their current and future needs and interests toward each other are concerned."[8]

The Ineffectiveness of Soft Power

American soft power has lost its influence in Russia for two principal reasons. First, since the early 1990s Russia has been neglected by the U.S. government. Second, Russia, after addressing tremendous challenges and transformations in its post-Soviet development, since 2003 has tried to diminish any U.S. impact on Russia's internal politics to avoid destabilizing effects in Russian society.

Why did once mighty U.S. public diplomacy fail to influence Russia? Given that hard power dominates in U.S.-Russia relations today, can we regard American public diplomacy as a failure?

Seeking reasons for the ineffectiveness of U.S. public diplomacy efforts, many researchers considered the successful U.S. soft power experience during the cold war. However, the cold war model of public diplomacy cannot be implemented today. In the bipolar world the United States had *one* ideological "enemy," so it aimed the mightiest informational weapon and hard power resources at *one* target. What about today? America needs to spread public diplomacy activities around the world, because strategically important regions are elsewhere: Iraq, Iran, Afghanistan, China, the European Union.... The list is long. This post-cold war world, "engaged in a vast remapping of the relationship of the state to images, messages, and information within its boundaries,"[9] demands new methods and principles of fulfilling state policies, including public diplomacy. Global net society made world leaders, policy makers, media, and nonofficial actors develop sophisticated strategies to create spheres of influence and markets for loyalties in the highly competitive information space. In the "global village," without information boundaries and strong ideological barriers, the implementation of effective public diplomacy is increasingly difficult.

The Internet and new media have complicated public diplomacy because they require special skills to define and find target audiences in a very fragmented communication field. Further, failures in strategic communication between nations occur because of transformations in geopolitics and increasing rivalry of great powers. In a fast-changing multicivilizational world or, as the *Economist* said, a "neo-polar world, in which old alliances and rivalries are bumping up against each other in new ways,"[10] public diplomacy's ability to influence a target state is difficult.

It makes sense to analyze U.S. public diplomacy through the prism of U.S.-Russian relations since the crucial historical point—the dissolution of the Soviet Union. The euphoria at the end the 1980s stimulated by freedom and convergence with the West has evaporated. Russia has entered a new decade that had been one of the most painful and desperate periods in its history. When Vladimir Putin called the collapse of the Soviet Union the greatest geopolitical catastrophe of the twentieth century, he did not mean he was nostalgic for the Soviet Empire, as many Westerners interpreted this statement. As Stephen F. Cohen noted, "No one in authority anywhere had ever foreseen that one of the twentieth century's two superpowers would plunge, along with its arsenals of destruction, into such catastrophic circumstances."[11] Ideological and economic decay after the end of the Soviet Union deprived Russia of its status and identity; people felt themselves disoriented and humiliated, many of them, including among the Russian intelligentsia, suffered from poverty. Western ideas promoted by United States and other Western public diplomats seemed elusive for the majority of disappointed Russians, who "experienced a collective inferiority complex."[12] It was the time of the next turn in the Russian mass consciousness, which shaped Russia's skeptical attitude toward Western ideas and democracy. Instead of a wealthy Western society, the nation, recently a superpower, plunged into severe depression and ideological turmoil. Nevertheless, in 1991–1993, a majority of Russians (approximately 70 percent) held positive views about the United States.[13] That was the appropriate moment for U.S. soft power to help Russia to recover from the post-Soviet fever.

But after the United States had declared itself the winner of the cold war, its attitude toward Russia began to change. Once a powerful rival, Russia was now plagued by political instability, economic crisis, and corruption, and no longer was viewed by the United States as a threat or a state of strategic importance.

During the early 1990s, a high priority for Western governments was (or should have been) to help Russia create its new political and economic environment. According to Lilia Shevtsova, "Most of the Western leaders, however, were not only unprepared for an ambitious program of assisting Russia's transformation, they failed to see how much was at the stake as the new Russian state took shape or to appreciate its potential impact on the world whether it succeeded or failed."[14]

Nevertheless, throughout the 1990s the United States funded hundreds of programs, including exchanges, technical assistance, and financial aid to promote democracy in Russia. U.S. officials hoped to facilitate "the transfer of democratic ideas into Russia."[15] Michael McFaul pointed out that the funds for democratic programs were limited while economic assistance for market promotion took the lion's share of U.S. budgets. This imbalance was a mistake, wrote McFaul, because "aid to stimulate market reforms without accompanying resources to foster democratic development is simply money wasted."[16]

Much of the democracy promotion came from American nongovernmental organizations (NGOs), which provided Russians with ideas about competitive elections, a multiparty system, and civil society. U.S. Agency for International Development with the National Endowment for Democracy funded the National Democratic Institute, the Free Trade Union Institute, the International Republican Institute, and sponsored various democratic assistance programs of such organizations as the Eurasia Foundation, Internews, and others. However, U.S. foreign policy strategies and public diplomacy efforts in Russia were inadequate and unsuccessful. McFaul noted that "while American NGO's may have been helpful in *designing* institutions associated with democratic states, to date they have done little to affect how these institutions *function*."[17]

The Clinton-Yeltsin era was marked by Russia's disastrous economic reforms based on Western programs and schemes. "Shock therapy" through radical economic measures resulted in national destabilization, corruption, the emergence of oligarchic clans, and mass poverty. Russians, disappointed by reforms, believed that the United States had intentionally imposed "wrong" ways of development to destroy its old rival. According to a survey of Russian adults, sponsored by the U.S. Department of State Office of Research, from 1995 to 2000 a majority of the Russian public believed "that the United States was utilizing Russia's weakness to reduce it to a second-rate power." Subscribers to this belief increased in impressive progression. In 1995, 59 percent of Russians believed this statement; in 1997, 71 percent; in 1999, 76 percent; in 2000, 81 percent.[18] Certainly, this public opinion was shaped mainly by messages of the Russian government openly blaming the United States for failed reforms in Russia.

Accusations that the United States has attempted to weaken and destabilize Russia have become a new mantra of Russia's foreign policy. This trend has led to negative consequences in U.S.-Russian relations, creating an atmosphere of mistrust and suspicion, fuelling various conspiracy theories, and presenting a challenge to U.S. public diplomacy.

In fact, after the dissolution of the Soviet Union and the demise of the Communist bloc, the U.S. government apparently regarded public diplomacy as a cold war relic. It reduced foreign operating expenses, cut academic and cultural exchanges, and funding of U.S. radio broadcasting. Along with the demolition of the USIA in 1998, these changes led to disarray in public diplomacy activity. Meanwhile, in Russia the VOA and Radio Liberty began to lose their exclusivity and popularity because of increasing competition with new Russian radio services and other media.

The Yugoslav war campaign initiated by the United States in March 1999 led U.S.-Russia relations to the crucial point: the Belgrade bombing and Serbia air strikes by NATO evoked deeply negative attitude to the United States among the Russian elite and broader public. The first NATO enlargement included former members of the Warsaw pact—the Czech Republic, Hungary, and Poland—and did considerable damage to relations between the United States and Russia. Dimitri K. Simes emphasized that "most Russians were prepared to accept NATO enlargement as an unhappy but unthreatening development—until the 1999 Kosovo crisis. When NATO went to war against Serbia, despite strong Russian objections and without approval from the UN Security Council, the Russian elite and the Russian people quickly came to the conclusion that they had been profoundly misled and that NATO remained directed against them. Great powers—particularly great powers in decline—do not appreciate such demonstrations of their irrelevance."[19] As a result, in a survey conducted in April 1999, Russia's attitude toward America reflected a dramatic change: only 33 percent of Russians kept their positive views about the United States while 53 percent expressed negative opinions.[20]

The Post-9/11 Opportunity

After the terrorist attacks on the United States on September 11, 2001, there was a real opportunity for improving relations between Moscow and Washington. Russia's president, Vladimir Putin was the first world leader who personally called George W. Bush to support him in a tragic moment. He provided intelligence assistance during the U.S. antiterrorist campaign in Afghanistan and coordinated with Central Asian nations to allow U.S. forces to use military bases of the former Soviet Union. Such an attitude seemed to mark a breakthrough in U.S.-Russian relations and gave a hope that both nations would cooperate not only in fighting the war on terror but also in other fields. Western and Russian policy makers welcomed this sudden turn in global affairs. When the NATO-Russia Council was created in 2002, the *Economist* noted, "After 70 years of blind-alley communism, and ten more of drift, Mr Putin is making a determined bid for Russia to end its self-estrangement and join the concert of developed, democratic countries, alongside America and Europe."[21] Unfortunately, mutual understanding between United States and Russia was short-lived, and Russia's movement toward a full partnership with the United States did not last.

Russia hoped Washington would estimate its support and therefore the relationship would be more balanced and productive. However, as Stephen F. Cohen stressed, "Instead, it got U.S. withdrawal from the ABM treaty, Washington's claim to permanent bases in Central Asia (as well as Georgia) and independent access to Caspian oil and gas, a second round of NATO expansion taking in several former Soviet republics and bloc members, and a still-growing indictment of its domestic and foreign conduct."[22] The Bush administration remained indifferent about Russian interests and needs and did not take into account Russia's reactions to the U.S. policy.

The Iraq war, initiated by the United States in 2003, became the next dramatic point in relations between Moscow and Washington and finally destroyed all hope for strategic partnership. An overwhelming majority of Russians condemned the American invasion. There was a huge decline in positive attitude toward America, reinforced by reports on Abu Ghraib cruelty incidents and misleading American statements about the threat of biological attacks posed by Iraq.

Remarkably, after September 11, 2001, U.S. public diplomacy activity in Russia continued to decrease. The United States shifted the main resources of soft power to the Middle East and the Islamic world. At the same time, the U.S. Broadcasting Board of Governors (BBG) cut funding for VOA programming in Eastern Europe, the Caucasus, and Central Asia. As Mitchell Polman noted, "While much energy and attention has gone to improve understanding of America and its policies in those regions, another important sphere has been neglected."[23] That important sphere was Russia.

Instead, in 2003–2004 the United States chose other strategic regions for the public diplomacy focus: Georgia and Ukraine. "Color" revolutions in former Soviet republics supported by the United States have widened the gap between Moscow and Washington. As Fyodor Lukianov noted, "the Russian authorities believe that American nongovernmental organizations can have a significant impact on political atmosphere in Russia. The 'orange' revolution in Ukraine in 2004 became a turning point in Russian government's perception and interpretation of US public diplomacy efforts. Obviously, that was a moment of disappointment for the Russian authorities admitted their own failures of soft power and official diplomacy. Then, they took into account all the lessons of 'orange' revolution and made those dangerous factors that deeply affected the situation in Ukraine to vanish from Russia's political and social environment."[24]

During the first decade of the new century, the first priority for Russian authorities has been the consolidation of power and stability inside Russian society. To make Russia stable and its internal politics invulnerable, the Kremlin developed strategies for defense from internal and foreign "enemies."

Attempts to dispose of all the possible and impossible enemies were made by Russian officials long before the "orange" threat. In 2002, the Peace Corps program that had more than 700 volunteers in programs such as teaching English and conducting business education classes was closed. Russia's Federal Security Service charged some Peace Corps volunteers with spying, accusing them of collecting information on the social, political, and economic situation in Russian regions. The U.S. Embassy dismissed the charges as groundless.[25]

As the *Guardian* wrote, "the Kremlin's 'political technologists'... have identified NGOs as the new soft-power battlefield between Russia and the West."[26] In 2006, Russia suspended the activities of Human Rights Watch, Amnesty International, the International Republican Institute, the National Democratic Institute, and more than ninety other foreign

NGOs, alleging they failed to meet the registration requirements of a new law governing the activities of NGOs. Under this law all foreign NGOs have to submit paperwork to win government approval for their continued activities. After selection by Russian lawmakers, ninety-nine foreign NGOs remained in Russia, including the American Chamber of Commerce, the Ford Foundation, and the Carnegie Moscow Center.[27]

Since 2005, Russia has begun to look more stable and assertive. It recovered after the years of instability, terror threats, and attacks, and Chechen war campaigns. The long-waited stability was followed by not only growing flows of "petrodollars" and dividends from high prices on energy resources but also centralization and a hard hierarchy of power that resulted in a lack of strong liberal opposition and democracy initiatives. Nevertheless, Russia's stability and self-sufficiency has improved lives of many Russians. Charismatic Vladimir Putin has become enormously popular. Being strongly supported by the Russian media, especially federal television, he was regarded as the most trusted Russian leader in the post-Soviet period. As Putin's power increased, the U.S. policy toward Russia toughened. This was reflected in Dick Cheney's Vilnius speech in May 2006, in which he highlighted undemocratic trends in Russia's policy.

Russia's disappointment in U.S. policies as well as irritation from endless harsh remarks of U.S. policy makers and media persuaded the Russian authorities to follow their own path without the West. As Dmitri Trenin described this process, "Russia saw itself as Pluto in the Western solar system, very far from the center but still fundamentally a part of it. Now it has left that orbit entirely: Russia's leaders have given up on becoming part of the West and have started creating their own Moscow-centered system."[28] Until recently, Russia's intention to be an equal rival of its historical opponent seemed unrealistic, and the United States and the rest of the West did not take it seriously. However, "Russia's ultimate interest is the status of a major world power, on par with the United States and China."[29]

The divorce from the West was enforced by assumptions that "as a big country, Russia is essentially friendless; no great power wants a strong Russia, which would be a formidable competitor, and many want a weak Russia that they could exploit and manipulate."[30] This approach has not emerged spontaneously. If "both the George H. W. Bush and Clinton administrations worked to give the Russians a place at the table" and tried to create government cooperation (the

Gore-Chernomyrdin Commission, the invitation to join the G-7), the George W. Bush administration "has long seemed to be sending the message that Russian interests were simply of no importance in Washington."[31] The strategic partnership, declared by the United States, turned out to be an illusion especially after the intentions to provide NATO membership for Ukraine and Georgia. Even the cold war Jackson-Vanik amendment remains in place "to punish Russians" despite American officials having promised to exempt Russia from this cold war legacy.[32]

These issues contributed to a huge deficit of trust between both states and at the same time encouraged Russia's independence and strength. American public diplomacy was unable to cope with U.S. "official" indifference to Russia and Russia's hostility toward foreign influence. Soft power has failed because the U.S. administration ignored Russia's changes and perceived Russia as a weak country that did not deserve much attention. The United States remained in the old paradigm of relations while Russia began to assert itself on the global stage. Russia's self-confidence reflected the Kremlin's perceptions of "the profound sense of disorientation in Western nations as how to build a new world order; the U.S. setback in Iraq and growing global hostility to American hegemony; and the crisis of 'color revolutions,' which so alarmed the Russian elite."[33]

Vladimir Putin reflected this in his speech at the Munich conference on national security on February 10, 2007, where without "excessive politeness" he explained Russia's vision of the world order under U.S. leadership. Although ideas about vulnerability of a unipolar world, where "no one feels safe anymore" and America's hegemony challenges were not new for Westerners, because all these issues were widely discussed in Western political circles and media, Putin's speech was regarded as harsh. "Munich signified above all a tactical change in Russian foreign policy, a change from grumbling about U.S. actions to very public opposition to the U.S. policy; from complaining about the way Russia's interests were being ignored to taking unilateral actions to protect and project these interests."[34]

Russian authorities regard many principles of today's world order as irrelevant and illegitimate. This has heightened tensions, so that "with every action that Russia takes to defy the existing order, there are stronger calls from Western countries to exclude Russia further from the international system. In return, Russian rhetoric has heated up."[35] The Georgia crisis in August 2008 again confirmed this trend.

Georgia 2008

The Caucasus five-day war, beginning with Georgia's attacks on Tskhinvali and ending with Georgia's defeat at the hands of the Russian Army, plunged U.S.-Russian relations to the iciest point in the post-Soviet era. Analyzing the aftermath of the Caucasus crisis, Michael McFaul admitted that "the U.S.-Russian bilateral relationship is largely empty... For too long, Russian and American officials have pursued policies unilaterally, without engaging in bilateral diplomacy beforehand."[36]

The escalation of the Georgia crisis was profound. Russia's military actions in a response to the Georgian-Ossetian conflict were condemned by U.S. officials as aggressive and disproportionate. The Kremlin's unilateral decision to recognize South Ossetia and Abkhazia as independent states impressed and alarmed the West, which decided that Russia wanted to "redraw the map of the strategically vital region on the Black Sea."[37] In return, Vladimir Putin, in an interview with CNN, suggested that the United States had orchestrated the conflict in Georgia. Russian experts did not understand "how could it happen that, given the heavy US presence and involvement in Georgia, including its military establishment, it did not know about Mikheil Saakashvili's plan of attack."[38]

Aggressive anti-Russian rhetoric dominated Western media coverage. Russia limited news media access to its official and war information, and failed to provide the West with credible reports. That allowed Mikheil Saakashvili, Georgia's president, to reach out to a worldwide audience. In global media reports Saakashvili repeatedly produced fake messages highlighting that it was Russia that started the war after the long-term planning of the Georgia invasion. Although there was evidence that he himself had brought about the war by attacking Tskhinvali, many people believed him and viewed Russia as the aggressor. Russia's actions were compared with the Soviet invasions of Hungary, Czechoslovakia, and Afghanistan, and even with Hitler's Germany. These absurd messages deeply influenced the global audience.

The conflict was complicated by misinformation from both sides. If one side highlighted the scope of Georgia's destruction and omitted reports about Ossetians, the other side exaggerated number of Ossetian victims. While hardline views were dominant, it is worth noting that U.S. ambassador to Russia, John Beyrle, tried to ease tensions. Interviewed by *Kommersant*, he said that the Russian army gave a well-grounded response to the Georgian attack on Russian peacekeepers although as he noted, Moscow had gone too far and violated Georgia's territorial integrity. Ambassador Beyrle also emphasized that Saakashvili acted without the consent of the United States and against the advice of the United States.[39]

Anatol Lieven noted, "U.S. society is much more open and democratic than Russian society; but this is no longer necessarily true of American politicians or Washington elites when it comes to key issues of foreign policy. As for most of the U.S. media, its response to the war over South Ossetia demonstrated that it can on occasion be every bit as hysterically one-sided and willfully inaccurate as the Russian one. Indeed, in this case it was parts of the U.S. media which told by far the biggest single lie—namely the outrageous suggestion, in the face of all the known facts, that it was Russia and not Georgia that started this latest war."[40]

As in all postmodern wars, this conflict instantly became a media war involving all the participants and global community in a struggle among contesting interpretations and claims about the consequences of the crisis. The main problem for Russia in this crisis was the inability to advance and defend its statements on the global stage, because it "has not yet developed effective mechanisms and strategies to win global recognition of its interests and actions."[41] In contrast with Western leaders, who supported their war operations with extensive public relations and media campaigns, Russia looked almost silent and in the end faced an informational blackout. As Dmitri Trenin noted, "Russia has not been able to make good use of its soft power. More than a set of slogans, it needs a positive international agenda of its own."[42]

After enduring anti-Russian campaigns in the Western political and media environment, Russia bounced back. Russian President Dmitri Medvedev and Prime Minister Putin gave numerous interviews to global media, explaining their views of the situation, and invited Western scholars and policy makers to the Valdai Discussion Club, which helped to reduce tensions.

In the Georgian conflict, hard power and government-to-government diplomacy dominated while soft power was downplayed. "The war in the Caucasus has been a tragedy with global and long-term consequences. Cataloguing the errors of judgment made by western policy makers, their failure to manage relations with Russia and who did what to start the South Ossetian war does not help to resolve the present crisis," admitted Denis Corboy, a former EU Ambassador to Georgia and director of the Caucasus Policy Institute at King's College in London.[43]

Meanwhile, U.S. policy makers attempted to cool the heated rhetoric between Moscow and Washington using soft power. Scholars and experts from the Brookings Institution, the Carnegie Endowment for International Peace, the New American Foundation, and the Nixon Center, as well as some media professionals focused their attention on U.S.-Russian relations in the context of the aftermath of the Caucasus crisis, and they began to discuss the situation and seek possible solutions to this crisis. Former Secretaries of State Henry A. Kissinger and George P. Shultz, contended that "isolating Russia is not sustainable long-range policy" and argued that the "drift toward confrontation must be ended." Instead, they noted, "the fundamental interests of the United States, Europe and Russia are more aligned today—or can be made so—even in the wake of the Georgian crisis, than at any point in recent history."[44] Michael McFaul, one of the leading experts on Russia, offered numerous comments in global media, including the Russian magazine *"The New Times."* Anatol Lieven contributed his viewpoints on the Georgia conflict and reported about the Valdai Club conference with Dmitri Medvedev and Vladimir Putin to various media. Such discussions helped to clarify reasons for the conflict and provided a better understanding of Russia's position.

Good examples of public diplomacy are the online debates in Oxford style at the *Economist* Web site that feature pro and contra speakers, featured guests, and more than 500 online participants, who in one instance voted on and commented on the proposition "The West should be bolder in its response to a newly assertive Russia." The "pro" speaker was Anne-Marie Slaughter, dean of the Woodrow Wilson School of Public and International Affairs at Princeton University, and the "con" speaker was Dmitri V. Trenin, deputy director of the Carnegie Moscow Center. The debates were emotional and controversial and ended with final vote 52 percent pro and 48 percent con. This kind of debate, which reaches a large audience, is one facet of modern public diplomacy.

Consolidating "smart" soft power produced by politicians, scholars, journalists, and businessmen has helped a broader public to understand U.S.-Russian tensions and consider ways to repair bridges between the two countries while they can still be fixed. This approach has room for varied viewpoints. Journalist Michael Zygar of *Kommersant* noted that "American public diplomacy often reflects mainly neoconservative viewpoints, expressed by the Bush administration, while it is essential to show the Russians another, pluralistic, America demonstrating a huge variety of opinions."[45]

The Georgia crisis revealed not only Russia's failure to use soft power's tools to advance its interests but also that U.S. public diplomacy could not find leverage for a constructive dialogue with Russia. The trend toward confrontation between the United States and Russia has accelerated in recent years and has underscored the communication gap between American and Russian political actors, opinion makers and publics that fostered misunderstanding about key policy issues in both countries. The conflict in the Caucasus revealed that twenty years after the cold war the two nations could not find a common language. This led policy makers to think about the vulnerability of any new world order.

Given the recent state of relations between Washington and Moscow, is there a chance for U.S. public diplomacy to promote U.S. national interests and shape Russian public opinion? How could public diplomacy cut through all the controversial issues in U.S.-Russian relations? What tools should public diplomats use to implement this task?

"Today's public diplomacy cannot reinvent all that has been done by officials,"[46] said Fyodor Lukianov. It is true, especially if we admit that there are few public diplomacy tools to carry out soft power's mission in Russia. Traditional public diplomacy agents such as U.S. radio services are almost invisible in the highly competitive and fragmented media environment and cannot attract a big audience. Moreover, their activity in Russia has diminished in recent years. In 2006, Russian regulators found license violations and unauthorized changes in programming of VOA and Radio Free Europe/Radio Liberty and forced more than sixty local stations to stop broadcasting news reports produced by both radio services[47]. In July 2008, under the U.S. BBG decision, the VOA Russian Service stopped broadcasting in Russia, leaving its Russian-language content only on the Internet.

Some American public diplomacy specialists were upset by this decision, but radio is not particularly popular in Russia, and so its influence is limited. According to a BBC/Reuters/Media Center Poll, the most important news source for Russians is television (mentioned first by 74 percent of those polled). Only 9 percent of Russian citizens give the priority to newspapers and 6 percent to radio. Television claims the highest level of trust: 84 percent of Russians trust "in television." Three federal TV channels considered most trustworthy are Channel One (mentioned by 36 percent), NTV (16 percent), and RTR (15 percent).[48]

As Walter Lippmann noted, "we cannot choose between true or false account... So, we choose between trustworthy and untrustworthy reporters."[49] To improve the U.S. image in Russia, the American media need to be trusted. So far, opinions about Russia and its policy in the American media reveal dramatic misunderstandings and misperceptions of Russian reality in the United State. Some publications about Russia are reminiscent of cold war reporting, filled with clichés, flawed analysis, and fundamental inaccuracies.

Stereotypes about Russia are amazingly widespread, and they result in biased and distorted media images that can influence global publics. "That Russia is often misunderstood, and worst-case scenarios are at the top of many people's minds, is not particularly surprising, in view of the Soviet Union's history, the cold war and more ancient prejudices. 'The Hun' lives on, only now he is known as the Russian bear."[50] After the Georgia crisis the Russian bear prowled through Western news media.

Cultural Linkage

During the cold war rival powers thoroughly studied their adversaries' politics, culture, and social life. The scope of research was very impressive. The Soviet books written by Americanists about American life, mass culture, and alternative cultural trends in music, movies, and literature were so interesting that they contributed, presumably unintentionally, to the promotion of the American way among Soviet citizens. In the United States, there were numerous research centers on Soviet studies. However, when the object of research—the Soviet Union—vanished, the attention to Russia was significantly decreased. Stephen Cohen noted that during the cold war his lectures at Princeton University were enormously popular; approximately 400 students attended his course about the USSR then, while in the 1990s only 145 students each semester were interested in Russia.[51] American Sovietologists included prominent scholars and policy makers such as Anders Aslund, Stephen Cohen, Anatol Lieven, Marshal Goldman, Rose Gottemoeller, Andrew Kuchins, Michael McFaul, and many others. They continue their research about Russia, but what about younger scholars?

Negative and sometimes nasty opinions about Russia emanating from America have affected the social and political atmosphere in Russia. The U.S. image hardly benefits from among this Russian intellectual elites and well-educated young people who are fluent in English and who regularly read the U.S. press and watch American television.

Thoughtful and competent reports about Russia in the American media strengthen the image of the United States in Russia. Certainly, interactive channels of communication between U.S. and Russian publics can be effective, especially for younger audiences. For instance, the Russian blog of the *New York Times* community presents reports about Russia translated into Russian. In return, comments from Russian bloggers in English are posted on the *Times* Web site. Discussions are devoted to various events in political and social life, involving many provocative issues, such as the Georgia conflict or Russia's economic problems. In August 2008, for example, Russian bloggers were invited by the *Times* to answer the following questions: (1) What should Russia's aims be in Georgia? (2) Did Russia overreact? (3) How much is America to blame? (4) Who is in charge: Putin or Medvedev? (5) What international leaders can Russia trust? The project is very attractive for Russian bloggers, who were given the opportunity to present their opinions on the Web site of the influential and respected American newspaper.

Influential federal Russian newspapers and magazines and television channels thoughtfully cover internal and foreign policy of the United States, and usually refrain from hostile commentary. As a rule, they provide detailed reports, although some controversial issues concerning global affairs and relations with Russia may be critical. For instance, reporting about the Serbia air strikes in 1999, the Salt Lake City Olympics judging in 2002 (allegedly biased against Russian athletes), the Iraq war, NATO expansion, and other such issues naturally hardened Russians' attitude toward the United States.

Public opinion about the United States in Russia is flexible and dependent on official positions articulated by Russian policy makers. The public's attitude toward Americans can be positive but if signs of deterioration in U.S.-Russian relations appear, the Russian people may at once change their attitude. So-called spontaneous anti-Americanism can seize Russian society for some time and then disappear. As Lev Gudkov, director of the Levada Center, a Russian independent polling service, has observed, Russians are easy manageable because they are receptive to stereotypes, including those crafted by the Russian government and media. As a result, the polarization scheme "we" and "they" is again alive. *They* are the Americans, not only an adversary in terms of wielding global influence, but also a powerful anti-Russian force.[52]

As a result of the deterioration in U.S.-Russian relations after the 2008 Georgia crisis, anti-American moods in Russia rose as never before since the beginning of the century. According to the Levada center,

67 percent of Russians had a bad opinion of the United States in mid-September 2008, while only 23 percent expressed a good opinion.[53] Another research center, the Public Opinion Foundation, revealed that 75 percent of Russians regarded the United States as "unfriendly state" (the highest point since 2001), and only 10 percent as "friendly" (the lowest point since 2001).[54] According to the survey, 71 percent believed that the United States played a negative role in today's world (those polled thought that the United States is a "hegemonic state that doesn't care about anybody"—21 percent; "aggressive state"—20 percent). Only 4 percent found a positive role of the United States.[55]

Meanwhile more Americans began to see Russia as a "dangerous" state. A 2008 Pew report revealed that the proportion naming Russia as top danger had significantly increased from 2 percent in February 2007 to 14 percent in September 2008. At the same time, the survey found that relatively few Americans (18 percent) view Russia as an adversary: far more (48 percent) say Russia is a serious problem but not an adversary.[56]

The Business Connection

In an unstable and multicivilizational world, where governments' soft power policies meet serious challenges, business and private actors as mediators of public diplomacy matter a lot. As a rule, sound educational and analytical background and professional competence make them ideal self-sufficient agents, independent from external, including official, influence. The convergence of business and public diplomacy activity can be successful because today's global business is deeply engaged in global politics and international affairs. As Dmitri Trenin noted, "in the age of globalization, any country's behavior is best moderated by the forces of the market."[57] For instance, global financial crisis in 2008, reached its apogee just after the Caucasus conflict, made all the sides— Americans, Russians, and others—feel that they all were in the same boat. Debates about a new cold war, sanctions against Russia, frightening scenarios of Russian aggression in Crimea, geopolitical games in Central Asia—all these dire prospects that seemed so menacing after the Caucasus conflict were pushed aside after the severe decline in world markets in September–October 2008. "Business first" has cooled and diverted pragmatic political leaders. In contrast with politicians, businessmen often just calculate consequences of a difficult situation and try to find the leverage they need to secure suitable outcomes.

Thus, Edward Verona, the president of the U.S.-Russia Business Council, in his comments to "Assertive Russia," the *Economist* online debates on the aftermath of the Georgia crisis, said, "In a sense, business has served as a stabilizing factor during difficult times, providing an avenue for co-operation and a force for positive economic and social change within Russia. We hope business activity will continue to exert a moderating influence between the two countries in this period of heightened tensions, certainly the worst that we have seen since the end of the cold war. Serious political differences between the two countries exist and will likely defy resolution in the near or intermediate term; and this will undoubtedly have economic repercussions."[58] He emphasized that "unilateral economic sanctions would likely be ineffective and potentially cause greater harm to our own business interests than to the intended target. Western trade and investment has exerted a generally healthy influence on Russian corporate governance and transparency, and enabled the emergence of a consumer-oriented middle class that is a catalyst for civil society and—one hopes—for eventual political reform. Business has engaged by and large with the more progressive elements of Russian society and politics. There is a risk that economic sanctions could inadvertently undermine those elements and reinforce the more reactionary ones."[59]

U.S.-Russian business communication and collaboration can enhance relations between nations, improve the political atmosphere, and make cooperation trustful. The American Chamber of Commerce in Russia, the largest foreign business organization in Russia, supports the trade and investment interests of more than 800 member companies and presses for regulatory improvements that could strengthen a business-friendly environment in the Russian Federation. The chamber offers assistance to individual company members in resolving problems, and it provides business development opportunities through its networking events.[60]

The Foundation for Russian American Economic Cooperation (FRAEC) serves as a forefront interconnected grassroots organizations, the private sector, regional officials, and federal decision makers. The Training and Exchanges Division of FRAEC educates and unites Russian, Eurasian, and American communities. U.S.-RFE Municipal Partnership Program is generously supported by the American people through the United States Agency for International Development. The Russian American Pacific Partnership encourages commercial cooperation between U.S. West Coast and the Russian Far East.[61]

A Washington-based trade association, the U.S.-Russia Business Council (USRBC) provides significant business development, government relations, and market intelligence services to its American and Russian member companies. The council also helps to resolve specific commercial disputes and to influence Russian policies that negatively affect their business in Russia. For Russian companies, the USRBC leverages relationships with major industry players, international finance organizations, and U.S. government agencies to assist in strategic planning and in partner searches.[62] Besides financial activity, the USRBC encourages conferences and cultural events. For instance, in October 2008 the USRBC agenda involved political discussions such as *"Can Perestroika Survive? A Conversation about the Changing Political and Cultural Reforms in Russia from Gorbachev to Putin"* and Woodrow Wilson Center offered *"Rethinking Russia and U.S.-Russian Relations: The Role of Russia in the Global World Order."* The council supports also cultural events, such as a celebrations week honoring Russia's great musician and Washington's beloved conductor Maestro Rostropovich on the occasion of the seventy-fifth anniversary of the National Symphony Orchestra.[63]

Public diplomacy exists in complex interdependent systems. If public diplomacy actors create structures and channels of communication between economists, businessmen, and politicians, then they can expect encouraging developments. Private agents, free from bureaucratic barriers, can significantly help in accomplishing public diplomacy tasks. "The best way to practice public diplomacy is through ordinary people. In many cases, only private actors have the credibility to make a difference."[64] Influential private actors provide venues for public-private diplomatic interaction, such as the World Economic Forum; public-private actors are involved in national brand-building; and private individual agents and firms are engaged in public diplomacy on behalf of governments.[65] "Engaging private actors in public diplomacy activity is one of the best strategies for today's public diplomacy," said Nina Belyaeva, head of the Public Policy Department at the Moscow High School of Economics. "The private sector free from bureaucratic obstacles can support multiple contacts with the public, reach target groups and carry out public diplomacy mission."[66]

Educational and cultural exchanges initiated by the U.S. government traditionally matter because they are mainly addressed to younger audiences and have a long-term effect, increasing understanding between Americans and Russians. Fulbright programs offer wide opportunities and an impressive range of research topics and fields for Russian and American students, teachers, scholars, educators, and professionals. Exchange programs include "The Future Leaders Secondary School Exchange" (FLEX) and Global Undergraduate Exchange Program funded by the U.S. government. The U.S. Embassy supervises a variety of people-to-people programs, involving citizens, research institutions, and NGOs; oversees "The Hubert H. Humphrey Program" for midcareer professionals and "Opportunity Initiative" that provides financial aid for highly qualified students. The community of Russian alumni of U.S. Government-funded exchange programs includes more than 55,000 people.

Besides educational programs, the U.S. Embassy organizes various cultural events, art exhibitions, concerts, American film festivals, supports American Centers (Libraries), and the American Corners—all these activities are a valuable contribution to cultural diplomacy that allows reducing stereotypes and promoting mutual understanding between the United States and Russia. Cultural diplomacy is an essential part of today's U.S. public diplomacy because it reaches younger, well-educated, talented Russians, creates a unique cross-cultural environment, and fosters common values.

Conclusion

In general, successful public diplomacy should be adjusted to each target state or region to meet challenges, use opportunities, and calculate possible outcomes and consequences for national interests and for world society.

In case of Russia, U.S. public diplomacy efforts are unlikely to be effective unless American attitudes and foreign policy toward Russia are changed. As Michael McFaul said, "The United States does not have enough leverage over Russia to influence internal change through coercive means. Only a strategy of linkage is available. However paradoxical, a more substantive agenda at the state-to-state level would create more permissive conditions for greater Western engagement with Russian society. A new American policy toward Russia must pursue both—a more ambitious bilateral relationship in conjunction with a more long-term strategy for strengthening Russian civil, political, and economic societies, which ultimately will be the critical forces that push Russia back onto a democratizing path."[67]

Without positive signs in U.S.-Russian relations, American public diplomacy will not be able to affect the Russians. Both the United States and Russia recognize it. Dmitri Trenin believes that "A strong relationship with the United States is indispensable to Russia's modernization, economic integration, and security"[68] while Steven Pifer emphasized that "the greater the interest that Moscow has in the bilateral relationship, the greater the leverage Washington has with Moscow."[69]

So, the first priority for successful U.S. public diplomacy in Russia is a tight relationship between countries based on mutual understanding, shared interests, economic cooperation, cultural, and social values. Public diplomats should create a U.S.-Russian communication infrastructure involving various politicians, economists, businessmen, experts, scholars, and media actors. As the Carnegie Moscow Center's experts said, "With the Cold War being history for over a dozen years, there is no sense in the Russo-American relationship continuing to be reduced to Kremlin-White House contacts alone."[70]

There is a need to foster bilateral efforts of soft power. Without Russian participation, strategic communication between the United States and Russia is impossible. Edward Lozansky, president of the American University in Moscow, underlined that "the dialogue between American and Russian expert community and publics can strengthen soft power of both nations. It is necessary to provide the Americans full and objective information about the most important events in Russia and U.S.-Russian relations, send press-releases in the American media, governmental organizations, think tanks, regularly hold seminars, conferences, briefings involving American and Russian experts, contribute reports of Russian scholars to the American media, publish and distribute in the United States Russian newspapers, magazines and books in English, and launch websites devoted to the U.S.-Russian relationship."[71] In return, the United States should do the same to support the truly bilateral relationship.

It is not the time for a confrontation; it is the time for partnership and collaboration. The Georgia crisis was a critical point in U.S.-Russian relations but it provoked state powers to reconsider their relations and analyze challenges and mistakes. As Albert Einstein noted, in the middle of difficulty lies opportunity. It would be good if this opportunity becomes a new chance for U.S.-Russian relations.

Notes

1. Hellene Keyssar, "Space Bridges: The U.S.—Soviet Space Bridge Resource Center," *Political Science and Politics*, June 1, 1994, http://www.jstor.org/pss/420280

2. Carnes Lord and Helle C. Dale, "Public Diplomacy and the Cold War: Lessons Learned," *Backgrounder*, no. 2070, September 18, 2007,http://www.heritage.org/Research/nationalSecurity/bg2070.cfm

3. Ibid.

4. Dimitri K.Simes, "Losing Russia: The Costs of Renewed Confrontation," *Foreign Affairs*, November/December, 2007, http://www.foreignaffairs.org/20071101faessay86603/dimitri-k-simes/losing-russia.html

5. "Not a Cold War, but a Cold Tiff," *The Economist*, February 15, 2007.

6. Lev Gudkov, "Attitude to the United States in Russia and the Anti-Americanism Issue," Polit.ru, May 22, 2002. http://old.polit.ru/documents/486669.html

7. Stephen F. Cohen, "The Missing Debate," *The Nation*, May 1, 2008, http://www.thenation.com/doc/20080519/cohen

8. Andrew C. Kuchins et al., "New Report on U.S.-Russian Relations: The Case for an Upgrade," The Carnegie Moscow Center, January 20, 2005, http://www.carnegie.ru/en/pubs/media/71958.htm

9. Monroe E. Price, *Media and Sovereignty: The Global Information Revolution and Its Challenge to State Power* (Cambridge, MA: MIT Press, 2002), 4.

10. Charlemagne: "A Worrying New World Order," *The Economist*, September 13, 2008, 40.

11. Stephen F. Cohen, "The New American Cold War," *The Nation,* July 10, 2006. http://www.thenation.com/doc/20060710/cohen/5

12. "The Hand that Feeds Them," *The Economist*, August 9, 2008, 27.

13. Gudkov, "Attitude to the United States in Russia."

14. Lilia Shevtsova, *Russia—Lost in Transition: The Yeltsin and Putin Legacies* (Washington, DC: Carnegie Endowment, 2007), 165.

15. Michael A. McFaul, "American Efforts as Promoting Regime Change in the Soviet Union and then Russia: Lessons Learned," Center on Democracy, Development, and the Rule of Law Stanford Institute on International Studies, no. 44, September, 2005, 44.

16. Ibid.

17. Ibid., 45.

18. Tom Bjorkman, "Russian Democracy and American Foreign Policy," The Brookings Institute. Brookings Policy Brief Series, July 2001, no. 85, http://www.brookings.edu/papers/2001/07russia_bjorkman.aspx

19. Simes, "Losing Russia."

20. Gudkov, "Attitude to the United States."

21. "To Russia for Love," *The Economist*, May 18, 2002, 11.

22. Cohen, "The New American Cold War."

23. Mitchell Polman, "We Need a Public Diplomacy Strategy for Russia," The Public Diplomacy Blog, comment posted August 20, 2007, http://uscpublicdiplomacy.com/index.php/newsroom/pdblog_detail/we_need_a_public_diplomacy_strategy_for_russia/

24. Olga Khvostunova, The Interview with Fyodor Lukianov, e-mail message to the author, September 17, 2008.

25. Jill Dougherty, "Russia Kicks Out U.S. Peace Corps," December 28, 2002. CNN.com./World, http://edition.cnn.com/2002/WORLD/europe/12/28/peace.corps/index.html

26. Timothy Garton Ash, "The Lesson that the West Must Learn from the Moscow Rock," *The Guardian,* January 26, 2006.

27. Peter Finn, "Russia Halts Activities on Many Groups from Abroad," *Washington Post Foreign Service*, October 20, 2006.

28. Dmitri V. Trenin, "Russia Leaves the West," *Foreign Affairs*, July/August, 2006, http://www.foreignaffairs.org/20060701faessay85407/dmitri-trenin/russia-leaves-the-west.html

29. Dmitri V. Trenin, "Russia's Strategic Choice," Carnegie Endowment for International Peace, Policy Brief, 50, May, 2007, 1. http://www.carnegieendowment.org/files/pb50_trenin_final.pdf

30. Trenin, "Russia Leaves the West."

31. Daniel Benjamin, "The Russians Moved Because They Know You Are Weak," The Brookings Institute, August 20, 2008, http://www.brookings.edu/opinions/2008/0820_russia_benjamin.aspx

32. Ibid.

33. Shevtsova, *Russia—Lost in Transition*, 165.

34. Dmitri V.Trenin, "Russia's Coercive Diplomacy," The Carnegie Moscow Center, Briefing, 10, no. 1 (January 2008), 3, http://www.carnegie.ru/en/pubs/briefings/PB%20_Jan_10_1_2008_Eng_web.pdf

35. Clifford G. Gaddy and Andrew C. Kuchins, "Putin's Plan," *The Washington Quarterly* 31, no. 2 (Spring 2008), 124, http://www.twq.com/08spring/docs/08spring_gaddy.pdf

36. Michael A. McFaul, "U.S.-Russia Relations in the Aftermath of the Georgia Crisis," House Committee on Foreign Affairs, September 9, 2008, http://foreignaffairs.house.gov/110/mcf090908.pdf

37. Ian Traynor, "Russia: We Are Ready for a New Cold War," *The Guardian*, August 27, 2008.

38. Dmitri V. Trenin, "The Opposition's Rebuttal Statement," on "Assertive Russia," *The Economist Debate Series,* September 12, 2008, http://www.economist.com/debate/index.cfm?action=article&debate_id=12&story_id=12070748

39. John Beyrly, "To the Last Moment, We Urged Georgia Not to Do It," *Kommersant*, August 22, 2008.

40. Anatol Lieven, "Lunch with Putin," *The National Interest Online*, September 17, 2008, http://www.nationalinterest.org/Article.aspx?id=19894

41. Silvio Pitter, "Local Win, Global Loss," *Russia Profile*, August 18, 2008. http://www.russiaprofile.org/page.php?pageid=International&articleid=a1219073336

42. Trenin, "Russia's Strategic Choices."

43. Denis Corboy, "EU Soft Power Best Agent to Solve the Conflict," *The Irish Times,* September 2, 2008.

44. Henry A. Kissinger and George P. Shultz, "Building on Common Ground with Russia," *The Washington Post*, October 8, 2008.

45. Olga Khvostunova, The Interview with Michael Zygar, e-mail message to the author, September 30, 2008.

46. Olga Khvostunova, The Interview with Fyodor Lukianov, e-mail message to the author, September 17, 2008.

47. Peter Finn, "Russia's Signal to Stations Is Clear: Cut U.S. Radio," *Washington Post Foreign Service*, July 7, 2006.

48. BBC/Reuters/Media Center Poll: Trust in Media. May 3, 2006, http://www.globescan.com/news_archives/Trust_in_Media.pdf

49. Walter Lippmann, *Public Opinion* (North Chelmsford, MA: Courier Dover Publications, 2004), 121.

50. Dmitri V. Trenin, "Opposition's Closing Statement" on "Assertive Russia," *The Economist Debate Series*, comment posted on September 17, 2008. http://www.economist.com/debate/index.cfm?action=article&debate_id=12&story_id=12070751

51. Veronika Krashenninikova, *America—Russia: The Cold War of Cultures* (Moscow: Europe Publishing, 2007), 350.

52. Victoria Kruchinina, Interview with Lev Gudkov, *Nezavisimaya Gazeta*, August 20, 2008.

53. "The Severe Deterioration of Russians' Attitude to the United States, the European Union, Georgia, Ukraine," The Levada Center, September 25, 2008, http://www.levada.ru/press/2008092501.html

54. "Russians' Attitude to America, The Public Opinion Foundation," September 4, 2008, http://bd.fom.ru/report/cat/inter_pol/_west_rel/Russia_USA/d083523

55. Ibid.

56. "Declining Public Support for Global Engagement," The Pew Research Center for the People and Press, September 24, 2008, http://people-press.org/report/453/declining-public-support-global-engagement

57. Trenin, "The Opposition's Closing Statement."

58. Edward Verona, Features Guest Comment on "Assertive Russia," *The Economist Debate Series,* comment posted on September 16, 2008, http://www.economist.com/debate/index.cfm?action=article&debate_id=12&story_id=12070657

59. Ibid.

60. The American Chamber of Commerce in Russia, http://www.amcham.ru

61. Foundation for Russian American Economic Cooperation, http://www.fraec.org

62. The U.S.-Russia Business Council (USRBC), https://www.usrbc.org

63. The U.S.-Russia Business Council (USRBC), https://www.usrbc.org/activities/councilevents/

64. Michael Holtzman, "Privatize Public Diplomacy," *The New York Times,* August 8, 2002.

65. Geoffrey Allen Pigman and Anthony Deos, "Consuls for Hire: Private Actors, Public Diplomacy," *Place Branding and Public Diplomacy* 4, no. 1, 90, Palgrave Macmillan, 2008.

66. Author interview. September 19, 2008.

67. Michael A. McFaul and James M. Goldgeier, "What To Do about Russia," Hoover Institution, *Policy Review,* October and November, 2005, http://www.hoover.org/publications/policyreview/2921316.html

68. Trenin, "Russia's Strategic Choice."

69. Steven Pifer, "What Does Russia Want? How Do We Respond?" The Brookings Institute, September 11, 2008, http://www.brookings.edu/speeches/2008/0911_russia_pifer.aspx

70. Kuchins, et al. "New Report on U.S.-Russian Relations."

71. Edward Lozansky, "Dialogue, Not a Confrontation," *Rossiyskaya Gazeta,* October 6, 2006.

CHAPTER FIVE

The View from China

GUOLIN SHEN

On August 8, 2008, U.S. President George W. Bush chose to attend the opening ceremonies of the Olympic Games in Beijing, an action that nullified any possibility for a U.S. Olympic boycott associated with the Chinese obstruction of antigovernment Tibetan protesters in March of that year. It was wise decision for him to come to Beijing at this pivotal juncture because the Olympic Games were extremely important to the Chinese government and its citizens. China viewed the games as a perfect opportunity to showcase the nation's emergence as a new world power and promote a positive national image to the international community. Thus, in working to achieve this "international recognition of China's social stability, economic progress and the healthy life of the Chinese people,"[1] the Chinese made a tremendous effort to orchestrate this prominent international athletic event, and they did not want to lose face in front of the world.

So save the Chinese face! President Bush is the first U.S. president to travel abroad and attend the Olympic Games in American history. Unlike British Prime Minister Gordon Brown and German Chancellor Angela Merkel, Bush never declined the opportunity to attend the Beijing Olympic Games, despite facing domestic and international pressure to punish China's government for the "crackdown" on Tibetan protesters. President Bush took a low-key position and did not respond to the criticism and thus the Chinese had an improved image of the U.S. government (when compared with countries like France and Germany). The Bush administration understood the importance of the political relationship between the United States and China. The White House's position was that any Olympic protest by the United States would run the risk of hindering a host of international efforts that the Bush administration needs China's help to solve. Those include confronting Myanmar's military junta and Iran's nuclear efforts as well as the continuing activities of North Korea.[2] In addition, when President Bush attended the dedication of the 600,000-square-foot U.S. embassy with his father, he also showed an effort to foster "trust" between China and the United States because the two countries have "built a strong relationship built on common interests."[3] By simply showing up at the first four days of the Beijing Olympic Games, President Bush, along with the other foreign leaders who attended, garnered substantial attention from the Chinese media and, consequently, earned enormous good will from the Chinese people.

New Face, Old Story

The Olympic Games are not only full of athletic stories of winning and losing, but they are also seen as a diplomatic stage for the winning or losing foreign people's minds and hearts. Edward R. Murrow, former director of U.S. Information Agency, cited the importance of "telling America's story." In the past few years, the Bush administration accelerated the pace on telling America's story to the Chinese people. On November 9, 2006, Michelle Kwan was appointed as a public diplomacy ambassador to represent American values especially to young people and sports enthusiasts over the world. Her parents were originally from China, and her first overseas trip was to China in 2007. When interviewed by the Chinese media, she expressed her desire to initiate dialogue with young Chinese people.[4] As a child of immigrants, Kwan grew up in a humble social situation. Dependent on her passion for figure skating and hard work, she has won nine U.S. championships, five World Championships, and two Olympic medals and has become the most decorated and successful figure skater in U.S. history.

As the first American Public Diplomacy Envoy, Kwan was a new face, but an old story to Chinese. It is the first time for the American government to appoint a sports star to play an active and valuable role in communicating with people abroad to present a good American image. Michelle Kwan, with Cal Ripken Jr., who was also named by the State Department as a special sports envoy to travel in China, represent an

American dream, depicted by James Truslow Adams as "that dream of a land in which life should be better and richer and fuller for everyone, with opportunity for each according to ability or achievement.... It is not a dream of motor cars and high wages merely, but a dream of social order in which each man and each woman shall be able to attain to the fullest stature of which they are innately capable, and be recognized by others for what they are, regardless of the fortuitous circumstances of birth or position."[5] This American dream is shaped as a fascinating scene based on liberal democracy, freedom, and modernization. Emphasizing individual achievement, which can be made without the restrictions of class, caste, religion, race, or ethnic group, the story of the American dream made the United States attractive to different kinds of people from all over the world. This attraction was fortified by the American mass communication arsenal and America's status as a superpower. Stories of America were spread throughout the world since World War II through publishing, broadcasting, cultural and educational exchange programs, and Hollywood movies.

Michelle Kwan and Cal Ripken Jr. are new examples for advertising the American dream. But this might not always work well in influencing Chinese opinion. Thirty years ago, when China emerged from the shadow of its cultural revolution, there was a fervent desire for opening to the outside and modernizing to catch up with developed countries. The United States represented both modernization and prosperity and thus became a dreamland of some young Chinese who wanted to attain success, look for freedom, and get better careers. Today, China is playing an important role on world stage as it continues on its path of substantial economic growth and social development. Lots of opportunities are booming for young people. More and more Chinese can tell stories of their own success in this new era, which has made the story of American dream seem outdated and less attractive. Individual achievement has been emphasized and media like to publicize China's own popular idols. With the rapid growth of many social aspects, China's youth now have more opportunities to develop themselves. In the Beijing Olympics, China replaced the United States as the world's premier sporting nation by winning fifty-one gold medals. Born in the 1980s, most of Chinese medalists came from common families and realized their Olympic dreams through hard work. The Chinese now have their own stories of sporting success and no longer have to admire American achievements. Winning the most gold medals on home soil has brought glory to China and encouraged youngsters to believe that they live in a great country that can provide for their dreams.

Aside from sports, China has successful stories in other fields. China has its own "Bill Gates." IT heroes like Yun Ma have made legendary stories in the IT field. A former teacher of English in Zhejiang, Ma started the country's first e-commerce Web site, Alibaba, in 1998. It has become the leader in its field, serving well more than 50,000 member traders in 200 countries and regions, with an annual business turnover amounting to approximately US$10 billion. Yun Ma is not the only Chinese entrepreneur who never let anyone deter him from his dream to succeed as a highly successful Chinese business leader. Another example is Yanhong Li who founded Baidu, the No.1 search engine in China as listed in NASDAQ in August 2005. This firm's success surprised the overseas capital market and boosted the confidence of Chinese IT colleagues. Although the young business leaders still have a long way to go before they can reach their dreams, their legends inspire Chinese youngsters, fueling hopes that they can achieve great things and realize their "Chinese dreams" rather than idolizing American figures.

With the growing influence of global media and communication networks, the Chinese public has received stories about the dark side of the American dream from the media. Not all immigrants can attain their American dream. Ethnic and racial discrimination is prevalent in the United States and thus, persistent hard work does not guarantee material prosperity and an improvement in social status. The gap between the American ideal and social reality made some Chinese doubt whether the American dream makes sense to everyone.

After the Olympic, Chinese now expects "respect" in global communications. The success of the Beijing Olympic Games led to soaring Chinese self-confidence. Before the opening ceremony, President Hu received eighty world leaders, including American President Bush, at a banquet that was described as the most important meal in Chinese history. Such a concentration of political influence let common people recall the memories of China's great dynasties spreading its culture and attracting surrounding states and peoples. The dignitaries attending this banquet will go some way to alleviating China's sense of inferiority. The 2008 Pew Global Attitudes survey in China finds that more than eight-in-ten Chinese are satisfied with their country's overall direction and their national economy, a significant increase in contentment from earlier in the decade.[6] David Shambaugh of George Washington University says the Olympic experience might allow Beijing to move on from what it saw as the century of humiliation at the hands of foreign powers. "That aggrieved nationalism was the dominant narrative for half a century, so the Chinese Communist Party staked its own legitimacy on overcoming all this humiliation. Now China has stood up in the world and it is clear for everybody to see. This offers China a chance to bury this aggrieved baggage they've carried with them, and stand more confidently in the world."[7] Meaning much more than gold medals, the Olympic Games proved to be a great opportunity for the nation to prove its prosperity. It spoke volumes about China's new soft power.

So, for its public diplomacy purposes the United States should redesign the story of American dream. U.S. policy makers should discover where the Chinese people and the American people wish their countries to be headed morally and focus not on what happened in the past but on the challenges ahead. For example, when I was studying at Yale in 2006, Wendy Kopp was invited to tell her story about launching Teach for America. I was deeply moved by the story and how she developed an innovative idea for helping to eliminate educational inequity in the United States. Today, Teach for America has proven to be very successful and applying for this program is very popular with seniors from some of America's elite colleges. In the fall of 2007, close to 18,000 individuals applied for an incoming corps of 2,900, who joined more than 2,100 returning teachers, and together these young teachers affected the lives of nearly 440,000 students.[8] In China, there are also efforts to improve education in poor areas, but most of these were initiated and funded by the government. It is difficult for ordinary people to launch an educational movement and make contributions to social development. So it would be beneficial for both the United States and China to introduce the story of "Teach for America" to show their citizens how common people can make their significant social contributions even in a developed country like the United States. To eliminate educational inequity demands the talent of a diverse group, which could continuously work from inside and outside the field of education for the fundamental changes necessary to ensure educational excellence and equity. The duty to give a brighter future to our children should be performed not only by the government but also by the people.

Divide of American Image

Public diplomacy aims to engage carefully targeted sectors of the foreign public to develop support for its goals. To reach these goals, policy makers should know what the foreign public's perspectives are. With this in mind, does the U.S. State Department understand the contemporary Chinese viewpoint?

In 2006, *Global Times* publicly submitted their report on Chinese perspective of Sino-U.S. relations. It is found that the total satisfaction rate on Sino-U.S. relations was as high as 79.8 percent and had increased by approximately nine percentage points since 2005. Related to this, nearly 80 percent of the respondents admitted that they like Americans in general, which was also an increase over 2005 by approximately 13 percent. At the same time, 56.3 percent considered the United States as their principal competitor, which was approximately 7 percent higher than in 2005. When asked the question that "what aspects of American society do you appreciate the most," the answer with the highest rate was "advanced technology." The results of the surveys for each year were almost the same at around 45 percent. The answer of "better off" accounted for 23.6 percent, more than the 17.9 percent in 2005. The respondents, who chose "personal development opportunities," only accounted for 7.9 percent. In determining whether the United States is containing China, nearly 60 percent of the respondents chose "yes," very close to the ratio of the year before. Chinese people weighed the Taiwan issue the most serious in Sino-U.S. relations, and cited as the most disliked U.S. policy, "arms sales to Taiwan."[9]

According to the survey, there is apparently a divide in America's image. Chinese people like Americans, but do not like the U.S. government and its policies. In another survey conducted by the Chicago Council on Global Affairs in 2007, 68 percent of Chinese people embraced the idea that the United States should play a cooperative role and do its share to solve international problems together with other countries; 77 percent said that the United States is currently playing the role of world police more than it should be; 61 percent rejected the idea that the U.S. government has a duty to enforce international law.[10] Apparently "the U.S." in the report refers solely to the U.S. government. Since September 11, unilateral foreign policy has been conducted and the war against Iraq became very unpopular throughout the world. In saying "either you are with us or with the terrorists," Bush effectively warned the rest of the world. No spin can camouflage or sweeten such threatening words that carry the weight of U.S. military, political, and economic might. Such a polarized view of the world leaves no room for dialogue or for a search for a middle ground.[11] The world's perception of America is very much dependent on American foreign policy, not only toward its own region, but also in other areas, like Iraq, Palestine, and Afghanistan.

The gap between American ideals and reality harms the American image all over the world. A WorldPublicOpinion.org poll of 907 urban Pakistanis revealed that most Pakistanis want Islam to play a larger role in Pakistani society. However, a majority also favors a more democratic political system, rejects Talibanization, and supports recent government efforts to reform the madrassah system by focusing more on science and mathematics.[12] The result creates a paradox for Americans. U.S. foreign policy often contradicts the principles of liberty and democracy, which are thought by American foreign policy maker to be spread to other parts of the world. The survey in Pakistan also found that Pakistani attitudes toward the United States are negative and that there was a growing perception that the United States is hostile toward Islam. This is also the case in China. The U.S. record of double standards on human rights has been deeply entrenched in the Chinese psyche. In response to the annual world human rights report released by U.S. State Department, China's government has published an annual report on American human rights every year, which reminds the Chinese and people from other countries of the longstanding malpractice and problems of human rights abuses in the United States. With Chinese media usually covering bad news of Uncle Sam, American government's brand as "the world human rights police" is often questioned and criticized. Chinese are aware of its human rights problem, but they do not want to solve it by being intervened by other superpowers. Any foreigner's criticism toward China's government is prone to be depicted as "Anti-China" or "Anti-Chinese."

On the other hand, China's social structure has undergone change. In the process of urbanization and industrialization, China's social stratification has evolved and it no longer possesses a distinct segregation of four social classes. The research by the Chinese Academy of Social Sciences divided China's society into ten social classes and indicated that new social classes, like private entrepreneurs, managers, and staff in foreign-funded and domestic firms and artistic and business free-lancers are increasing their economic and political clout as they accrue personal wealth.[13] With more wealth and accountability, China's rising middle class could make their voice louder and influence broader public opinion. What do they really want? What are their perspectives of the West and the United States? To what extent can the middle class influence domestic and foreign policy making? What kinds of stories do they prefer? No doubt the emerging social classes will have a significant impact on the sociopolitical structure in China. Furthermore, 21.4 percent of China's 1.3 plus billion people were aged from fifteen to twenty-nine.[14] In China, discussions have been triggered about the post-80s generation, who were born in the 1980s and are also China's first generation of one-child policy. They were sent by their parents to schools, colleges, and universities overseas and formed a different perspective of the outside world from that of their parents. These young people are also very active online. Not only surfing the Web, an estimated 47 million people also try blogging.[15]

It is also evident that China's general public and its elites display disparity on some issues in Sino-U.S. relations. C-100's survey illustrated that elites not only differ from the general public in both countries in terms of their views of the other nation, but also tend to misperceive the general public's views of each other. In China, opinion leaders and business leaders hold a far more favorable opinion of the United States than the general public does. Among the general public, better-educated and wealthier people are more likely to hold favorable views of the United States. Chinese Communist Party members (74 percent) hold a more favorable opinion of the United States than those non–Party members (60 percent).[16] There is also a divide between Chinese elites and the general public in perspectives of Sino-U.S. relations. Elites might embrace the principles of liberalism and democracy to push forward the reform, while the general public prefers American prosperity in economics and technology.

Is VOA Influential?

Voice of America (VOA), the most famous international media operation of the U.S. government, broadcasts more than 1,250 hours of programming in 45 languages every week. But it is not as influential as before in China. In December 1941, with the Japanese attack on Pearl Harbor and Germany's declaration of war against the United States, the United States began to launch its international broadcasting. VOA began broadcasting in February 1942 to provide a trusted source of news and information and to tell the truth. By the end of the war, VOA had thirty-nine transmitters and provided service in forty languages, including Mandarin and Cantonese. After winning the war, VOA was redesigned to counter Soviet propaganda directed against American policy. During the cold war, VOA, along with other American international broadcasts, played an important role in spreading the idea of American democracy and mobilizing local people to turn against their government in communist occupied areas. In China, although Chinese-language VOA broadcasts were jammed by the Chinese government, some Chinese could receive the signals of VOA via shortwave. Especially during the spring of 1989, VOA was the only international source from which Chinese people could get forbidden information. According to VOA Director Richard Carlson, during the crisis in 1989 between 60 and 100 million Chinese people listened to its programs every day.[17] Despite China's isolation from the outside world during the Tiananmen crisis, many Chinese still looked for information from external sources to get a complete picture of the political turmoil, which they could not get from purely internal sources due to the government's censorship. The VOA's Chinese-language broadcasts at the time were a key source of information for student demonstrators, the *Washington Post* reported in 1986. These students relied on VOA news programs for information about their own demonstrations and about similar protests in other Chinese cities.[18]

After the defeat of Soviet communism, American public diplomacy was retested and given a lower status in American foreign policy making. But VOA was deemed as a valuable vehicle of public diplomacy and continues to broadcast around the globe to support young democracies, free markets, ethnic tolerance, and other American values and interests. Its listenership, however, has gradually been shrinking. A mere 2 percent of Arabs listen to VOA.[19] In China, it is hard to calculate the exact rate, but the study led by Liqing Zhang demonstrated that the VOA now faces a significant challenge in China. VOA listenership has dramatically declined in recent years. This study employed fifty-one face-to-face field interviews to investigate the role the Internet has played in the declining listenership in China for Western shortwave radio broadcasts like the VOA. Findings suggest that the Internet has become the primary information source for the VOA's targeted audience in China. The growth of the Internet has led to a new pattern of media consumption. The continuing evolution of media liberalization and globalization in China forced by the Internet has also reduced the audience's demand for foreign radio.[20] Today's China is not the same as the China of the 1980s. All sorts of resources and information are now provided through the Internet. People can find foreign media online despite government censorship. Among those media, the BBC, the *New York Times,* the AP, and Reuters and so on are now more prestigious than the VOA.

In the 1990s, the VOA did not stop the development of its Chinese programs. New programs were launched one after another. Radio and TV simulcast *China Forum, American Issues, To Your Health, Pro and Con,* and *Cultural Odyssey* have been beamed into China by satellite and shortwave radio. However, the signal of VOA has been jammed since 1956 in China. In September 10, 2001, the VOA's Chinese Branch officially launched its new Web site for China at www.voachinese.com that replaced the branch's former site, available since 1995. Both are blocked by Chinese authorities. Limited access to foreign listeners is a formidable problem. As an arm of the U.S. Government, VOA is seen in China as not just a journalistic entity but also a symbol of official American influence. The perceived image of the VOA as an "enemy radio station" and Western value purveyor is challenging its role in China. Furthermore, after the Tibetan crisis in March, 2008, all the Western media's credibility are now being questioned and regarded as hostile to a rising and increasingly powerful China.

Covering the story of Chinese dissidents and the Dalai Lama will not increase prestige of the VOA in China. "It is not possible to get the truth from domestic Chinese sources. To get the truth in China, one has no choice but to become a faithful listener to the VOA," said Chinese democracy activist Jinsheng Wei, shortly after his November 1997 release from prison and expulsion to the United States. His praise of VOA can only hurt VOA's reputation as a credible news organization. Although it rejects allegations that its reporting is distorted or propagandistic, the network has been depicted as an ideological propaganda machine due to the rising nationalism in China. The VOA Charter drafted in 1960 and signed into law in 1976 reads, "The long-range interests of the United States are served by communicating directly with the peoples of the world by radio. To be effective, the Voice of America must win the attention and respect of listeners. These principles will therefore govern Voice of America broadcasts. 1. VOA will serve as a consistently reliable and authoritative source of news. VOA news will be accurate, objective, and comprehensive; 2. VOA will represent America, not any single segment of American society, and will therefore present a balanced and comprehensive projection of significant American thought and institutions; 3. VOA will present the policies of the United States clearly and effectively, and will also present responsible discussions and opinion on these policies."[21] The charter cannot avoid contradiction that exists in itself and make VOA less persuasive. If a so-called global media network presents the policies of one country clearly and effectively, how can it be accurate, objective, and balanced? In late 1993 and early 1994, VOA had worked with WorldNet to develop a pilot weekly television news and discussion program in Mandarin Chinese called *Pacific Horizons*. However, the attempt was scuttled when USIA's Office of East Asian Affairs insisted on approving topics for the program and selecting guests for it. Bureau of Broadcasting director Joseph B. Bruns and Director of Programs Sid Davis refused on principle to move forward with the project.[22]

The most effective VOA program now is its language program. In December 1999, VOA's Special English Division celebrated forty years of broadcasting. In China, many Chinese learned English through this simple form of English (a 1,500-word vocabulary, a single idea per sentence). American history, science and technology, literature and culture are taught in those programs, which present American characteristics. According to BBG's report, VOA's English teaching programs are sold widely throughout China.[23] Actually, VOA provides free English teaching programs to some radio and organizations. Some schools would like to take them as subsidiary materials for teaching English. Walking around university campus, VOA's English book, mp3s, and video can be purchased. Through teaching its language, this program has proven to be an effective way to spread U.S. culture.

Privatization of American Public Diplomacy

The U.S. government is by no means the only actor on the public diplomacy stage abroad. Sometimes the voice of government is questioned and found to be not credible. Nongovernmental organizations (NGOs), private foundations, transnational corporations, commercial media, and even individuals can make public diplomatic achievements by pursuing their goals in public venues around the world with skill and success. In the 2007 Edelman survey, NGOs were seen as either the most credible institutions or tied for the most credible institutions in ten of eighteen countries. This places NGOs even with businesses, which also leads or ties for the most trusted actors (above media and government in seven of eighteen countries). In the 2006 survey, NGOs were also the most trusted in seven of eleven nations surveyed.[24] And the fact that U.S. Undersecretary of State for Public Diplomacy and Public Affairs Karen Hughes has made the "empowerment" of private sector entities and individuals a fundamental tenet in her plans to transform U.S. public diplomacy also suggests that public diplomacy is well on its way to becoming "privatized." According to Hughes, such efforts recognize that "the voices of government officials are not always the most powerful nor the most credible."[25]

Actually American private foundations and NGOs began to play an active role in China as early as the beginning of the twentieth century. In 1913–1914, the newly formed Rockefeller Foundation created a commission to financially support the Peking Union Medical College, one of the most prestigious medical educational organizations in China. The foundation also sponsored James Yen's mass educational movement to raise the educational, social, and economic standards of rural China. After 1949, the Ford Foundation was the first American private foundation to set up an office in Beijing in January, 1988. Cooperating with the China Social Science Academy since 1985, Ford Foundation projects emphasize economic, legal, international relations, environment, education, and reproductive health initiatives. These projects are frequently welcomed by various regions and groups in China.

Chinese scholar Zhongjun Zi argues that American private foundations run programs in China for several purposes: (1) as part of their philanthropy; China is treated as a third world country that should be developed gradually; (2) to help Americans understand Chinese culture, which is at the heart of a major world civilization and a reason for funding China studies in America; (3) to stimulate changes of the U.S. government's China policy because it is a disadvantage for the American government to formulate policies toward China without knowing China much beyond the background of the cold war; (4) to push forward reform, democratization, and modernization in China. This is the American elite's dream.[26] Foundations and NGOs do not represent the interests of the U.S. government, but reflect the values of American elites and mainstream society. They are more flexible and thus can work with China's government and be more receptive to the Chinese people than the American government is.

The American public welfare foundation and NGOs that work in China have a good reputation. For fifteen years, the Ford Foundation's program has been the largest of its kind in China. Its notable activities have included: strengthening teaching and research capacity in economics, international relations, law, gender studies, and development studies; support for a number of research centers, think tanks, and NGOs working on social, agricultural, and environmental policy and legal reform; the introduction (especially in Southwest China) of participatory approaches to natural resource management and poverty alleviation; support for a cluster of pioneering public interest law centers and so on.[27] Many universities, agencies, local governments, and NGOs are their local counterpart. With a budget of 288 million U.S. dollars in China, the Bill and Melinda Gates Foundation has provided

2.9 million U.S. dollars for the World Association of Children and Parents to work with orphaned and disabled children in Henan and 7.3 million U.S. dollars for PATH to work on adolescent reproductive health and AIDS prevention.[28] It is estimated that the number of international NGOs working in China is between 3,000 and 6,500.[29] Other famous foundations and organization includes Rockefeller, Hands On, Heifer and AmeriCares Foundation, and so on. It is hard to calculate how many NGOs are headquartered in the United States. Most of the activities held by NGOs have brought the Western values of environment protection, human rights, animal protection, preventing disease, and eliminating poverty.

Despite these successes, color revolutions in Central Asia have sent a warning to China's government. It is noteworthy that a number of foundations and NGOs like National Endowment for Democracy, the International Republican Institute, the National Democratic Institute for International Affairs, Freedom House and Open Society Institute of George Soros were heavily involved in the anticommunism revolutions in post-Communist countries. Some of them were directly supported by USAID. The U.S. government spent 41 million in Yugoslavia and 14 million in Ukraine in organizing and funding year-long operations to serve American interest.[30] Regarding the great impact of international NGOs, China's Foreign Ministry has established a special unit, known as the Foreign NGOs Management Office, within the Bureau of International Organizations, to review the work of all foreign NGOs in China. Analysts say that China has sent intelligence experts from various social science academies to Uzbekistan, Kyrgyzstan, the Ukraine, Belarus, and Georgia to study the processes of political change, and especially the NGO role.[31] Some scholars also warned that perceived black hands of America have played an important role in Eastern Europe and Central Asia through NGOs' efforts.[32] On August 22, 2008, USAID Administrator Henrietta Fore visited Georgia to meet with President Mikheil Saakashvili, providing humanitarian assistance to the people of Georgia, which was a good opportunity to gain the friendship of individual citizens in this country, but was also seen as promoting American national interests. In China, the ideological stances of international NGOs are often examined, so that American public diplomacy and any possible U.S. agendas will easily hit a wall.

Although the report of the United States Advisory Commission on Public Diplomacy suggested American public diplomacy is a class of activity that somehow exists and operates independently of bilateral relationships, rather than an activity that is organic, or at least closely tied, to the management of those relationships,[33] the U.S. government has taken public diplomacy into consideration in Sino–U.S. relations. In July, 2007, U.S. Treasury Secretary Henry Paulson visited Qinghai to call attention to environmental issues, showing that the United States did care about other parts of China besides big cities. In 2008, the Bush administration won a public diplomatic success in China. Between 2003 and 2008, the American government has made efforts to increase the number of diplomats in China. Apart from the renovation and expansion of the American embassy in Beijing, in the coming years the number of diplomats in China will be increased and some of these individuals will be pushed into the front lines of diplomacy. Much of the public diplomatic behavior of governments is intended to "win hearts and minds," but actually there is neither a winner nor a loser on the public diplomatic stage. As Lamis Andoni pointed out, in the era of "us against them" and the absolute battle between "good and evil," the United States has no room for another worldview and little if any inclination to consider the victims of U.S. economic, political, and military dominance.[34] If the United States still embraces the notion of "Win-lose" in the field of public diplomacy, how can it build up a diversified, democratic, and amenable image in such a complicated global context? As the Fulbright-Hays Act states, the U.S. government must conduct activities that lead to "mutual understanding," instead of using the simplistic either black-or-white, either friend–or–enemy attitude that will cost a lot of flexibility in its public diplomacy. The perspective of "good or evil" might help the United States to win the cold war, but will not work out in the post-9/11 era.

Notes

1. Li Lanqing, the vice premier of China, when interviewed by CCTV, declared "The winning of the 2008 Olympic bid is an example of the international recognition of China's social stability, economic progress and the healthy life of the Chinese people," July 13, 2001.
2. "Bush to Attend Opening Rites of Olympic Games in China," *The Associated Press*, July 4, 2008.
3. "Bush speaks of free expression at U.S. Embassy dedication," *CNN* http://edition.cnn.com/2008/POLITICS/08/07/bush.china.olympics/index.html
4. Yanna Le and Wen Zhang, "GUAN Yinshan: Very Lucky to Have Two Cultural Background, No Wedding Ring on the Finger," *Globe*, February 6, 2007, http://sports.sina.com.cn/o/2007–02–06/11262741069.shtml
5. James Truslow Adams, *The Epic of America* (Boston: Little, Brown, and Company, 1931), 214–215.
6. "The Chinese Celebrate Their Roaring Economy, As They Struggle With Its Costs," *Pew Global Attitudes Project*, http://pewglobal.org/reports/display.php?ReportID=261

7. Louisa Lim, "With Olympics Over, China's Self-Confidence Soars," *NPR,* August 25, 2008, http://www.npr.org/templates/story/story.php?storyId=93947241

8. "Teach For America Places Largest-Ever Corps, Expanding Its Impact to 26 Regions Nationwide," *Teach For America,* http://www.teachforamerica.org/newsroom/documents/081507_Largestcorps.htm

9. "Global Times Survey: Chinese Are Optimistic on Sino-US relations," *Global Times,* March 20, 2006, http://www.chinadaily.com.cn/jjzg/2006–03/20/content_547090.htm

10. "World Publics Reject US Role as the World Leader," *Chicago Council on Global Affairs and WorldPublicOpinion.org,* 2007.

11. Antony J. Blinken, "Winning the War of Ideas," *The Washington Quarterly* 25, no. 2 (2002): 101–114.

12. "Pakistanis Want Larger Role for Islam and Democracy," *World Public Opinion,* January 4, 2008, http://www.worldpublicopinion.org/pipa/articles/brasiapacificra/440.php?lb=bras&pnt=440&nid=&id=

13. Xueyi Lu ed., *Report on Social Stratums in Contemporary China* (Beijing: Social Science Literature Press, 2002).

14. National population survey 2006, *China Family Planning Commission.*

15. "FACTBOX: The ABC's of China's Post-1980s Generation," *Reuters,* June 4, 2008, http://www.reuters.com/article/inDepthNews/idUST26422020080605?pageNumber=2&virtualBrandChannel=0

16. "Hope and Fear: C-100's Survey on American and Chinese Attitudes Toward Each Other," *Committee of 100,* 2007.

17. B. Shelley, "Protest and Globalization: Media, Symbols and Audience in the Drama of Democratization," *Democratization* 8, no. 4 (2001), 155–174.

18. Patricia Sullivan, "VOA Journalist Mark W. Hopkins," *Washington Post,* October 11, 2006, B07.

19. Blinken, "Winning the War of Ideas."

20. Lena Liqing Zhang, Are They Still Listening? Reconceptualizing the Chinese Audience of the Voice of America in the Cyber Era, *Journal of Radio Studies* 9 (2002): 317.

21. "VOA Charter," http://www.voanews.com/english/Africa/VOACharter.cfm

22. Alan L. Heil, *Voice of America: A History* (New York: Columbia University, 2003), 344.

23. "Voice of America", *Broadcasting Board of Governor,* http://www.bbg.gov/broadcasters/voa.html

24. "Business More Trusted Than Media and Government in Every Region of the Globe," *Edelman Trust Barometer 2007,* http://www.edelman.com/news/ShowOne.asp?ID=146

25. Karen P. Hughes, *Major Public Diplomacy Accomplishments*, U.S. Department of State report, 2006, quoted in Kathy R. Fitzpatrick, Privatizing U.S. Public Diplomacy: Issues and Implications (paper presented on International Studies Association Conference, Chicago, Illinois, February 28, 2007).

26. Zhongjun, Zi, *The Destiny of wealth: Study on American Modern Public Welfare Foundation* (Shanghai: Shanghai People Press, 2006), 219.

27. "The Ford Foundation," *Directory of International NGOs,* http://www.chinadevelopmentbrief.com/dingo/Sector/Gender/2–14-0–64-0–0.html

28. "Bill and Melinda Gates Foundation," *Directory of International NGOs,* http://www.chinadevelopmentbrief.com/dingo/Sector/HIV--AIDS/2–49-0–70-0–0.html

29. Xiaode, "Neither Angel Nor Devil: International NGO's Two Faces," *International Herald Leader,* June 16, 2008.

30. Ian Traynor, "US Campaign behind the Turmoil in Kiev," *Guardian,* November 26, 2004, World News edition.

31. Paul Mooney, "How to Deal with NGOs—Part I, China," *YaleGlobal,* August 1, 2006, http://yaleglobal.yale.edu/display.article?id=7902

32. Guolin Shen, *Controlling Communication: U.S. Government Propaganda Via Media* (Shanghai: Shanghai People Press, 2007), 178.

33. "Getting the People Part Right: A Report on the Human Resources Dimension of U.S. Public Diplomacy," *The United States Advisory Commission on Public Diplomacy,* 2008.

34. Lamis Andoni, "Deeds Speak Louder than Words," *Washington Quarterly* 25, no. 2 (2002): 85–100.

CHAPTER SIX

The View from Egypt

HUSSEIN AMIN

American public diplomacy in the Middle East was a focus of renewed interest following the terrorist attacks on the World Trade Center on September 11, 2001. Despite an initial outpouring of public sympathy for America following the 9/11 attacks and dramatically increased funding for public diplomacy efforts, favorable ratings have dropped precipitously. Egyptian—and Arab—public opinion of the United States has reached new lows. America is losing the battle to win the "hearts and minds" of Arabs and Muslims in the Middle East.

Almost all Arab polls show widespread disapproval of American policies regarding Iraq, Israel, and Palestine and negative images of the United States, especially since the beginning of the war in Iraq. An annual opinion poll, conducted in 2008 by Zogby International, surveyed more than 4,000 people in Egypt, Jordan, Lebanon, Morocco, Saudi Arabia, and the United Arab Emirates. The results of the survey show that 83 percent of the Arab public has an unfavorable view of the United States and 70 percent express no confidence in the United States. Both numbers represent increases over the previous survey in 2006.[1] A 65 percent of respondents do not believe that democracy is America's real objective in the Middle East, and only 8 percent believe that the American efforts to spread democracy in the Middle East is an important objective that will make a difference in the region.

A 50 percent of respondents replied that the most important factor driving American policy in the Middle East was controlling oil. Respondents would choose to live in France (39 percent) over the

United States (7 percent) and would prefer members of their family to study in France (36 percent) over the United States (11 percent) and increasingly believe that Israel (95 percent) and the United States (88 percent) are bigger threats than Iran (7 percent).[2] An earlier poll, conducted in January 2007 by the University of Maryland, shows a 93 percent unfavorable rating regarding the current U.S. government. This is among the very worst ever recorded from any Arab public. The same poll showed that three-quarters of Egyptian respondents agreed strongly with a statement that "America pretends to be helpful to Muslim countries, but in fact everything it does is really part of a scheme to take advantage of people in the Middle East and steal their oil."[3]

Much of the hostility toward America is driven by opposition to American foreign policy. The Iraq war is deeply unpopular as is the overall U.S.-led war on terrorism. Media coverage of abuses at Abu Ghraib and Guantanamo Bay, civilian deaths in Iraq and Afghanistan, rendition, references to the Crusades and clash of civilizations, and ethnic profiling contribute to the feelings of ill will. Overwhelmingly, Muslim publics believe that the United States ignores their interests when making foreign policy. In addition, there is widespread fear of American power, exacerbated by discussions of the Bush doctrine of preemptive strikes against perceived threats to the United States. In a 2007 Pew Global Attitudes survey, a large majority of Muslims in every predominantly Muslim country said they are worried the United States could become a military threat to their country someday.[4] Asked their opinion at a coffee house near Midan Talaat Harb in downtown Cairo, residents said they simply do not trust Bush. If he cared about human rights, they said, he would help the Palestinians. Distrust of the Bush administration's intentions is so prevalent and strong in Egypt that U.S. support for human rights groups, media, nongovernmental organizations, and other institutions is interpreted as interfering in domestic politics.[5]

The good news for the American government is that these negative views do not, apparently, arise from a deep cultural divide or rejection of American values but are primarily the results of a dislike of American foreign policy. Polls show that parts of the Arab world are increasingly rejecting terrorism, voicing support for democracy, and signaling that a clash of civilizations is not inevitable. An 80 percent of the Arabs surveyed responded that their attitudes toward the United States were based more on American policy than American values.[6] Arabs continue to rank the United States among the top countries with freedom and democracy for their own people, and the 2007 Maryland poll found that 82 percent of Egyptians say democracy is a good way of governing Egypt. In addition, despite al Qaeda's best efforts to the contrary, only 6 percent of Arab respondents selected Osama bin Laden as the leader they admire the most.[7]

Given the depth of opposition to current U.S. foreign policy in much of the Muslim world, American public diplomacy is facing tremendous challenges. Public diplomacy activities, led by the U.S. Department of State, are designed to counter negative opinion by explaining American foreign policy, countering misinformation, and promoting mutual understanding between America and other countries.[8] Following the attacks on 9/11, the challenge to U.S. public diplomacy in the Arab world was to make it clear that the United States was a victim of an unjustified act of terrorism; that the United States is not engaged in a war against Muslims and is not against Islam; and that terrorist networks, both those that planned and carried out the 9/11 attacks and all others, will be brought to justice. The question facing the State Department was how to prevent terrorists from gaining ground with their ideas and, at the same time, provide hope as well as visions of alternative futures based on tolerance and prosperity to young and rapidly growing Arab and Muslim populations.[9] At the very least, the task was to find an answer to the question, "Why do they hate us?"

Washington's immediate response to the attacks of 9/11 was to try to figure out how best to communicate its message and find an answer to this question. The State Department expanded its public diplomacy efforts around the world but particularly focused on countries in the Arab and Muslim world, prime recruiting areas for al Qaeda and other terrorist networks and critically important in the war on terrorism.[10] The administration had already targeted Egypt for reform, since it was the most populous Arab country and a recipient at the time of $2 billion a year in American aid. One of its first acts was to appoint a communications professional to head the public diplomacy efforts. Advertising Executive Charlotte Beers, former chairperson of advertising agency, J. Walter Thompson, and former head of public relations firm Ogilvy and Mather, was appointed undersecretary of state for public diplomacy and public affairs. Her task was to design a comprehensive strategy for marketing the United States in the Arab and Islamic worlds. Washington turned to the media to get its message to audiences in the Middle East.[11]

Public diplomacy strategies traditionally call for media campaigns and cultural exchanges as well as increased dialogue with media and various publics. While the Fulbright scholars program and others continued their important work in promoting cultural and scholarly exchanges, these programs were challenged by new visa requirements and onerous, and sometimes insurmountable, security requirements. Many Egyptian and Arab scholars of all ages were denied visas or were subjected to intimidating and intrusive security procedures at embassies and airports. One effective way of addressing both mass audiences and the cultural and economic elite in the Arab world has been through the Arabic-language satellite TV networks popular with Arab viewers. U.S. secretaries of state, national security advisors, and other senior administration officials have been interviewed by Al Jazeera, Egypt TV, and other networks to present the United States' point of view.

The State Department launched, in 2002, a new public diplomacy strategy called "Shared Values." Five video segments were produced for the campaign, attempting to counter stories of hate crimes and discrimination against Muslims in the United States. The segments were broadcast to several countries in the Middle East and to Indonesia. The $15 million campaign was abandoned by early 2003 amid questions about its effectiveness and impact and raised some serious concerns about how the impact of these public diplomacy efforts can and should be measured.[12]

Critics of the campaign observed that while advertising and propaganda were well known to have an impact on short-term decisions, they have very little impact on more fundamental beliefs. Other critics added that the leadership of the public diplomacy efforts was operating on the belief that anti-American feelings were based primarily on a misunderstanding of America—that if only citizens of the region knew and understood American values, they would love the country once again. The reality was that a large majority of the people in Egypt and the Arab world were quite familiar with American values through television, the media, and travel and that their opinions—and dislike—toward America were based primarily on U.S. foreign policy.[13]

Hi Magazine

In July 2003, the State Department launched an Arabic-language magazine targeted at young men and women aged between eighteen and thirty-five years old in fourteen Arab countries. *Hi* Magazine was produced entirely in Arabic by an Arab-American staff hired by the magazine's publisher, the Washington-based Magazine Group, and constituted one part of a three-part $62 million annual effort to counter anti-American sentiment in the Egypt and the Middle East. Intended as a nonpolitical, lifestyle magazine, *Hi*'s goal was to "build bridges of communication" between Arabs and the United States.[14] To complement the print publication, the Magazine Group launched an Internet site, *himag.com,* in July 2003. The interactive site enabled visitors to view magazine content, respond to polls, submit poetry in monthly contests, and ask questions about America.[15]

According to traditional public diplomacy theory, conflict between the United States and other nations can be greatly lessened if foreign populations can be made to see that Americans are people just like them. For that reason, the magazine focused nearly exclusively on cultural matters and avoided topics where there was expected to be great difference between the U.S. government and Arab readers. With an initial budget of $4.1 million, the magazine hoped to capture enough market shares to support itself through advertising. The magazine's ads, however, were directed to the kind of elite readership who would most likely have already been exposed to American culture, and the magazine's content reflected this Western orientation. The magazine reported to young Arabs on affluent Western lifestyles, with stories on Internet dating, rock-climbing, yoga, and sand surfing, a pastime limited to a tiny subset of Western tourists in the Arab world.[16] Articles were relentlessly optimistic, portraying, for example, the lives of Arab students on U.S. campuses as without difficulty or complications; Egyptian youth knew differently from stories in U.S. and Egyptian media as well as firsthand reports from returning students.

Despite being priced at a relatively inexpensive LE5 (US$1=LE5.3) in Egypt, the magazine's trendy layout and high-quality photography have not managed to attract readers. According to newsstand dealers, the magazine is not widely available, and newspaper vendors say *Hi* does not sell. Calling it the "American magazine," one dealer said that no one was interested in buying it. Of the 55,000 copies distributed, only 2,500 were purchased on any given month, according to the State Department. After the first couple of issues, the Middle East Report wrote that "At a time when the US really ought to be engaging in frank dialogue and genuine debate about ideas with people from the Middle East, it is hard to imagine *Hi* failing more spectacularly."[17]

Critics have called *Hi* "soft-sell propaganda," whose nonpolitical content fails to close any gaps with Arab youth. Prominent columnist for Egypt's *Al-Ahram* newspaper Salama Ahmed Salama described *Hi* (and Radio Sawa) as being "useless, since they both fail to answer important questions regarding the US presence in Iraq and the US's Israeli-biased policies." He added that it "is too naïve and superficial to bridge any gaps, not even cultural ones."[18] Adel Hammouda, former editor-in-chief of the Egypt's independent weekly *Sawt Al-Umma* newspaper, agreed with Salama that "*Hi* magazine is already off point since Egyptians are already widely exposed to American culture via different media channels." He added that "Arab youths already like American culture but are seriously at odds with US foreign policy."[19] Hammouda said that although Egyptian youths may not be politically well-read, they have formed strong opinions regarding U.S. policies in the Middle East. "The whole US media campaign shows the American inability to understand Arab culture and mentality."[20]

On December 22, 2005, the State Department announced that it was suspending publication of *Hi*, acknowledging that the dialogue it had sought to create with youth in the Arab world had become one-way. The decision to suspend publication was made by Karen Hughes, the new undersecretary of state for public diplomacy, replacing Charlotte Beers. Steven Cook, a Middle East expert at the nonpartisan Council of Foreign Relations, commented that the magazine was not seen as being credible but was instead seen as U.S. propaganda. He noted that the magazine had two strikes against it from the beginning, since it was known that it was being published by the U.S. government.[21]

Voice of America

The United States formally began broadcasting to the Middle East in 1950 when the Voice of America (VOA), the broadcasting organization established in 1942 to counter Nazi propaganda in Europe, started transmission of its radio programs in Arabic. The United States Information Agency (USIA) was charged with the task of conducting international advocacy, broadcasting and information activities, and coordinating the U.S. government's exchange programs, and broadcasts were aimed at countries the United States feared would fall under Soviet influence. The VOA's mission was to present the news, good or bad, to people who could not receive accurate, unbiased information.[22]

Following Iraq's invasion of Kuwait in 1990, the Bush administration began the complex process of building a coalition of countries that would send troops to Saudi Arabia to prevent further aggression and prepare to liberate Kuwait. The USIA's VOA radio network initiated a series of emergency program measures to support these ends. The VOA

Arabic Service expanded from seven to nearly ten hours and then later moved to fifteen and a half hours of broadcasts a day. VOA doubled English-language programming to the Middle East, borrowing transmitter space from Radio Free Europe and Radio Liberty. During the course of the Gulf War, the USIA increased its medium wave capacity in the Gulf region further, borrowing transmitter time from Russia. VOA ran news reports in Arabic in seven Arab nations, including Egypt, Saudi Arabia, Jordan, and Bahrain. VOA also created a dial-in service to allow anyone to access its news feed in Arabic, and in its first year, the service received more than 200,000 calls. Programming on VOA's Arabic Service at the start of the conflict included full coverage of the UN Security Council debate on Iraq in forty-three languages, as well as interviews with U.S., Iraqi, Kuwaiti, and Egyptian diplomats.[23]

Radio Sawa

The impetus for revamping and strengthening the VOA's Arabic broadcasting service was not the attacks on the 9/11. The failure of the Camp David discussions and the start of the second Palestinian *intifada* led the United States to reevaluate its broadcasting to the Middle East and begin planning for a 24/7 Arabic network. The State Department believed that the United States must play a role in strengthening the peace process and providing a forum for the forces of moderation and tolerance in the region. At the time, the VOA, with a staff of thirty-five Arabic-language professionals, broadcast seven hours a day on outdated shortwave and medium wave transmitters into the Middle East and was losing its audience. While the network's news and information were considered to be highly credible and well produced, the formats had grown outdated and rather dull and there was a general lack of dynamic, interesting programming.[24] Data showed that listeners were increasingly turning to medium wave and particularly FM frequencies. Acknowledging these problems, VOA's management developed a plan in 2001 to expand transmission capabilities, lease FM frequencies, and improve programming, but the Arabic service was eliminated before the plan could be put into effect.[25]

The attacks on 9/11 changed VOA's mission. Critics of the VOA's Arabic service said that it was failing to reach a young audience, and there was widespread agreement among the staff that the service needed to change the programming to appeal to the region's increasingly young population. The demographics in the region were changing, with more than 50 percent of the population of the region less than 35 years of age,[26] and the government hoped to appeal to those young men who were at risk of being recruited by Islamic terrorist organizations. The station was rebranded as Radio Sawa, "Together" in Arabic, and replaced the widely respected brand of the VOA's Arabic Service, which had for more than fifty years provided the region with news, music, educational, and cultural programming.[27]

The moving force behind the establishment of the network was Norman Pattiz, who, until his resignation at the end of 2006, was a member of the Broadcasting Board of Governors (BBG), an independent U.S. federal agency. Some criticism of this independence is that the BBG has been not only autonomous but truly independent of influence even from the State Department, despite the fact that the secretary of state has a seat on the BBG and theoretically state has some input (but in fact it has almost none). Broadcasting decisions are made by the BBG, with the Congress being the only check on what they want to do. The BBG is responsible for all nonmilitary U.S. government-funded broadcast outlets.[28] Pattiz felt that a new approach was needed to respond to the changing demographics of the Middle East, and that one way to win the hearts and minds of Arab youth and turn them into loyal listeners to the station was to play pop hits from both the United States and the Arab world.[29] Rather than reformulate the VOA's Arabic Service, Pattiz and other founders were convinced that the new network needed to separate from the VOA, whose mandate and charter imposed undesirable restrictions. The VOA charter, adopted in 1976, was the foundation of the VOA's credibility and required that the network "provide accurate, objective and comprehensive news; a broad and balanced picture of American institutions, thought and values; and a thorough discussion of U.S. policies on a broad range of issues."[30]

To run the new station, the BBG created the Middle East Broadcasting Network (MBN) as a nonprofit corporation. MBN also operates Al Hurra, America's satellite TV channel that broadcasts to the Middle East. Sawa went live in March 2002, transmitting on FM frequencies to most Arab countries and using a powerful medium wave transmission to the rest. The new station cost $34 million in its first year; in contrast, the VOA's Arabic service cost the U.S. government less than $5 million annually. Reacting to the cancellation of the VOA Arabic Service, more than a third of VOA employees signed a petition in 2004 protesting the "dismantling" of the agency and the replacement of its news and cultural programming in Arabic with a service focused primarily on pop music.[31]

Radio Sawa was praised by Bush administration officials, but U.S. diplomats stationed in the Middle East were more critical, complaining about the poor quality of the newscasts and newsreaders and the lack of credibility of the news programming.[32] The only nonmusic broadcasts are brief segments called *The World Now,* which included hard news, light news, topical features and interviews, and sports, and a daily thirty-minute news program, called *Iraq and the World,* which presents news related to the situation in Iraq.[33] The network also provides access to a live, streaming feed of its programs from its Web site.[34] These critics claimed that the network never identifies itself as an American station or states from where its broadcasts originate, that artists and songs are not identified, and that no informative narrative is provided to describe the types of songs played, the dates of issuance, their background or popularity, and other items of interest to educate the listener.[35] Commentators and critics also complained that the short newscasts relied too heavily on statements from Washington and that there were no breaking news stories. They labeled the station a U.S. propaganda tool.

A true assessment of Radio Sawa's broadcast content and performance has been difficult for researchers and government administrators to obtain, because the station has in the past resisted any outside, independent review of its programs. The station has also refused to accept the findings reached by the Government Accountability Office (GAO) and the State Department Inspector General's office.[36] Radio Sawa's management says that it is aware of the problems the network faces and has taken steps to improve its programming and effectiveness. The network reports that it has increased news and information programming to approximately seven hours a day, including live coverage of key speeches, news conferences, and congressional hearings from Washington. Radio Sawa staffers agree that the station is improving its content but report that it is hard to shake the network's image as a shallow rock 'n' roll station.[37] Radio Sawa reports that it has more than seventy employees divided between its headquarters in Virginia and its Middle East Program Center in Dubai, UAE. In addition, the network says it employs ninety stringers based in forty-three major cities in the Middle East, Europe, and other countries. Stringers in Washington, DC, and Detroit, Michigan cover U.S. news.

Radio Sawa's goal is to broadcast six dialect streams targeting different areas of the Middle East with more localized news in Egypt/Levant, the Gulf, Iraq, Morocco, Jordan/Palestine, Lebanon, and Sudan/Yemen. As of 2007, Radio Sawa has added only one of these streams—an Iraqi dialect stream—to supplement the pan-Arab broadcast; however, the network is continuing development of the other localized news broadcasts.[38]

As for the VOA in the Middle East, audiences in the region can no longer hear VOA reports in Arabic or English, except from the service's Web site. Other than a few hours of English broadcast in Baghdad, Mosul, and Kuwait, VOA can only be heard in non-Arabic languages on the periphery of the region. The VOA Web site's audio links to correspondents' reports is now the only way for VOA English to penetrate the Middle East. The Bush Administration's budget request for 2008 calls increased funding for Radio Sawa and Al Hurra Television. To offset the increase, the budget requests calls for the reduction or elimination of services in other languages, as well as the VOA English flagship service, VOA News Now. English will be reserved for a few hours a day of targeted programming to Africa. A Senate panel is currently working to reinstate some of this funding.[39]

Al Hurra

As discussed in chapter three of this book, Al Hurra, Radio Sawa's sister network, is an Arab-language television network founded and funded by the Bush administration to promote a positive image of the United States. Run by the same MBN nonprofit that is responsible for Sawa, both networks were developed to provide Arab audiences with an American perspective on world events and help reverse the steep rise in negative public sentiment that has been building against the Bush administration since the launch of the war on terrorism following 9/11.

Al Hurra has become America's most expensive public diplomacy effort. The network's initial start-up budget called for $67 million budget in 2004. Its budget request for 2009 is $112 million.[40] The BBG has invested more than $200 million in the MBN organization that runs Radio Sawa and Al Hurra Television.[41] Both Radio Sawa and Al Hurra are on the air 24/7 in Arabic and, according to a January 2006 MBN press release, together claim a weekly audience of approximately 35 million,[42] although this has had no independent confirmation.

The network was designed not only to counter Al Jazeera but also to provide Arab viewers with reliable, objective, high quality, and credible alternatives to state-owned television news broadcasts that were rigidly controlled by the governments of Arab countries. With generally poor production values and a mobilization type of broad-casting format, where the primary coverage is of the activities of the head of state and generally "safe" topics, state-owned news stations were not answering the needs of viewers, who were rapidly turning to satellite news stations. By the time of its launch in 2004, however, the Arab world had a surfeit of relatively high-quality and open sat-ellite television networks, including MBC networks, Egyptian Nile Networks, and Orbit Networks, as well as satellite channels Dream TV, Al Mehawar TV, and OTV, and others, with multiple sources of information and talk shows that already discussed all the issues that Al Hurra planned to introduce. By 2008, the list had expanded to include MSNBC in Arabic, ONTV, and the public diplomacy efforts of the United Kingdom (BBC Arabic), France (France 24), Russia (Russia Al Youm), Germany (Deutsche Welle), and more. In the past several years, governments in Egypt and the Gulf have loosened restrictions on programming and allowed private ownership of satellite networks. Although Al Jazeera remains the most popular network for news in both Egypt and the region, Orbit and Egyptian TV, among others, have some of the region's most highly rated and controversial programs and talk shows, discussing topics as wide-ranging as election coverage, women's rights, civil society, democracy, legal decisions, controversial laws, and policy proposals, as well as a constant menu of economic, government, business, and celebrity scandals.

Al Hurra, with its stigma of U.S. funding, never had a chance to be more than a rather obscure satellite network, particularly as its pro-gramming failed to generate much political debate or controversy. Al Jazeera continues to hold the largest share of the Arab news market, with 53 percent of Arabs surveyed in a 2008 poll identifying it as their first choice for news, with practically no change from 2007. Egyptian TV is the next most popular source of international news, with 17 percent of Arabs choosing it as their primary source. In 2008, audience share increased for Egyptian Television and Al Arabiya 2007. Egyptian audi-ences also prefer Al Jazeera for international news, followed by Egyptian networks (31 percent).[43]

The challenge that Al Hurra has not been able to overcome is that viewers continue to see it as an American propaganda station, unwilling to cover controversial stories in the region. On the one hand, critics say the reason Arab audiences are not more receptive to Al Hurra is the perception that it is biased because it is funded by the U.S. State Department, regardless of whether these people have viewed the channel.[44] Only 2 percent of the Middle East audience rate Al Hurra as their preferred source of news, about the same percentage that Al-Manar, Hezbollah's channel, receives. Although Al Hurra has a separate, localized broadcast for Iraq and enjoys a larger audience share, it is still the number four network in the country. Researcher Shibley Telhami says that Al Hurra's impact on public opinion has been less than zero. "For most people in the region," he said, "it's simply not on the radar."[45]

According to William Rugh, one of America's most respected experts on the Middle East, Al Jazeera's coverage of the United States is more in-depth than Al Hurra's and it covers issues and encourages debate in ways that Al Hurra does not.[46] James Glassman, who replaced Karen Hughes as the person leading the State Department's public diplomacy efforts, holds a more optimistic view of Al Hurra's success, observing that government polling shows that more than 8 percent of the Arabic-speaking population of the Middle East watch Al Hurra for at least some period of time each week, constituting millions of people that the network has an opportunity to influence.[47] The question remains, who is watching?

Most independent observers agree that Al Hurra is largely irrelevant to Arab viewers, with little market share and almost no political impact. The station faces a number of challenges in addition to the general perception of the region's audiences that the station exists to propagate the views of the U.S. government. Some of those challenges are managerial, while others relate to its structure and the nature of its mission. In 2006, founding director Mouafic Harb left after a harsh report by the USGAO that criticized the station's management and performance and cited serious deficiencies in transparency and accountability. The removal of Harb, along with the replacement of Kenneth Tomlinson as chairman of the BBG, created an opportunity for the channel to correct some of its deficiencies. Larry Register, formerly of CNN, was hired to try and save the station. When Register took over, he tried to increase Al Hurra's audience by covering issues of interest to Arabs, featuring a wider, more diverse range of voices, and trying to establish a reputation for Al Hurra as a model of uncensored, objective broadcasting rather than American propaganda. Register also increased coverage of American politics, focusing on one of Al Hurra's few points of comparative advantage. Whether all of this might have won Al Hurra any increase in market share is unknown. In June 2007, Register announced his resignation. His departure followed a campaign by conservative journalists and members of Congress, angered at some of Register's programming.[48]

The conservative anger over Register's attempts to broadcast more balanced content that presents diverse viewpoints on the issues, some in opposition to official U.S. policy, demonstrates one of the great difficulties facing Al Hurra and other attempts at American public diplomacy broadcasting the Middle East. To be a credible source of information for Arab audiences means allowing critics of American policy to speak and reporting news that might not be completely positive about America. For example, one of the main attacks on Register was that he allowed the broadcast of a speech by Hezbollah leader Hassan Nasrallah. The reality is that every network news station in the Middle East covered this speech because it was important and newsworthy; not covering it would have reinforced the public's perception of Al Hurra as a propaganda machine for the U.S. government. An example of this occurred under Harb's leadership, when Al Hurra notoriously continued broadcast of a cooking show instead of breaking in with news of the assassination of Hamas leader Ahmed Yassin.[49]

The other major challenge facing the network is its lack of transparency and accountability. The network operates with little oversight from its board of governors and the U.S. government. The network's leaders generally do not speak Arabic and so have difficulty understanding what is broadcast. In addition, programming experts have made choices that are not attuned to the culture and concerns of the network's audience. For example, in March 2008, the network aired a documentary on the Crusades. Some of the Muslim staffers, and viewers, saw the program as an unfortunate reminder of Bush's 2001 comment that the war on terrorism would be a "crusade."[50]

For Congress and government oversight bodies, information about Al Hurra's content has been hard to obtain. Al Hurra has no live feed to the United States and does not provide transcripts of its programs in Arabic or English (unlike Al Jazeera and Al Arabiya, both of which offer full transcripts of their programs online).[51] Despite its difficulties and lack of accountability, Al Hurra's budget has steadily increased.

A New Public Diplomacy Czar

In 2005, Karen Hughes was nominated by President Bush to become the new undersecretary of state for public diplomacy, replacing Charlotte Beers. A former television news reporter, Hughes served as Bush's director of communications while he was governor of Texas, planned the 2004 Republican Convention, and was a member of the

White House Iraq Group, the task force charged with increasing public support for the Iraq war.[52] After taking office, Hughes established a strategic framework for U.S. public diplomacy efforts. The framework calls for offering a "positive image of hope," isolating and marginalizing extremists, and promoting shared values and common interests. Hughes stated that she intended to achieve these goals using five tactics: engagement, exchanges, education, empowerment, and evaluation, as well as traditional public diplomacy programs.[53]

One of her first acts was to schedule a visit to several countries in the Middle East. Her trip, billed as a "listening tour" stopped first in Cairo, where she denounced Islamic militancy and defended administration policies in Iraq. During her time in Cairo, she also met with Sheikh Muhammed Sayed Tantawi, the mufti, or spiritual leader, of Al Azhar University, the leading Sunni Muslim center. She praised the sheikh as a respected moderate voice in the Islamic world and noted that he was one of the first among the Muslim leaders to condemn the attacks of 9/11. Her audiences were generally composed of people friendly to her message and included a group of Egyptian high school students who had been exchange students in the United States, as well as students at the American University in Cairo.[54]

Her trip to the region was similar to others taken by senior American diplomats and included meetings with senior government officials, press conferences, and interviews with local media. The reception she got, however, was often angry.[55] The media were critical and tagged several of her remarks as incorrect or insensitive and said that the selection of Hughes as spokesperson to the Arab world was problematic, as she had spent no time in the Arab world, possessed no knowledge of Arab or Egyptian history or culture, and didn't speak Arabic.[56] In Cairo, as the U.S.-led invasion of Iraq was condemned, U.S. commentator Fred Kaplan described the visit as a "fiasco." She travelled next to Saudi Arabia, where she repeatedly spoke about the strength and importance of President Bush's religious beliefs, a particularly dangerous tactic given Bin Laden's message that the United States was on a religious crusade, using force to transform Muslim societies according to a Christian agenda.[57]

Hughes resigned her position in 2007. James Glassman, a conservative commentator and journalist who was chairman of the BBG, was named as her replacement. Columnist Rhami Khouri of the *Lebanon Daily Star* said that Hughes's tenure was "a political catastrophe, ineffective and probably counterproductive"[58] although she received praise from other quarters, including the observation that she implemented some of the 2003 recommendations of the Advisory Group on Public Diplomacy and that she created a rapid response team of Arabic-speaking analysts to appear on Middle Eastern media and send talking points to diplomats worldwide.[59]

In 2006, the U.S. government's GAO reviewed performance plans and fieldwork in Egypt and concluded that the post's public diplomacy work lacked important elements of strategic communication planning. It found that there was no detailed, country-level plan, that there were too many competing messages and that the staff needed to do a better job of clarifying and defining the program's message as well as establish clear, measurable objectives. Officials in Egypt said that there was rarely sufficient time to strategize, plan, or evaluate programs and that it was difficult to find time to travel outside the capital. Tours of duty for public diplomacy professionals were too short—tours in the Muslim world are, on average, 22 percent shorter in length than tours in other countries. In addition, the report found that 30 percent of public diplomacy positions in the Muslim world were filled by officers without sufficient language skills.[60] Although much criticism was directed toward Karen Hughes, it is fair to state that she was handed an extremely difficult task made some quiet progress.

The Way Forward

Polls have consistently shown that audiences in Egypt and the Middle East already know and understand American values and that they share those values as well as the aspirations of Americans. Egyptian and Arab respondents tell the pollsters that they admire not only American educational achievements and technology, but also the freedom of expression that is enshrined in the U.S. Constitution. Public diplomacy efforts need to shift their focus from educating the region's audiences about American values to creating dialogues about the issues and ideas that are blocking improved relations. Public diplomacy has to be about more than just one-way communication; it must include convincing the people in the region that the information they are hearing and seeing is not only accurate and truthful but also that the United States understands and respects Egyptian and Arab culture and values in return. For example, it is critical that the United States counter claims by Bin Laden and others that the United States is engaging in a crusade against Islam. Successful public diplomacy efforts require a sustained investment in listening first, and then acting on what is heard.

The Independent Task Force on Public Diplomacy, sponsored by the Council on Foreign Relations, and the Bush administration's Advisory Group on Public Diplomacy for the Arab and Muslim World, developed a list of recommendations for improving the effectiveness of public diplomacy efforts in the region. The most important of these include assessing the ways in which U.S. actions will be received by the rest of the world before major new international initiatives are undertaken and building in communication strategies to proactively reduce criticism, increasing Arab-language and Muslim culture expertise in all U.S. agencies that are involved in the region, and enlarging cultural and academic exchange programs.[61]

The United States has worked for many years in the region quietly building a deep understanding of core American values through academic, professional, and cultural exchanges. These programs have a history of demonstrated success and continue to be a powerful tool to create positive feelings toward the United States. Public diplomacy efforts should recognize the importance of these exchanges and continue to expand and fund programs like the Fulbright scholarships and the International Visitor program. In addition, new exchange programs that focus on youth, education, and dialogue should be explored, as well as programs that include a component of shared experience: Americans visiting Egypt and the Arab world, as well as Egyptians and Arabs travelling to the United States. This positive achievement is attributable both to Karen Hughes and to Dina Powell, an Egyptian–American who headed the education and culture bureau at the State Department.

International broadcasting has a vital role to play in communicating with the people of the Middle East. Unfortunately, the United States is doing little to engage those policy makers and the academics and professionals that once tuned in to news and information, in English and Arabic, on the respected VOA.[62] There are two contradictory options facing proponents of public diplomacy broadcasting: produce a rather boring, uncontroversial, pro-U.S. propaganda product which nobody watches and which has no news credibility for its audiences or produce a competitive, high quality, popular product, which might anger Congress or conservatives who object to its taxpayer-funded programs airing views that are in opposition to the official government position.[63]

VOA, before its dissolution, developed a plan to reinvigorate its broadcasts. In developing this plan, VOA professionals consulted with Middle East experts in the State Department as well as specialists with knowledge of the Middle East and Arab academicians, who agreed that there was a demand for programming on American news, politics, social and cultural trends, and lifestyles. The plan calls for renewed adherence to the tenets of the VOA charter, calling for objective and balanced reporting. The plan also calls for programming that combines an exciting format of music, news, and other types of programming broadcast 24/7 and hosted by well-informed, personable, identifiable, and professional on-air personalities. News reports would be carefully sourced, objective and accurate to increase credibility, and news and news-related discussion and call-in programs, originating locally in locations like Cairo, Amman, Dubai, Baghdad, and Jerusalem, would focus on conflict resolution, peace, and dialogue among the people of the Middle East. Disc jockeys with an understanding of national and international issues, as well as pop music and entertainment, would host the music and segments between programs and segments that deal with American life, culture, education, and thought. Programming would be developed by professional journalists based in Washington and New York, in major Arab-American communities, and through-out the Middle East.[64]

Al Hurra has undergone a number of changes, including replacements of some of the network's leadership. The new leadership may be more willing to take a more critical look at the network's programming and operations and make needed improvements. During 2008, for example, the network provided extensive coverage of the U.S. presidential election campaigns, including live broadcasts of the U.S. presidential and vice presidential debates and expert analysis following each broadcast. The network broadcast live coverage including simultaneous translation of key speeches and interviews of Congressmen, experts, journalists, and others who discussed topics of regional interest.[65] Congress has raised issues related to the Bush Administration's 2008 budget request, including calling for greater accountability and transparency and hopefully will take a fresh look at international broadcasting, especially to the Middle East. The network needs to greatly increase transparency, by, among other things, providing a live feed to the United States and transcripts of its programs on a greatly expanded Web site. This transparency would protect against attacks by critics and will provide some context to controversial programming. This increased access might also strengthen the network's impact with, for example, the millions of Egyptians and Arabs who routinely visit the Web sites of Al Jazeera and Al Arabiya.[66]

The challenge is clear, and the timing is critical. The image of the United States has plummeted in key Arab countries over the past few years. Respect for the U.S. leadership role and its ability to promote issues related to human rights, the environment, the fight against corruption, democracy, and even the economy has declined drastically in the wake of the U.S. war on terrorism, the lack of progress at resolving the Israeli/Palestinian conflict, Guantanamo Bay and Abu Ghraib, and three Arab and Muslim country invasions by the United States in the last fourteen years.[67] American strategic interests in the region are also at a critical juncture, given the fragility of the progress in Iraq, a resurgent Iran exploring its position in the regional power structure, the price of oil at unprecedented heights, and restive populations wanting hope and empowerment.

Efforts at countering the steep decline in America's image through international broadcasting efforts have been mostly fruitless, but there may be some new opportunities for dialogue and audience engagement on several policy fronts: growing popular opposition to most forms of terrorism against civilians, particularly following attacks against local citizens and important tourist industries in Egypt and Jordan, and support for a peaceful, two-state solution to the Palestinian-Israeli problem.

Those responsible for U.S. public diplomacy efforts must do a better job of understanding Arab culture, values, history, and public opinion. They need to develop plans, programs, and programming tailored to individual countries rather than for the region as a whole and greatly increase the number of Arabic-speaking staff members. They need to do a better job of communicating with Arab audiences, focusing more on wide-ranging, balanced, and honest discussions of the issues that divide the countries, rather than educating Arabs about American values.

Finally, true progress on improving the image of the United States will only occur when the substantive issues that have angered Egyptian and other Middle East publics are recognized as legitimate and important, and the United States takes action to explain, debate, and resolve the issues in ways that demonstrate that Americans value the Arab world and its citizens.

Notes

1. Telhami, *2008 Annual Arab Public Opinion Poll* and Zogby, "Arab Public Opinion and the US in 2008."
2. Ibid.
3. Pollock, "Arab Public Opinion."

4. Wilke, "Karen Hughes' Uphill Battle."
5. Craft. "US Arabic Channel a Turn-Off."
6. Telhami, *2008 Annual Arab Public Opinion Poll.*
7. Ibid.
8. Ford, "US Public Diplomacy."
9. Lussenhop, "Creativity and Patience."
10. Ford, "US Public Diplomacy ."
11. Hoffman, "Beyond Public Diplomacy."
12. Plaisance, "The Propaganda War on Terrorism."
13. Ibid., 250–251.
14. Cola and Toensing, "Never Too Soon to Say Goodbye to Hi."
15. "Hi Magazine," *Source Watch.*
16. Colla and Toensing, "Never Too Soon to Say Goodbye to Hi."
17. Ibid.
18. Harper, "US Shelves Arabic 'Propaganda' Mag."
19. Ibid.
20. Shahine, "Hi Is Not Enough."
21. Harper, "US Shelves Arabic 'Propaganda' Mag."
22. Kassman, "Voice of America Versus Radio Sawa."
23. Cull, "The Perfect War."
24. Whitworth, "America's Voice as It Could Have Been."
25. Kassman, "Voice of America Versus Radio Sawa."
26. Ibid.
27. Linzer, "Lost in Translation."
28. Hilmy, "Radio Sawa."
29. Kassman, "Voice of America versus Radio Sawa."
30. Whitworth, "America's Voice as It Could Have Been."
31. Hilmy, "Radio Sawa."
32. Linzer, "Lost in Translation."
33. Hilmy, "Radio Sawa."
34. Lynch, "The Alhurra Project."
35. Hilmy, "Radio Sawa."
36. Ibid.
37. Kassman, "Voice of America versus Radio Sawa."
38. Ibid.
39. Whitworth, "America's Voice as It Could Have Been."
40. Ibid.
41. Heil, "2007: A Fateful Year for America's Voices?"
42. Ibid.
43. Telhami, *2008 Annual Arab Public Opinion Poll.*
44. Cochrane, "Is Al-Hurra Doomed?"
45. Linzer, "Lost in Translation."
46. Ibid.
47. Ibid.
48. Lynch, "The Alhurra Project."
49. Ibid.
50. Linzer, "Lost in Translation."
51. Lynch, "The Alhurra Project."
52. Weisman, "In Egypt, Hughes Defends US Policy."
53. Ford, "US Public Diplomacy."
54. Weisman, "In Egypt, Hughes Defends US Policy."
55. Jones. "Karen Hughes' 'Listening Tour' and Its Aftermath."

56. Weisman, "In Egypt, Hughes Defends US Policy."
57. ones, "Karen Hughes' 'Listening Tour' and Its Aftermath."
58. Fry, "US Public Diplomacy Chief Departs Amid Praise, Criticism."
59. Ibid.
60. Ford, "US Public Diplomacy."
61. Brown, "Public Diplomacy."
62. Whitworth, "America's Voice as It Could Have Been."
63. Lynch, "The Alhurra Project."
64. Whitworth, "America's Voice as It Could Have Been."
65. "Al Hurra Brings the Presidential Debates to the Middle East," E-mail press release from Middle East Broadcasting Networks, September 26, 2008.
66. Lynch, "The Alhurra Project."
67. Snow, "Anti-Americanism and the Rise of Civic Diplomacy."

Bibliography

Aboul-Enein, Youssef. "Spymaster: Former Egyptian Intelligence Chief Discusses Psychological Warfare." *Infantry Magazine*, July—August 2006. http://findarticles.com/p/articles/mi_m0IAV/is_4_95/ai_n17154167 (accessed September 1, 2008).

"Al Hurra Brings the Presidential Debates to the Middle East," E-mail press release from Middle East Broadcasting Networks, September 26, 2008.

Brown, Seyom. "Public Diplomacy: Restoring Legitimacy to US International Leadership." *Center for American Progress*, November 1, 2004. http://www.americanprogress.org/issues/2004/11/b237877.html (accessed September 5, 2008).

Cochrane, Paul. "Is Al-Hurra Doomed?" Worldpress.org, June 11, 2004. http://www.worldpress.org/Mideast/1872.cfm (accessed September 4, 2008).

Colla, Elliott and Chris Toensing. "Never Too Soon to Say Goodbye to Hi." *Middle East Report Online*, September 2003. http://www.merip.org/medo/interventions/colla_interv.html (accessed September 16, 2008).

Craft, Matthew. "US Arabic Channel a Turn-Off." *Guardian.co.uk*, February 16, 2004. http://www.guardian.co.uk/media/2004/feb/16/broadcasting.usnews (accessed September 1, 2008).

Cull, Nicholas. "'The Perfect War': US Public Diplomacy and International Broadcasting During Desert Shield and Desert Storm 1990/1991." *Arab Media & Society* (Fall 2006). http://www.arabmediasociety.com/topics/index.php?t_article=87 (accessed September 16, 2008).

Ford, Jess T. "US Public Diplomacy: State Department Efforts Lack Certain Communication Elements and Face Persistent Challenges." Testimony before the Subcommittee on Science, the Departments of State, Justice, and Commerce, and Related Agencies, House Committee on Appropriations, May 3, 2006. http://www.gao.gov/new.items/d06707t.pdf (accessed September 16, 2008).

Fry, Jim. "US Public Diplomacy Chief Departs Amid Praise, Criticism." *VOANews.com* December 11, 2007. http://www.voanews.com/english/archive/2007–12/2007-12-11-voa30.cfm?CFID=44718695&CFTOKEN=39678023 (accessed September 6, 2008).

Harper, Tim. "US Shelves Arabic 'Propaganda' Mag." *CommonDreams.org News Center*, December 23, 2005. http://www.commondreams.org/headlines05/1223–06.htm (accessed September 16, 2008).

Heil, Alan L., Jr. "2007: A Fateful Year for America's Voices?" *Arab Media & Society*. http://www.arabmediasociety.com/topics/index.php?t_article=76 (accessed September 17, 2008).

"Hi Magazine." *Source Watch*. Center for Media and Democracy. http://www.sourcewatch.org/index.php?title=Hi_Magazine (accessed September 10, 2008).

Hilmy, Sam. "Radio Sawa: America's New Adventure in Radio Broadcasting." *Arab Media & Society*, May 2007. http://www.arabmediasociety.com/index.php?article=187&p=1 (accessed September 4, 2008).

Hoffman, David. "Beyond Public Diplomacy." *Foreign Affairs* 81, no. 2 (March/April 2002). http://www.foreignaffairs.org/20020301faessay7974/david-hoffman/beyond-public-diplomacy.html (accessed September 10, 2008).

Jones, Lucy. "Karen Hughes' 'Listening Tour' and Its Aftermath." *Report on Middle East Affairs* (December 2005): 24–26. http://www.washington-report.org/archives/December_2005/0512024.html (accessed September 10, 2008).

Kassman, Laurie. "Voice of America Versus Radio Sawa in the Middle East: A Personal Perspective," *Arab Media & Society*, May 2007. http://www.arabmediasociety.com/?article=184 (accessed September 16, 2008).

Kohut, Andrew. "American Public Diplomacy in the Islamic World." *Remarks to the Senate Foreign Relations Committee Hearing*, February 27, 2003. http://foreign.senate.gov/testimony/2003/KohutTestimony030227.pdf (accessed September 16, 2008).

Linzer, Dafna. "Lost in Translation: Alhurra—America's Troubled Effort to Win Middle East Hearts and Minds." *ProPublica* June 22, 2008. www.propublica.org/feature/alhurra-middle-east-hearts-and-minds-622 (accessed September 15, 2008).

Lussenhop, Matt. "Creativity and Patience: Public Diplomacy Post-Sept. 11." *Foreign Service Journal* (April 2002): 29–32. http://www.afsa.org/fsj/Apr02/Lussenhop.pdf (accessed September 16, 2008).

Lynch, Marc. "The Alhurra Project: Radio Marti of the Middle East." *Arab Media & Society*, June 2007. http://www.arabmediasociety.com/?article=268 (accessed September 16, 2008).

Plaisance, Patrick Lee. "The Propaganda War on Terrorism: An Analysis of the United States' 'Shared Values' Public-Diplomacy Campaign after September 11, 2001." *Journal of Mass Media Ethics* 20, no. 4 (2005): 250–268.

Pollock, David. "Arab Public Opinion." Testimony at the Joint Hearing of the Committee on Foreign Affairs Subcommittee on the Middle East and South Asia and on International Organizations, Human Rights, and Oversight, United States House of Representatives. May 3, 2007. http://www.globalsecurity.org/military/library/congress/2007_hr/070503-transcript.pdf (accessed September 17, 2008).

Rugh, William A. *American Encounters with Arabs: The "Soft Power" of U.S. Public Diplomacy in the Middle East*. Westport, CT: Greenwood, 2006.

Satioff, Robert. "Devising a Public Diplomacy Campaign toward the Middle East (Part I): Basic Principles," *Policy Watch* #579. The Washington Institute for Near East Policy. October 30, 2001. https://www.washingtoninstitute.org/templateC05.php?CID=1457 (accessed September 12, 2008).

Shahine, Gihan. "Hi Is Not Enough." *Al-Ahram Weekly On-line*, no. 656, September 18–24, 2003. http://weekly.ahram.org.eg/2003/656/eg8.htm (accessed September 16, 2008).

Snow, Nancy. "Anti-Americanism and the Rise of Civic Diplomacy." *Foreign Policy in Focus*. December 13, 2006. http://www.fpif.org/fpiftxt/3795 (accessed September 14, 2008).

Telhami, Shibley (principal investigator). *2008 Annual Arab Public Opinion Poll*. Survey of the Anwar Sadat Chair for Peace and Development at the University of Maryland (with Zogby International), March 2008. http://www.brookings.edu/topics/~/media/Files/

events/2008/0414_middle_east/0414_middle_east_telhami.pdf (accessed September 10, 2008).

Weisman, Steven. "In Egypt, Hughes Defends US Policy." *International Herald Tribune* September 26, 2005. http://www.iht.com/articles/2005/09/26/news/hughes.php (accessed September 1, 2008).

Whitworth, Myrna. "America's Voice as It Could Have Been." *Arab Media & Society*, May 2007. http://arabmediasociety.sqgd.co.uk/topics/index.php?t_article=118 (accessed September 10, 2008).

Wilke, Richard. "Karen Hughes' Uphill Battle." Pew Research Center Publications. November 1, 2007. http://pewresearch.org/pubs/627/karen-hughes (accessed September 1, 2008).

Zogby, James. "Arab Public Opinion and the US in 2008." *The Huffington Post*. May 9, 2008. http://www.huffingtonpost.com/james-zogby/arab-public-opinion-the-u_b_101073.html (accessed September 1, 2008).

PART III

Where We Go from Here

CHAPTER SEVEN

Public Diplomacy 2.0

AMELIA ARSENAULT

In 1969, Dr. Robert F. Delaney, Director of the Edward R. Murrow Center of the Fletcher School of Law and Diplomacy told participants of the Emergency Committee for a Reappraisal of United States Overseas Information Policies and Programs that the global dispersion of radio and television platforms represented "nothing less than a new diplomacy, a new weapons system" that could ameliorate America's declining world image in the wake of international dissatisfaction with the Vietnam War and U.S. racial policies.[1]

Just less than forty years later, a "new diplomacy" based on one-way radio and television communications appears both outmoded and naïve. From the printing press, to the telegraph, to the radio, to the television, to the Internet, new communication technologies have influenced the form and content of public diplomacy—challenging existing institutional practices and presenting new opportunities for engaging and/or alienating foreign constituencies. Today, the Internet, mobile phones, and other participatory platforms often referred to as "Web 2.0" or "social media" have emerged as the locus for discussion about American public diplomacy inviting a reimagination of how international messaging strategies are produced, distributed, and consumed.[2]

End users from around the world now engage in collaboration and dialogue on a host of topics and disseminate information and/or disinformation with unprecedented ease, cost, and speed, largely unfettered by governmental control. Pundits and politicians struggle with how to engage with this more diffuse and often chaotic global communications sphere. Whether these technologies offer a panacea or poison for global cross-cultural relations remains speculative. However, large-scale adoption of participatory technology and culture, the blurring of mass communication and digital communication networks, and corresponding changes in end-user behaviors necessitate a parallel shift in discussions about public diplomatic practices. New technologies have not replaced traditional modes of outreach. They are, however, making them more germane and at the same time more unpredictable as mechanisms for shaping foreign public opinion and cross-national relationships. In short, the rise of a transnational, transmedia, and transmodal public sphere has further devolved state influence over its national image while simultaneously offering new tools for the practice of public diplomacy. A 2.0 world[3] necessitates a public diplomacy 2.0 strategy characterized by more nuanced reactive and proactive outreach strategies that consider three broad and interrelated developments in the contemporary media and communications environment: (1) the technological convergence of communication networks, (2) related problems of information delivery and visibility, and (3) an incorporation of participatory and collaborative models of interaction. This chapter evaluates contemporary U.S. public diplomacy activities in light of these trends and points to future considerations and possible new directions.

Convergence

In September 2006, as a uniformed Chinese officer gunned down a line of Tibetan refugees hiking across a snowy Mount Everest pass, a member of an unrelated mountaineering expedition took out his cellphone and recorded the events as they unfolded. Upon returning home, he delivered the footage to a Romanian TV network, where it aired, and then quickly disappeared from the news cycle. That is, until a viewer decided to repost the video on YouTube. To date, individuals from around the world have watched the video 106,000 times in its Romanian version and an additional 1.5 million times in English, French, and Chinese translations on sites like AOL Video, MySpace, and Trueveo.com. Television outlets like CNN and BBC world also syndicated the YouTube video. These rebroadcasts were then reposted on YouTube garnering tens of thousands of more viewers. Pressed by mounting public concern, diplomats from around the world voiced formal and informal objections to China's treatment of refugees.

This story is just one of many examples underscoring how national reputations are increasingly negotiated across multiple media and information platforms. The digitization of all forms of information means that mobile, media, and Internet networks are increasingly converging into one porous, information rich, and chaotic global information sphere. Technological convergence has many implications for the behavior of target populations, many of which will be discussed later in this chapter. This section focuses on how technological convergence has altered the information environment at large.

First, the barriers to entry are significantly lowered. The 2.0 world is not limited to Westerners with broadband Internet connections. Mobile phones, which are more widely accessible than the Internet, provide both indirect and direct points of entry. Many phones offer short-messaging-system (SMS) applications, cameras, and Internet browsers. If a photographer does not have Internet access, he or she can send these images via SMS to someone who does. These mobile devices also link users to the online sphere in more traditional ways. Many communities that lived previously in isolation can now tap into global diasporic networks or communities of interest with a phone call to another user who may have Internet access. In this environment, traditional economies of scale no longer hold true. An activist with an SMS enabled phone can create international news. For example, in the postelection violence in Kenya in 2008, Kenyan activists bypassed government media crackdowns by creating the Ushahidi.com Web site that geo-mapped instances of political violence, looting, voter intimidation and the like on the basis of text-message reports sent from around the country. And sometimes a hacker with a cause can disrupt and/or deface communication channels, as was the case in April 26, 2008, the anniversary of Chernobyl, when a cyber attack put eight Internet sites operated by the U.S. international broadcaster Radio Free Europe/Radio Liberty out of commission for several days.

Communication flows are thus multidirectional and multiproductional. Brian McNair posited that the proliferation of information sources has opened a "chaos paradigm" for international journalism and telecommunications companies.[4] The shift toward participatory modes of information production and dissemination has opened a similar chaos paradigm for public diplomacy professionals. Negative stories, images, and messages circulate unfettered in today's converged information environment. While practitioners can use new technologies to reach out to and engage with specific communities of interest, boundaries between communication spheres are increasingly anachronistic. Almost all communication material is universally available. Indeed, national media spaces are increasingly defined by an "imagined community" that includes both global and diasporic actors rather than a territorially bounded information space.[5] Traditional one-to-many communication platforms provide a common culture and the web and Internet provide more localized channels for responding to that culture.[6] These responses often find their way back into more traditional media platforms leading to a cycle of cocreation and coproduction of content. For example, the Digital Outreach Team, a component of the Department of State's online strategy that engages in targeted dialogue sessions with Muslim bloggers, engaged in a long exchange of posts with Ali Akbar Javanfekr, Iranian president Mahmoud Ahmadinejad's media affairs adviser. The results of the online conversation were then republished in *Iran Newspaper* on the subject of nuclear proliferation where it then filtered outward into other outlets.[7]

YouTube, the world's largest streaming video site embodies the unpredictable nature of a converged communication environment. In recent years, people have begun to talk about the "YouTube effect," what Moises Naim describes as a phenomenon "whereby video-clips, often produced by individuals acting on their own, are rapidly disseminated throughout the world" and often instigate sociopolitical responses in the off-line world.[8] Videos of President George Bush rubbing German Chancellor Christina Merkel's shoulders and of Coalition soldiers committing violence against Iraqi civilians are just two examples of YouTube videos that have affected foreign public opinion as well as elicited responses from government actors. Streaming video is not the only delivery mechanism by which unintended or misdirected images circulate. In April 2008, faced with a Freedom of Information Act request by the *New York Times*, the Pentagon released documents and audio-files onto the web detailing the Department of Defense (DOD) military analyst program, whereby experts either paid by or closely affiliated with the department served as "expert commentators" about the Iraq War on media programs across America.[9] Once public, these documents provided fertile fodder among the blogosphere for theories about American international propaganda activities around the world.

The unbounded nature of the international communication environment means that legal safeguards designed to protect U.S. citizens from propaganda are increasingly anachronistic. The 1948 Smith-Mundt Act restricts the dissemination of information specifically tailored for international audiences within U.S. borders. Today, U.S. government departments struggle to respect the spirit of the Smith-Mundt restrictions and the realities of a converged environment. The Department of State maintains State.gov, a public affairs Web site and America. gov the international information portal for foreign audiences. Given the sheer scope of Web sites, social networks, and general information available to end users maintaining multiple Web sites and replicating content across them is both inefficient and at times counterproductive. In reality, the domestic/international dichotomy is little more than a useful fiction. Only 42 percent of State.gov traffic originates inside the United States and more than 20 percent of visitors to America.gov are domestic residents. Hundreds of sites operate within U.S. borders contain links to the America.gov Web site. State.gov is comparatively much more popular in countries like Iran and Nigeria than America. gov. State.gov ranks as the 388th most popular web destination in Iran while America.gov comes in at 4,202.[10] In the Internet age, applying a 1948 regulation that demands a clear domestic/international separation is all but impossible.

Regardless of how new technologies are regulated and deployed by public diplomacy practitioners, negative information will continue to circulate. Officials must wrestle with information and misinformation circulating online, off-line, and every manner of in between. The State Department launched the Rapid Response Unit in 2007 and maintains Rumors, Myths and Fabrications blog, both of which are designed to disseminate accurate information. However, while posted comments are not necessarily a direct reflection of the size of readership, the lack of feedback suggests that the site has gained little traction within the blogosphere. This underscores the fact that more than ever, delivering corrective information is not simply a process of one-to-many communication.

Monitoring all 27 billion web pages and the estimated 2.3 trillion SMS messages transmitted every year is all but impossible.[11] Governments cannot simply assume that information once released will gain traction and/or remain unfiltered. End users actively participate in both selecting and redistributing information, creating new issues for packaging and delivering information so it is heard amidst the cacophony of alternate information sources.

Customization and Universalization

While digitized information moves fluidly across delivery platforms, end users are largely responsible for the breadth and depth of its transfer. Because customary delivery mechanisms for information have been upended, accessibility, credibility, and resonance are even more important. Particularly when it comes to the United States, target communities around the world struggle with *too* much not too little information. As Princess Rym Ali of Jordan stated at an Arab-U.S. media conference, "With all the blogs available, with all the access to images depicting all sides and with all the willingness in the world to bring about mutual understanding, one would think there was no room for misunderstanding. The overflow of information is such that it becomes like a tower of Babel—and making sense of it all can be challenging, to say the least."[12]

Accessibility

Utilizing multiple platforms and delivery mechanisms customized according to the preferences and the connectivity of the target populations is fundamental to public diplomacy 2.0. Internet penetration remains low in the majority of the world. However, particularly in the last few years the digital divide has shrunk rapidly. The ratio between Internet access in developed and developing economies dropped from 80.6:1 in 1997 to 5.8:1 in 2007. As developed economies approach saturation, the future of Internet and mobile growth lies predominantly outside the West.[13] To give a small indication, 66 percent of the world's Internet users resided inside the United States in 1996 as compared to 21 percent in 2008.[14] In 2008, China surpassed the United States as the largest Internet market in the world with 253 million users by the end of June 2008; 84.7 percent of those users were broadband users.[15] Social media applications are also increasingly popular. For example, 72 percent of Saudi and 46.5 percent of UAE netizens now regularly participate in social media activities such as blogging and social networking.[16] Facebook, the world's most popular social network regularly attracts more than 125 million unique visitors per month, only a fifth of whom are American.[17]

When looking at new technologies' impact on public diplomacy, it is no longer necessary to speak about reaching out across the digital divide. It is more useful to talk about customizing delivery mechanisms according to levels and preferences for access to information. Of course some individuals find it easier to participate in the Web 2.0 culture either due to training, inequalities of access, or comfort levels with new technologies. However, while those with broadband connections find it easier to upload images and videos, maintain a blog, or participate in a virtual meeting, limited access no longer presents the same barriers to entry. Mobile Internet looks to be the future in many countries. In the United States, 62 percent of Americans have used mobile phones to engage in such nonvoice activities as search the Internet, watch or record a video, and send and receive instant messages.[18] ComScore estimates that mobile search grew by 68 percent in the United States and 38 percent in Europe between September 2007 and September 2008.[19] The mobile surge is not limited to the West; 29 percent of China's Internet users have accessed the Internet via mobile phones.[20] And India's mobile network is so advanced that Bollywood films are now regularly delivered via streaming mobile.

Still, in most parts of the world, access to the digital information sphere is secondary, tertiary, or constrained by low-bandwidth. Thus, public diplomacy practitioners must critically evaluate how to tailor programs for multiple levels of access. Voice of America now provides Special-English programs via mobile phones and in the summer of 2008 the Planning, Budget and Applied Technologies Directorate (PBAT) in the Public Diplomacy Information Technology Office (IT) launched the first of a series of online chats using Adobe connect, a software that requires very little bandwidth. The central point is that whatever the initiative, it must be easily accessible across multiple levels of access. Corporate actors have learned that the future is in "transmedia" production whereby an anchor product such as a movie or television show is supplemented with consumer products, video games, comic books, virtual worlds, and mobile applications.[21]

By mid-2008, 80–90 percent of the world's population lived within range of a cellular network.[22] The ubiquity of mobile networks and differing levels of mobile phone availability also suggests potential synergies between communication technology development programs generally managed by USAID and public diplomacy initiatives. Widening access serves development goals, stands as a goodwill gesture, and brings interactive potential to new communities that the U.S. government can engage with and potentially learn from. Still, accessibility does not guarantee success.

Credibility

The expanded information environment has amplified the importance of ensuring that all public diplomacy messages and programs are accurate, credible, and stringently ethical. Just as participatory technologies have been pivotal in expanding the size of the Internet, they have also broadened the range of actors capable of playing a watchdog function.

Although many actors capitalize on the anonymity of the digital world, government actors cannot, without risk of furthering already popular theories about U.S. disinformation and propaganda activities. There have been several instances where the DOD has been caught violating these principles. For example, the Pentagon was caught paying reporters to place complimentary articles in Iraqi newspapers and maintains several newspaper-like sites including Mawtani.com where the site attribution deeply buried. In justifying the distribution of this information, Michael Vickers, the assistant secretary of defense in charge of special operations and stabilization efforts explained that "our adversaries use the Internet to great advantage, so we have the responsibility of countering (their messages) with accurate, truthful information, and these websites are a good vehicle."[23] Truthful and accurate information should be a key priority for U.S. public diplomacy. However, proper source attribution is a main component of truthful dissemination of information. These stories are precisely the ones that undermine U.S. credibility in an environment already overcrowded with information.

Resonance

Radio, television, and cinema must also attract viewers, but consumers often watch television channels or listen to radio programs because "nothing else is on." They may also consume these media while engaging in numerous other activities. The Internet, on the other hand, relies almost entirely on pulling audiences to different applications, programs, and sites. Web sites live or die based on whether they can convince users to visit their pages either through cross-linking, search-engine placement, and/or viral popularity. Web 2.0 technologies have changed the dynamics of attraction. There were 50 pages on the World Wide Web in 1993 and no more than 150 by 1994; as of September 2008 the indexed web contains at least 27.6 billion pages.[24] Every month, YouTube alone receives more than 66 million unique visitors, who amass 16 billion page views, and post between 150 and 200,000 new videos each day.[25] However, viewership of individual videos and for Internet sites in general is heavily uneven. If a particular site is not compelling or credible, then there are million more options available. Nielsen Netratings estimates that the average user visits 1,522 web pages each month, but spends only an average of 48 seconds on each site.[26] Due to bandwidth restrictions, mobile users are even more discerning than computer users. When looking at the U.S. market, the average the mobile user visited only 6.4 sites per month.[27] For every video or Web site that spreads virally from user to user, thousands languish in obscurity.

This is certainly true for many public diplomacy initiatives. Although no U.S. international broadcaster currently maintains a YouTube presence, a picture of the traffic rankings of other comparable broadcasters provided in table 7.1 gives an indication of the difficulties in attracting audiences.

As table 7.1 illustrates, the number of visitors varies widely by broadcasting outlet. Outlets with strong off-line brand recognition like Al Jazeera and BBC World also have the highest online traffic. However, the limits of proactive public diplomacy 2.0 should be realized. To put this in context, between June 2006 and September 2007, Lonelygirl 15, a fake web diary of a 15-year-old girl, received 70 million combined hits and a 1.40 minute video of a baby sitting in a highchair laughing is ranked as the sixth most popular video of all time.[28] And in the first week of its launch the Oprah YouTube Channel received almost 5 million views. Al Jazeera English's comparative online success thus pales in comparison.

Largely due to Smith-Mundt restrictions, the earliest State Department uses of YouTube and similar technologies took place within the domestic Bureau of Public Affairs. Under the initiative of Digital Media Lab Director Heath Kern, Public Affairs launched its own YouTube channel, StateVideo in February 2007.[29] As of September 2008, the channel had been viewed 32,211 times and had 525 subscribers. However, while the YouTube channel remains relatively unremarked, individual videos have resonated with audiences. A three-part series on the murder of journalist Daniel Pearl were the most watched videos, with more than a quarter of

Table 7.1 International broadcaster viewership on YouTube (September 2008)

Broadcaster	Date Joined	November 2007		September 2008	
		Subscribers	Channel Views	Subscribers	Channel Views
Al Jazeera	3/26/2007	964	82,173	8,738	909,300
Al Jazeera English	11/23/2006	11,420	642,443	30,901	1,735,932
BBC World News	7/3/2006	4,196	213,221	12,228	579,994
CCTV International	6/20/2007	12	851	312	10,322
Deutsch Welle	4/4/2007	254	28,052	1,101	86,259
France 24	4/4/2007	306	47,085	1,190	126, 292
France 24 English	4/4/2007	178	7,239	1,474	59,596
Russia Today	3/28/2007	739	39,719	7,295	349,242
Telesur TV	6/08/2007	131	7,825	460	15,329

a million views. DipNote, the Bureau's blog authored by Foreign Service officers around the world has also achieved modest success.

Because they are run by Public Affairs, DipNote and StateVideo are not defined as public diplomacy programs. However, data released by the DipNote team recording total page view records stress the site's international presence. In March 2008, visitors from 173 countries visited the blog. As the site has also become a forum for discussion and debate among Foreign Service officers, it is likely that a significant portion of that traffic originates from American government employees abroad. However, given the traffic volume, the site is attracting audiences outside the U.S. diplomatic corps and scholars of public diplomacy. A significant number of visitors to the site came from countries of particular concern for public diplomacy practitioners, including China (6,539 page views), Saudi Arabia (554 page views), Morocco (280 page views), and Iran (167 page views).[30] Admittedly, StateVideo and DipNote have attracted relatively small audiences. However, DipNote's international audiences coupled with numerous Web sites designed to promote dialogue with the United States such as theworldvotes.org and apologiesaccepted.com provide evidence of an unmet demand for engagement via the Internet.

A seemingly infinite number of social media sites exist and more appear every day. It is impossible for the State Department to engage with every one of them. In addition to the aforementioned online video sites and social networking outlets, blogs and online journals number in the millions. Technorati, the largest blog tracker on the Internet, tracks more than 112 million blogs and more than 175,000 new ones are created each day. The State Department launched a Digital Outreach Team in 2007 in an attempt to participate in dialogue in the blogosphere. Rather than engage with "extremists," team members focus on "swing voter sites" such as the discussion forums accompanying current news posts on BBC Arabic.[31] However, given the vast size of the digital territory to be covered, the small size of the staff, and the limited language capabilities (only two team members speak Arabic), this outreach strategy is largely symbolic. However, as the team's leader Brent Blatchkey argues, "There is no guarantee that we will influence anyone; but we won't influence anyone if we're not there."[32]

Cocreation and Collaboration

The circulation of national reputations through interconnected media and communication spheres increasingly depends on the active participation of end users.[33] While audiences have always been more active than they are typically given credit for, bringing their own opinions, preconceptions, and cultural positions to whatever content they may consume, 2.0 technologies have empowered consumers to produce and distribute their own content as well as perform watchdog functions previously the domain of the traditional news media. The issues of credibility, visibility, and delivery identified in the previous section may be rectified to a certain extent by a wider incorporation of the participatory and collaborative dimensions of 2.0 applications. However, the trick, as Kern puts it, is "not just using technology for technology's sake."[34] Cowan and Arsenault argue that practitioners should conceive of public diplomacy in terms of three layers: monologue, defined as one-way informational communications; dialogue, defined as multidirectional interaction; and collaboration, conceived of as working with target populations in joint ventures or projects.[35] Each of these "layers" represents useful forms of outreach that may be enhanced through a more nuanced adoption of participatory technologies.

One-Way Communications

When designing ways to successfully distribute press releases, information campaigns, and corrective information, an appreciation of the pervasiveness of the participatory dynamics of the digital world is essential. Social media and other 2.0 technologies have not replaced Web 1.0; just as public diplomacy 2.0 will not supplant the need for more traditional forms of engagement. Largely informational "read-only" Web sites are still prevalent and many Web sites, particularly government and mainstream media Web sites use a combination of 1.0 and 2.0 features. However, users now expect and depend on both levels of interaction. A visitor to America.gov, for example, may seek transcripts of speeches made by a particular politician, and/or upload user-generated videos and/or participate in social networking or chat rooms. Increasingly users may also expect to be able to access content produced by official U.S. government sources through their Web site portal of choice both on their computers and/or on their mobile phones.

It is important to note that end-user behavior varies widely. Recent Pew studies find that just 3 percent of individuals send video links on a daily basis to each other. More people (75 percent) receive video links than send them (57 percent). This suggests the certain individual users may serve as critical nodes in socially configured distribution networks.[36] Already, U.S. government agencies have begun to engage with the blogosphere. The DOD maintains the Bloggers Roundtable and the State Department regularly hosts online chats with bloggers.[37] Identifying and expanding communication with these nodes and others and aiding others in bridging participation gaps may help to improve the circulation of constructive messaging.

Second, recognition of this participatory ethos may also help public diplomacy practitioners to target a community of users that are traditionally more skeptical of mass media information and exhibit more independence and self-reliance when constructing opinions.[38] As Sey and Castells point out, "it is not that the Internet makes people want autonomy. It is that people searching for autonomy turn to the Internet as their medium of choice."[39] Strategies that capitalize on this need for autonomous information seeking and construction may therefore be more successful. Providing mechanisms for fact checking, feedback, and direct participation in tandem with packaged one-way communications may resonate with skeptical end users. Almost every major news organization offers site visitors the opportunity to upload content that, if compelling enough, will be featured online and in an ever-increasing number of television programs that feature user-generated content (e.g., CNN's IReport & CBS's EyeMobile). Similarly, newspapers now regularly cite and depend on members of the blogosphere as sources of cutting edge social and political news. Government Web sites might benefit from similar initiatives.

Third, the Googlearchy, defined as the positioning of search items in search results, is fundamental to facilitating a successful online and off-line presence.[40] Searching for information is a principal activity if not the principal activity of most Internet users. ComScore estimates that as of 2006, four out of five Internet users now access government information and search for government Web sites using Google and other search engines.[41] However, government sponsored sites are consistently outranked by information from outside sources. Search engine users simultaneously consume information and help to determine the accessibility and dominance of that information source for other users in the Internet sphere. Google, Yahoo, Baidu, and others use a combination of keyword relevance, the popularity of search terms, links to other sites, and the behavior of end users to determine the order of search results. As more and more users follow particular links, the higher these sources rise in the Googlearchy. This instigates a domino effect. Users are most likely to click on a link in the first pages of results. Relevance thus breeds relevance. As public diplomacy practitioners vie to deliver their messages to target audiences over the web and to use the web to permeate off-line information platforms, they should be mindful of the dynamics of these powerful information gatekeepers.

In reaction to the "indexical bias" inherent in Web 2.0 search engines, social activists and corporate actors have utilized several strategies to influence search results. Bloggers have participated in multiple instances of what is popularly referred to as "Google bombing," or "spamdexing." As search results are determined by a combination of user behavior and of links to other sites, creating dense linkages between certain terms can alter the rankings. By creating dense crosslinks, bloggers have set off Google bombs linking Tony Blair to the word "liar," George Bush to the words "miserable failure," and conservative U.S. Senator Rick Santorum to homosexual sex.[42] Of course, ethically speaking public diplomacy practitioners should not set off Google bombs, but they should make every attempt to ensure that their sites include relevant search terms, and where appropriate, to recognize that their ability to reach broader audiences depends in part on their links with other sites and online communities. State governments such as Virginia, Arizona, California, and Utah have collaborated with Google to improve their search engine optimization (SEO) strategies, editing and organizing their content to contain key words that will help their sites to appear higher on search engine results listings.[43] In 2008, the U.S. State Department learned the hard way that indexical bias can be difficult to overcome. In overhauling its international portal, it shifted the URL from UsInfo.gov to America.gov, thereby losing its previous position within the Googlearchy. Expanding the reach of U.S. government information programs in the new media environment is important, but so too is exploring ways to deepen cross-national relations through dialogue and collaboration.

Dialogue

Since 9/11, calls for increased dialogue between cultures and nations have abounded. Dialogue in its most basic definition refers to a conversation between two people. Dialogue as a model for public diplomacy 2.0 necessitates a more flexible interpretation of the term. According to Martin Buber, true dialogue occurs when both parties enter the relationship with respect and a willingness to listen and most importantly view their interactions as the goal of the relationship.[44] In other words, the benefits of dialogue are most pronounced when communicative interaction is the goal not a means to an end. In many ways, social media platforms, in which users are encouraged to share both information and opinions about themselves and the world around them, is a hybridized form of dialogue.

As Philip Seib notes, social media technologies are helping to foster a web culture based on conversation.[45] He cites the success of Korea's OhMyNews, a populist news and information site that relies on thousands of citizen journalists around the world to collect information. Jean K. Min, OhMyNews head of international operations, observed, "contrary to initial thinking, the Internet is not just another channel for news to travel along. Instead it's a space that everyone can use, and that means that journalism is going to stop being a lecture given by a few 'special' people, and start being a conversation."[46] There are many Web 2.0 applications that might also help public diplomacy become more conversational. "Social-broadcasting" sites like Nowlive.com and Ustream.tv allow that users to create their own live on air call-in radio and TV talk shows have become increasingly popular. Other users can "call-in" to these programs using other 2.0 applications such as Google Chat and Skype. Shows are then archived online much the same as mainstream media organizations now stream television over their sites. These are just a few examples of conversational communities that might present fertile ground for facilitating dialogue.

Individuals and departments across the United States government have begun to use social media technologies to open up dialogue about how to better use these technologies. They have formed interest groups like "Government 2.0" within larger social networking sites like LinkedIn and Facebook. In 2008, Steve Ressler, an information technology officer in the Department of Homeland Security Immigrations and Customs Enforcement Office of the Chief Information Officer founded GovLoop.com, a social network for government 2.0 but with no formal government support or funding. Government members are encouraged to connect across departments and share information through blogs and postings. The PBAT maintains a Digital Digest blog that keeps State Department members apprised of cutting edge developments in new technologies. These social media applications present real opportunities not only to brainstorm about how to utilize new technologies but also to invite target populations to actively participate in creating public diplomacy programs and projects.

Countries around the world are beginning to take heed of the opportunities for dialogue afforded by the Internet and mobile phones. The German government has sponsored an online portal called Qantara ("The Bridge") and the Egyptian government launched IslamOnline to promote cross-cultural dialogue. In 2008, the State Department

launched a Democracy Dialogues Web site that included a video con-
test asking users to submit their own video short about "Democracy
is...." However, regulatory restrictions codified before the advent of
social media applications stand in the way of incorporating these technologies on a broad scale. The PBAT has dedicated much attention to
identifying the legal conditions necessary to implement social media
initiatives.[47] At the time of writing, federal law prohibits the use of
tracking cookies on all Web sites. Full use of social media applications
requires the use of these cookies because they provide site moderators
with feedback about how often and how long users engage with different dimensions of the site giving an indication of overall interest levels.
Understandably, government programs are also restricted by stringent
privacy regulations. Every government site includes a privacy statement
and restrictions on collecting personal identifiers. As practitioners strategize how to expand their use of social media platforms like YouTube
and Facebook, issues have arisen about how to negotiate federal privacy
regulations with those of the host site, particularly in social networks
where users freely choose to provide personal information.

A public diplomacy 2.0 implies using social media technologies to
provide a conduit for feedback, as a platform for citizen-to-citizen dialogue, and as a mechanism for listening to and incorporating viable
opinions and critical information both through expressed opinions
and through end-user behaviors. These restrictions were conceived
of before the introduction of social media applications and should be
reformed if public diplomacy actors are to use them effectively.

Collaboration

Cowan and Arsenault argued that a public diplomacy strategy that
includes a strong relationships-building component holds greater promise than one tethered to foreign policy promotion and can ultimately
serve foreign policy goals by improving trust and credibility between
foreign publics and nation states even when policies remain unpopular.[48]
Collaboration can provide a critical tool not for reaching consensus
about a nation's foreign policy but for furthering understanding about
those policies and the society from which they originate.

Virtual worlds such as Second Life are by nature collaborative
endeavors in that users in the form of avatars help to create the customs, cultures, and even the virtual real estate that they inhabit.
Virtual worlds are already a supranational meeting place. Their citizens are international, and they represent a diverse range of ages and

socioeconomic backgrounds who visit virtual worlds for both entertainment and often to engage with pressing social-issues. For example,
following the London Bombings, netizens from around the Second
Life galaxy attended virtual memorials. In September 2008, on the
UN International Day of Peace, War Child, an organization dedicated
to raising awareness about the impact of war on children around the
world, hosted one of the largest virtual rallies for global peace to date in
Habbo Hotel, an online community geared toward teenagers popular
in Europe and Australasia. Footage of the march was then posted on
YouTube where more than 30,000 others viewed the demonstration.

Already, major media groups such as Reuters, NBC, and MTV have
presence posts in Second Life. Many educational institutions own virtual property in world and numerous embassies have set up Embassies
(e.g., Estonia, the Maldives, and Chile). Illustrating the potential of
real-world /in-world synergies, Vodafone InsideOut now provides a
service that allows subscribers to use virtual mobile phones to make
calls and text messages to real life phones. The IIP began exploring
the potential of Second Life in 2007, when it cohosted a virtual Jazz
concert—a virtual rendition of Dizzy Gillespie and other's jazz tours
during the 1950s—attended by 250 Second Life citizens from around
the world. Of course, not all outreach programs either through Second
Life or other online participatory technologies will work. Finding the
right formula(s) will take time and trial and error; but luckily virtual
experimentation is far cheaper than comparable real-world programs.
Moreover, the impact of dialogue platforms, virtual communities, and
platforms for feedback cannot be measured by attendance alone but in
the strength of the relationships that they engender. As R. S. Zaharna
notes that, in an era of ubiquitous global communication platforms,
"the quality of [governmental] relationships with key publics rather
than the quantity of viewers or listeners" for foreign policy message
campaigns provides the key to successful public diplomacy.[49]

Conclusion

While the laptop is almost certainly mightier than the machine gun,
most pundits agree that communication strategies alone, no matter
how cutting edge or well deployed, will not solve America's international image problem. Policy remains paramount. New technologies
both support and undermine public diplomacy. They provide a tool for
circulating corrective information, for engaging in dialogue and collaboration; and for their undoing. Writing in 1993, Michael J. O'Neill,

former editor of the New York Daily News and past president of the American Society of Newspaper Editors warned that in today's media rich environment "it is no longer the statesman who controls the theater of power but the theater which controls the statesman."[50] Although this may be an overstatement, certainly the decentralization and universalization of the communication technologies will continue to have pronounced and long-term implications for the nature, depth and breadth of America's international reputation and relationships among foreign publics.

An open and transparent embrace of the participatory ethos of the contemporary information environment is in America's best interest and reflects a renewed support for free and open access to information, a fundamental component of U.S. democracy since its inception. Participatory communication is not only a tool, but also a fundamental American value that though not always perfect in practice can be a critical means of promoting U.S. ideals abroad. At the first State Department Conference on the impact of new technology and diplomacy, NetDiplomacy 2000, the Under Secretary of Economics, Business and Agriculture, Alan P. Larson reminded the audience that "a digital world is one that is largely friendly to American interests and values."[51] There have been initiatives designed around this concept. The IIP has hosted online chats for bloggers and cyber dissidents on the subject of Internet censorship. The State EJournal produced a special issue on the Internet as an agent of social change.[52] America.gov also includes a blog launched in April 2008 maintained by journalist Stephen Kauffman on the subject of freedom of expression.[53]

These programs represent a step in the right direction and should be expanded. Supporting free and open access to information, whether it is critical or complimentary of American policy and programs, reinforces one of the most attractive features of American culture—agreement on the right to disagree. As American public diplomacy is upgraded, this principle should be embraced.

Notes

1. Arnold H. Lubasch, "US Is Criticized on Overseas News," *New York Times*, October 26, 1969, 31.
2. Examples of Web 2.0 or social media applications include: video upload sites like YouTube and ifilm, social networking sites such as MySpace and Facebook; collaborative information generation sites like Wikipedia, and numerous hybridized platforms like Xanga, LiveJournal, and Twines that combine social networking with functions like blogging and mobile communication.

3. Dale Dougherty of O'Reilly Media coined the term Web 2.0 in 2004, as a way of describing the shift of Internet technology and applications toward a participatory model.

4. Brian McNair, *Cultural Chaos: Journalism, News, and Power in a Globalised World* (London: Routledge, 2006).

5. Benedict Anderson, *Imagined Communities* (London: Verso, 1983); Philip M Seib, *The Al Jazeera Effect: How the New Global Media Are Reshaping World Politics*, 1st ed. (Washington, DC: Potomac Books, 2008), 65–71.

6. Henry Jenkins, *Convergence Culture: Where Old and New Media Collide* (New York: New York University Press, 2006), 211.

7. A translation of the exchange is available from Matt Armstrong "Debating in the New Media: State Department Dialogues with Ahmadinejad's media advisor." September 16, 2008. http://mountainrunner.us/2008/09/debating_Ahmadinejads_media_advisor.html (accessed September 17, 2008).

8. Moises Naim, "The YouTube Effect How a Technology for Teenagers Became a Force for Political and Economic Change," *Foreign Policy* 158, no. January/February (2007).

9. The documents are available on http://www.dod.mil/pubs/foi/milanalysts/

10. Statistics from Alexa.com (Accessed August 1, 2008).

11. UNCTAD, *WSIS Follow-Up Report 2008*, A Report of the United Nations Conference on Trade and Development (New York: United Nations, 2008).

12. Arab-US Media Forum, *Dead Sea Scrolling* (Aspen, CO: Aspen Institute, 2008), 5.

13. ITU, *World Information Society Report 2007: Beyond WSIS* (Geneva: International Telecommunications Union / United Nations Conference on Trade and Development, 2007).

14. ComScore, "Press Release 'Digital World: State of the Internet' Report Highlights Growth in Emerging Internet Markets," ComScore, http://www.comscore.com/press/release.asp?press=2115 (accessed March 20, 2008).

15. China Internet Network Information Center, *Statistical Survey Report on the Internet Development in China Abridged Edition (July 2008)* (Beijing: Chinese Academy of Sciences, 2008), 10.

16. Numbers from the Arab Advisors Group, republished in Arab-US Media Forum, 3.

17. Caroline McCarthy, "Comscore: Facebook Is Beating MySpace Worldwide," *CNET News,* The Social (2008).

18. John Horrigan, "Mobile Access to Data and Information," Pew/Internet & American Life Project, (2008), http://www.pewinternet.org/PPF/r/244/report_display.asp.

19. ComScore, "Press Release 'ComScore M:Metrics Reports Mobile Search Grew 68 Percent in the U.S. and 38 Percent in Western Europe During Past Year," ComScore, http://www.comscore.com/press/release.asp?press=2469

20. China Internet Network Information Center, 20.

21. Jenkins, *Convergence Culture.*

22. UNCTAD, 3.

23. Peter Eisler, "Pentagon Launches Foreign News Websites," *USA Today,* April 30, 2008.

24. Worldwidewebsize.com provides daily account of the size of webpages that are indexed. This figure does not include an untold number of sites in the so-called deep web that are not indexed by the major search engines.

25. Michael Arrington, "Alexa Says YouTube Is Now Bigger Than Google. Alexa Is Useless." *Techcrunch,* August 13, 2007; Michael Wesch, "YouTube Statistics," *Digital Ethnography,* March 18, 2008, http://mediatedcultures.net/ksudigg/?p=163 (accessed September 3, 2008)

26. Nielsen Netratings, "Global Index Chart, Month of August 2008," The Nielsen Company, http://www.nielsen-netratings.com/press_fd.jsp?section=pr_netv&nav=3 (accessed September 15, 2008).

27. Nielsen Mobile, "Critical Mass: The World Wide State of the Mobile Web," The Nielsen Company, www.nielsenmobile.com/documents/CriticalMass.pdf.

28. Davey Winder, "YouTube Lonelygirl Matures into Bebo KateModern." Daniweb.com, July 30, 2007, http://www.daniweb.com/blogs/entry1564.html (accessed February 3, 2008).

29. See the State Department YouTube site on http://www.youtube.com/profile?user=statevideo; DipNote is available on: http://www.blogs.state.gov/

30. Log data for March 2008 provided by DipNote.

31. Brent Blatchkey, interview by author, written notes, Washington, DC, March 19, 2008.

32. Ibid.

33. Jenkins, *Convergence Culture,* 3.

34. Heath Kern, Interview by author, written notes, Washington, DC, March 15, 2008.

35. Geoffrey, Cowan, and Arsenault Amelia, "Moving from Monologue to Dialogue to Collaboration: The Three Layers of Public Diplomacy," *The ANNALS of the American Academy of Political and Social Science* 616, no. 1 (2008): 10–30.

36. Pew, *Social Networking and Online Videos Take Off: Internet's Broader Role in Campaign 2008* (Washington, DC: Pew Research Center for the People and the Press, 2008); Manuel Castells, "Communication, Power and Counter-Power in the Network Society," *International Journal of Communication* 1, no. 1 (2007): 238–266.

37. Available on http://www.defenselink.mil/blogger/Index.aspx

38. Bruce A. Bimber, and Richard Davis, *Campaigning Online: The Internet in U.S. Elections* (New York: Oxford University Press, 2003).

39. Araba Sey and Manuel Castells, "From Media Politics to Networked Politics: The Internet and the Political Process," in *The Network Society: A Cross-Cultural Perspective,* ed. Manuel Castells (Cheltenham, UK: Edward Elgar, 2004), 370.

40. Matthew Hindman, et al., "'Googlearchy': How a Few Heavily-Linked Sites Dominate Politics on the Web" (Paper presented at the Midwest Political Science Association, Chicago, IL, 2003).

41. Elad Segev, "Search Engines and Power: A Politics of Online (Mis-) Information," *Webology* 5, no. 2 (2008).

42. Heather Greenfield, "Political Bloggers Coordinate Google Bombs," *National Journal* (2006). For an example of Google Bomb instructions, see http://bigpicture.typepad.com/writing/2006/07/google_bomb_san.html

43. Barbara Quint, "Google Burrows into State Government Data," *News Breaks Today,* May 7, 2007.

44. Maurice S Friedman, *Martin Buber: The Life of Dialogue* (New York: Harper, 1960).

45. Seib, *Al Jazeera Effect.*

46. David Mattin, "We Are Changing the Nature of News," *Guardian,* August 15, 2005, also quoted in Seib, *Al Jazeera Effect,* 55.

47. William May and Lovisa Williams, interview by author, written notes, Washington, DC, March 14, 2008.

48. Cowan and Arsenault.

49. R. S. Zaharna, "The Network Paradigm of Strategic Public Diplomacy," *Foreign Policy in Focus* 10, no. 1 (2005): 1–2.

50. Michael J O'Neill, *The Roar of the Crowd: How Television and People Power Are Changing the World,* 1st ed. (New York: Time Books, 1993).

51. Alan P. Larson, "Plenary Remarks (as Delivered)" (Paper presented at the NetDiplomacy 2001 Conference, Washington, DC, 2001).

52. U.S. Department of State International Information Programs, "Making Media Change," *EJournalUSA* 12, no. 12 (2007).

53. http://blogs.america.gov/freepress/

CHAPTER EIGHT

Privatized Public Diplomacy

KATHY R. FITZPATRICK

This chapter identifies key issues and questions that should be addressed as public and private entities attempt to define an "ideal" privatization scheme for U.S. public diplomacy. For example, what is "privatized" public diplomacy? What should be the roles and responsibilities of private entities in advancing the public diplomacy mission—and who defines them? Given the trend toward increased private sector involvement in American public diplomacy, caution and thoughtfulness are essential in the development of public-private partnerships, as is consideration of both positive and negative implications of relegating public diplomacy responsibilities to private parties. Although the private sector contributes significantly to U.S. international relations, the innovations needed for U.S. public diplomacy to be successful over the long term must come from within—not outside—government.

In early 2007, U.S. Under Secretary of State for Public Diplomacy and Public Affairs Karen Hughes hosted "The Private Sector Summit on Public Diplomacy" at which 150 top public relations professionals and U.S. State Department leaders discussed opportunities for greater private sector participation in U.S. public diplomacy.[1] Suggestions ranged from developing business practices that make public diplomacy a core element of international corporate public relations, such as naming a corporate officer responsible for public diplomacy, to promoting understanding of American society, culture, and values through community relations efforts to creating a corps of business "foreign service officers" to supporting international exchanges. To encourage such efforts, Secretary of State Condoleezza

Rice announced the creation of the "Benjamin Franklin Award" to be presented annually to honor a company, academic institution, or other nongovernmental entity that does the most to promote the U.S. image abroad through intercultural understanding.

Later that year, when Hughes announced her retirement from government service, she cited her efforts to expand the government's diplomatic partnerships with the private sector, including the establishment of an office charged with overseeing public/private public diplomacy initiatives, as a signature accomplishment.[2]

Such actions suggest that U.S. public diplomacy may be among the latest government functions to be swept up in the privatization revolution.[3] As Paul R. Verkuil observes in *Outsourcing Sovereignty*, the increased use of contractors who have displaced functions normally performed by government officials has resulted in unprecedented delegations of power being awarded to the private sector.[4] Government operations involving prisons,[5] healthcare,[6] education,[7] military,[8] security,[9] even peacekeeping,[10] have been turned over to private entities in recent years, ushering in what some have called an "era of privatization."[11]

Is Public Diplomacy Next?

Certainly, the dozens of post-9/11 recommendations from both government agencies and private entities for greater private sector involvement in American public diplomacy suggest a move in that direction.[12] The fact that Rice and Hughes made the empowerment of private sector entities and individuals a fundamental tenet in their efforts to transform U.S. public diplomacy also suggests that public diplomacy is well on its way to becoming "privatized." According to Hughes, such efforts recognize that "the voices of government officials are not always the most powerful or the most credible."[13]

In observing public diplomacy's recent shift to the private sector, Crocker Snow, Jr., Director of the Edward R. Murrow Center of Public Diplomacy at The Fletcher School of Law and Diplomacy, echoes such thinking: "In large part, public diplomacy's shift to the private sector is a function of the diminished credibility of the U.S. government in the eyes of the world due to its unpopular undertakings." According to Snow, "The best and most effective public diplomacy initiatives have come from the private, non-governmental sectors." A primary reason, he suggests, is that Washington experienced a "change of focus" after the end of the cold war and the collapse of communism, which resulted in the dissolution of the United States Information Agency (USIA) and the marginalization of the public diplomacy function.[14]

Involving nonstate actors in public diplomacy is believed to provide government the ability to accomplish what it might not have the resources or ability to do on its own. For example, in commenting on the Private Sector Summit, Hughes's deputy Dina Powell explained, "Public diplomacy is not the government's job alone, and we will be much more successful as American citizens if we work together with corporations, NGOs [nongovernmental organizations], academic institutions and everyday Americans to amplify our efforts."[15]

According to Bruce Gregory, Director of the Institute of Public Diplomacy at George Washington University, "[p]ublic diplomacy could not function without private sector partnerships."[16] Gregory points out that nongovernmental organizations have long been involved in administering and funding international exchanges and democratization programs. U.S. public diplomacy officials, he says, now seek "to leverage private sector talents and creativity to enhance operational capacity in knowledge domains, product identification and development, services and skills, and evaluative feedback."[17]

Before the privatization of U.S. public diplomacy is fully embraced, however, some important questions should be answered. For example, what exactly do we mean by "privatization"? As Barry Fulton, Research Professor and Director of the Public Diplomacy Institute at George Washington University, has pointed out, "Practically every study [on U.S. public diplomacy] has recommended engaging the private sector, but what this means has not been thoroughly explored."[18]

In addition, can the benefits believed to be gained from increased private sector involvement in U.S. public diplomacy be fully realized? Or are they offset by potential problems associated with or created by increased private sector participation? Most importantly, how can the U.S. government reap the benefits of private sector support while diminish any potential liabilities? Such questions could have significant impact on determinations regarding both the desirability and proper role of the private sector in American public diplomacy.

Defining "Privatization"

Privatization generally refers to private entities performing government functions. In most cases, privatization involves the contracting out, or outsourcing, of government services to private—in most cases profit-making—enterprises that assume full responsibility for administering those services. Autonomy and decision-making authority generally accompany such transfers.

Viewed more broadly, privatization includes the development of partnerships between government agencies and private sector entities that are engaged to support government efforts. Privatization expert E. S. Savas defines these "public-private partnerships"—which, he notes, are "less contentious" than "privatization"—as "any arrangement between government and the private sector in which partially or traditionally public activities are performed by the private sector."[19] In such arrangements, autonomy and decision-making authority become less clear-cut.

In fact, part of the difficulty in analyzing the privatization of public diplomacy is the lack of a precise definition of exactly what privatization entails. For example, is the hiring of public relations and advertising firms by the government to support the implementation of a public diplomacy campaign a kind of "privatization"?[20] Is the appointment of public relations and/or advertising professionals to head U.S. public diplomacy efforts another aspect of "privatization"? Are the international public relations efforts of corporations to improve the image of "American" brands among foreign publics still another facet of "privatization" of U.S. public diplomacy?

It is questionable whether "privatization" as generally understood is even the right term to describe the types of arrangements either existing or being contemplated in U.S. public diplomacy. For example, diplomacy scholar Brian Hocking has observed that the multifaceted and expanding role of private actors in contemporary diplomacy "is a more complex one than the idea of 'privatization' implies."[21] Not only is such a view "misleading and simplistic," Hocking says, but it "fails to recognize the significant role that agents of the state continue to play in the context of the emergent structures of global governance."[22]

Political scientist Nicholas Henry has also noted the limitations of "privatization" in describing arrangements in which a government works with profit and nonprofit entities, as well as other governments. Henry suggests that a better term for such collaborations is "intersectoral administration," which recognizes the decreasingly hierarchical and increasingly networked environment in which governments operate.[23] According to Henry, "privatization" is a subset of "intersectoral administration," which he defines as "the management and coordination of the relations among government agencies and organizations in the private and nonprofit sectors for the purpose of achieving specific policy goals."[24]

Although it would seem that "intersectoral administration" better reflects the reality of private sector involvement in U.S. public diplomacy today, the point here is not to sort out what private sector involvement in public diplomacy should be *called*. Rather it is to suggest the need to better understand what "privatization" of public diplomacy actually *means*. For example, it is unclear just how "empowered" the U.S. government would like its private sector partners to be in advancing the public diplomacy mission.

At the same time, it should be recognized that not all attempts at privatization in public diplomacy have been—or will be—initiated by the government. In the years since 9/11, for example, business corporations have observed a need for "corporate diplomacy" designed to address harms to business caused by America's declining image in the world. In a special 2006 issue of the *Journal of Business Strategy* devoted to examining the role of business in public diplomacy, Michael Goodman, director of the Corporate Communication Institute at Fairleigh Dickinson University, writes that businesses have been called to respond to the eroding global trust in American businesses brought about by "global scandals, the perception of globalization as an American initiative, and a widespread disagreement with U.S. policy abroad."[25] According to Goodman, "[t]he role of business now includes public diplomacy."[26]

Such thinking is manifest in entities such as Business for Diplomatic Action (BDA), a private sector task force spearheaded by U.S. advertising executive Keith Reinhold. Recognizing that "[a]nti-Americanism is bad for business," BDA's mission is "to enlist the U.S. business community in actions to improve the standing of America in the world with the goal of, once again, seeing America admired as a global leader and respected as a courier of progress and prosperity for all people."[27] Toward that end, BDA brings professionals in media, political science, marketing, communications, and global development together to offer guidance to the U.S. government on "communication and perception issues that U.S. businesses are uniquely positioned to address."[28] The group characterizes its work as "A New Brand of American Diplomacy."[29]

State and local governments have also expanded their representation abroad, and nonprofit organizations have become involved in efforts to influence foreign perceptions of America. For example, Layalina Productions, led by Marc C. Ginsberg (ambassador to Morocco during the Clinton administration) and financed primarily by foundations with no government support, produced a reality television series broad-cast throughout the Middle East that follows a group of young Arabs on an educational tour of the United States. According to a *New York Times* report, the objective of the series, as well as other media projects sponsored by Layalina and directed to Arab audiences, is to "help sooth the rage on all sides" that followed 9/11 and to "correct whatever damage has been done to America's standing in the Middle East by the Iraq war and the nearly four-year American military presence in that country."[30]

Of course, it has long been recognized that the U.S. government does not hold a monopoly on global practices intended to combat anti-Americanism and improve America's image in the world. For exam-ple, Edmund Guillion, former dean of the Fletcher School of Law and Diplomacy at Tufts University—who is credited with coining the phrase "public diplomacy" in 1965—indicated at the time that public diplomacy encompassed "the interaction of private groups and interests in one country with those of another." While some might argue that such interactions are not public diplomacy per se, the fact that private parties influence U.S. international relations has been widely recog-nized throughout the history of the nation.

What is new, however, is the *degree* of involvement by nonstate actors in U.S. public diplomacy. Certainly, recent efforts such as those noted earlier demonstrate a heightened level of international public relations activities designed to influence foreign publics' views of the United States. They also show that the private sector may have a great deal of influence on defining the future "privatization" of U.S. public diplomacy.

In envisioning diplomacy's possible futures, Alan K. Henrickson of Tufts's Fletcher School of Law and Diplomacy offers one scenario in which state-run diplomacy "with its formal structures and bureaucratic procedures" may be "disintermediated," or "bypassed by non-state actors who establish their own international relations functions and processes."[31] If the "9/11 effect," or the perceived need for state pro-tectionism, wanes, Henrickson suggests, "the 'privatization' of foreign policy and diplomacy...may become more prevalent" and professional diplomacy could undergo a "profound adaptation, or reformation."[32] Accordingly, Henrickson concludes, "the consequence for 'disinterme-diated' diplomacy might be that, as a result of stronger competition, the diplomatic professional will be required to mimic private enterprise and its methods."[33]

There appears to be some agreement, at least among U.S. observers and policy makers, that American public diplomacy's salvation may lie in private hands. Whether because the government can't do it or simply won't do it, many believe that "fixing" U.S. public diplomacy is partially—if not fully—a job for private entities. According to public relations executive Michael Holtzman, "Public diplomacy is much too important to leave to professional diplomats."[34]

Potential Pros of Privatization

The mantra of privatization proponents is that private entities can perform government functions faster, better, and cheaper than the government can perform the same functions. In the context of public diplomacy, the advantages cited most frequently relate to efficiency, expertise, credibility, and cost.

Efficiency

If you ask former USIA officials who experienced the dissolution of USIA in 1999 and the subsequent integration of public diplomacy functions into the State Department what they miss most about operating as an independent agency, many would say autonomy and flexibility, or the ability to respond quickly and effectively to situations as they arise on the ground. Less red tape in the agency meant fewer bureaucratic roadblocks to slow down programs and projects and impede their effectiveness.

As an example, Cari Eggspuehler, who worked in the State Department after 9/11 and now represents the BDA, contends that the problems with the "Brand America" campaign implemented in the wake of the terrorist attacks—and widely criticized as a public diplomacy failure—derived from the "rigid and bureaucratic" institutional roadblocks rather than strategic deficiencies.[35] Thus, it is believed, shifting public diplomacy functions to "independent" entities and/or relying on private actors for certain public diplomacy tasks could provide the flexibility needed to be more effective—particularly in a dynamic 24/7 global news environment that requires constant monitoring and rapid responses.

Expertise

Private companies also could provide sorely needed expertise required for strategic planning and effective communication in U.S. public diplomacy. Best practices in business translate into best practices in government, it is argued. Goodman, for example, points out that business professionals are well-attuned to the sensitivities of diverse cultures and the world at large. "Global companies and their brands touch the lives of more people than government representatives ever could."[36]

In addition, outside experts can help counteract the "brain drain" in U.S. public diplomacy that resulted from significant retirements after the end of the cold war and the dissolution of USIA. Many specialists in public diplomacy today lack the skills needed to meet the challenges of an information society, a problem that could be solved by looking to the private sector, according to David Morey, chairman of the Independent Task Force on Public Diplomacy sponsored by the Council on Foreign Relations and chief executive of a private strategic and communications consultancy. Morey observes that "the private sector—think Hollywood, Madison Avenue and Silicon Valley—is where the most advanced communications tactics are developed."[37]

Partially to take advantage of such expertise, the Council on Foreign Relations proposed the establishment of a Corporation for Public Diplomacy (CPD) (modeled on the Corporation for Public Broadcasting) that would be responsible for producing content and helping distribute U.S. public diplomacy programs abroad through television, books, magazines, public speakers, and the Internet. According to Peter G. Peterson, chairman of the Council, such a public-private partnership "could attract and nurture top talent, people who might not choose to work direct for the U.S. government."[38]

Private entities—particularly corporate and academic institutions—also are viewed as better able to provide the research and diplomatic "intelligence" needed to develop effective public diplomacy programs and campaigns, an area that has long been neglected by the government. For example, in recent years, the research budget for U.S. public diplomacy has been approximately $5 million a year, a fraction of what multinational businesses spend on research for corporate marketing communication programs. Morey points out that the U.S. private sector spends $6 billion annually on foreign public opinion and market research.[39]

Credibility

Perhaps more important than efficiency and expertise is the perceived credibility factor. Advocates of privatization in public diplomacy argue that because people abroad trust nongovernmental sources more than they trust the U.S. government, foreign publics will be both more receptive and more responsive to messages coming from private parties. In making this case, some point to studies such as the "Annual Trust Barometer" sponsored by Edelman Public Relations Worldwide, which found in 2006 that with respect to trust in institutions, NGOs ranked first, business second, and government third.[40]

According to Holtzman, regular citizens and private institutions can do far more to create goodwill for America than the U.S. government can. About the Middle East specifically, Holtzman observes that "[m]erely branding a public diplomacy initiative with the imprimatur of the United States government is enough to conjure instant distrust in a region whose people have long perceived Washington's hand in their national affairs and for whom anti-Americanism is the only outlet for expressing strong political feeling."[41] Rather than creating new government agencies, Holtzman says, the United States should cultivate nongovernmental relations between Americans and the Middle East. "In many cases, he contends, only private actors have the credibility to make a difference."[42] According to Eggspuehler, "the federal government is just not a credible messenger."[43]

Alternatively, private faces promoting American values and ideals are believed to lessen the hostility directed at government officials and government policies. As Peterson puts it, private sector participation would provide "a 'heat shield' that could help in controversial issues that might have negative political or diplomatic repercussions if the government's hand were too visible."[44]

Cost

Another argument for privatization is that farming out public diplomacy tasks to organizations that can perform the same functions more efficiently both lowers taxpayers' costs and provides additional resources to support the public diplomacy mission. For example, the proposed CPD could accept private donations and raise additional funds from private sources. According to Peterson, "Private-sector partnerships working through the CPD would effectively mobilize and use America's rich and diverse resources."[45]

Toward that end, James Murphy of the Public Relations Council, who heads global marketing and communications for Accenture, also points out that U.S. companies and individuals donate significantly more money overseas than the overall U.S. aid budget, which could provide significant resources in advancing the public diplomacy mission.

Given the insufficient funding earmarked by U.S. leaders for public diplomacy since the cold war, such contributions could be significant.

Finally, training costs for public diplomacy specialists could be reduced if private sector experts are involved. Although the U.S. Foreign Service Institute has increased training in public diplomacy significantly since 9/11, such efforts are still perceived as inadequate to meet current needs. Thus, private sector support could help fill the gaps.

Making the Case for Privatization ... or Not?

Certainly, the potential for increased efficiency, expert resources, enhanced credibility, and lower costs makes a strong case for privatizing U.S. public diplomacy. However, these perceived benefits should not go unexamined.

For example, do "business best practices" really translate directly into "government best practices"? In that regard, critics of the post-9/11 "Brand America" campaign, which involved corporate marketing techniques, argued that nations are not products or services and should not be treated as such. As the *Wall Street Journal* observed, "the U.S. can't be sold as a 'brand,' like Cheerios."[46] Or as Matthew Grimm, writing from *Brandweek*, put it, "Marketing tools don't work in public policy."[47] According to Grimm, "it is a profoundly frivolous assumption that one can ameliorate stark problems of civil society with heart-felt imagery, a couple catch phrases and some swelling music."[48]

Even if some "best practices" do translate, there is some question about whether and how private sector expertise can best be used to advance U.S. public diplomacy. As Fulton observes, although "the American private sector has no equal in media production, marketing and survey research ... [i]t is far less evident that the government knows how to exploit this knowledge apart from short-term political campaigns."[49]

With respect to credibility, the long-term implications of allowing private sector surrogates to carry U.S. messages to people abroad are unknown. An important question is whether private sector "fronts" ultimately will hurt as much as help in accomplishing American public diplomacy objectives. For example, while business support may quell some anti-American backlash against American products and services, how effective will it be in developing good relations between the *United States of America* and people abroad?

Cost savings is another issue that should be looked at closely. Certainly, given the Bush administration's track record in privatizing other government functions—and the significant financial losses incurred—it should not be assumed that delegating public diplomacy practices will result in financial windfalls.[50] Rather, various approaches to public-private partnerships should be carefully evaluated to determine cost effectiveness.

Finally, even if efficiency and costs are decreased by private sector involvement in public diplomacy, will the government have to sell its soul to reap these operational and financial rewards? In other words, will the public diplomacy mission be compromised by allowing those with *private* interests take the lead on diplomatic initiatives purported to serve the *public* interest?

Potential Cons of Privatization

The potential disadvantages of increased private sector involvement in U.S. public diplomacy have received scant attention in either the scholarly or professional literature. One notable exception is the *Middle East Quarterly* that, in reviewing recommendations by the Council on Foreign Relations calling for the partial privatization of U.S. public diplomacy, found that "despite its august auspices," the council's report which, according to the *Quarterly*, represented "conventional thinking in the American policy elite," was "a profoundly controversial statement" over the direction of U.S. public diplomacy.[51] The *Quarterly* observed, "The 'consensus' of the task force represents only one point on the spectrum of informed ideas about how the United States should explain itself and its actions to the world."[52]

Indeed, before privatization is accepted as the model paradigm for American public diplomacy, a number of potential disadvantages should be addressed. Matters related to control, accountability, and mission could be particularly significant in evaluating the desirability and long-term benefits of privatization.

Control

None of the post-9/11 proposals recommending increased private sector involvement in U.S. public diplomacy have suggested completely turning over the function of public diplomacy to private entities. Nor do existing State Department initiatives cede total control to nonstate parties. However, the ambiguous nature of public-private relationships in this area raises a key question with significant implications for the strategic direction and effective practice of U.S. public diplomacy: Who is in charge?

Although only government officials have the authority to speak or act on behalf of the U.S. government, government officials have little power to control either the messages or the means used by private parties to communicate with people abroad. Hocking notes, for example, that "the role of the diplomat in the context of a diplomacy where the public and the private become intermeshed is increasingly focused on a coordinating role defined not so much in the assertion of control over policy processes but in facilitating information flows and sharing the management of complex issues with a range of governmental and nongovernmental actors."[53]

According to Hocking, this new diplomatic environment raises an important question: "What do national diplomatic systems do in such an environment?"[54] Perhaps a better question with regard to privatization is how can—or should—U.S. officials influence the direction and intensity of private sector public diplomacy efforts? What is the appropriate scope of authority and responsibility that should be—can be—afforded private sector partners? And what criteria will be used to gauge the effectiveness of private sector performance?

Organizational issues also must be addressed in evaluating public-private partnerships. In discussing public diplomacy's weaknesses, for example, Fulton points out the need to develop an institutional structure that reflects the realities of the world today. Noting the significant effects of new media, nonstate actors and globalization on the diplomatic environment, he asks, "[H]ow can the [State] Department effectively engage non-state actors when it is currently organized to focus on other governments?"[55]

Accountability

For much of its history, U.S. public diplomacy has operated outside the view of the American public. Although not necessarily the intent, the Smith-Mundt Act enacted in 1948, which prohibits the domestic dissemination of American public diplomacy materials, virtually guaranteed U.S. citizens would be ignorant of their government's efforts to influence foreign public opinion and to build supportive relations with people abroad. As a result, oversight of American public diplomacy has fallen to a congressionally confirmed advisory body (historically ignored by U.S. public diplomacy officials) and to the news media, which exhibited little interest in public diplomacy functions before 9/11.[56] Even today, media scrutiny of the U.S. military and other areas of government claim far more media attention than does diplomacy.

Will privatization make matters worse? For example, would increased involvement of private entities in U.S. public diplomacy make it more difficult for U.S. citizens to gain access to information about the public diplomacy policies and practices of the government?[57] A central concern here is whether the Freedom of Information Act (FOIA) applies to private-sector public diplomacy efforts. For example, in what situations would private firms have the "functional equivalency" or "degree of control" over various activities required for FOIA to apply?[58] Would the authority afforded nonstate actors engaged in public diplomacy allow private partners to skirt government regulations? Also, could U.S. public diplomacy officials hide behind private firms to avoid congressional oversight of their work? What safeguards are in place to ensure the transparency and disclosure needed for U.S. citizens to monitor the performance of their government in the area of public diplomacy?

Mission

An important question concerning private sector participation in U.S. public diplomacy is whether the public diplomacy mission would be compromised by private sector involvement in public diplomacy. Specifically, what effect will the potentially conflicting missions of public and private entities—especially profit-making corporations driven by the bottom line—have on public diplomacy?

A State Department effort to involve corporate CEOs in international relief efforts illustrates the problem. When interviewed by the *Wall Street Journal*, Robert Lane, chief executive of Deere & Co., who accompanied the U.S. Under Secretary of Public Diplomacy and Public Affairs on a trip to Guatemala following an earthquake there, admitted that the motivations of CEOs involved in such efforts weren't "purely patriotic."[59] Rather, according to Lane, "[o]ur mission is to provide quality products and services...So, if we're asked to do things that go beyond what our mission is, that's where we may have to say it has gone too far."[60]

In fact, could the appointment of private "envoys" who know little about the U.S. government's nature, motivations, or policies to represent U.S. interests abroad do more harm than good?[61] Certainly, the routine appointments of individuals to key government posts chosen on the basis of their contributions to political war chests rather than on their professional credentials and experience provide some evidence of potential harms. Thus, a key question with regard to public-private partnerships in U.S. public diplomacy is: What safeguards are in place to ensure that the government's private sector partners uphold the *public* mission?

Even if private parties are successful in developing positive relations with foreign publics, who reaps the benefits of those relationships? Clearly, one serious disadvantage of allowing private sector entities to take the lead may be that the resulting relationships will be between *private* entities—rather than the U.S. government—and people abroad, a result that effectively defeats public diplomacy's primary mission.

The most significant negative impact of increased private sector involvement in U.S. public diplomacy, however, may be on the function itself. By looking elsewhere for solutions to public diplomacy problems, U.S. officials may believe they can avoid the difficult task of building a sophisticated, twenty-first-century public diplomacy operation capable of combating the hostile anti-Americanism that fuels global terrorism and threatens the nation's political and economic interests. Here, the central question is: Will increased private sector involvement in U.S. public diplomacy provide an excuse for U.S. officials to avoid making the changes—and providing the resources—needed to improve public diplomacy's long-term success?

Toward a Paradigm of Privatization

Proposing a privatization paradigm that defines the "ideal" role of the private sector in U.S. public diplomacy is beyond the scope of this chapter. Rather, the purpose here is to identify issues that should be considered as public and private entities evaluate the desirability and proper function of the private sector in American public diplomacy practices. The next step is to develop a strategic approach to U.S. public diplomacy that recognizes the growing prominence and influence of nonstate actors in foreign affairs.

Toward that end, it will be important to keep in mind that, by definition, "diplomacy" is "the conducting of relations between *nations* [emphasis added]."[62] *Public* diplomacy is a nation's efforts to build positive relationships with the *people* of other countries. Efforts by the U.S. government to increase private sector involvement in U.S. public diplomacy—and efforts by the private sector to become more involved in American public diplomacy—should be grounded in that reality.

At the same time, the involvement of corporations and other private parties in international public relations efforts, along with other private activities (e.g., cultural and entertainment), have tremendous impact on U.S. international relations and, therefore, on the ultimate success of American public diplomacy.[63] Thus, it is in the interest of the U.S. government to work with the private sector to ensure that private sector efforts support, rather than undermine, public diplomacy's long-term effectiveness.

As private actors gain increasing influence in world affairs, this challenge will become more difficult. As Michael A. Cohen and Maria Figueroa Kupcu observe in the *World Policy Journal* about the privatization of foreign policy, "finding the proper balance between the responsibilities and accountability of public and private actors may well become the foremost policy challenge of the twenty-first century."[64]

In searching for new ways of relating to foreign publics, U.S. leaders might recall the counsel of one of the nation's most prominent former diplomats. In a 1997 *Foreign Affairs* article entitled "Diplomacy without Diplomats?" former U.S. Ambassador to the Soviet Union George F. Kennan wrote about uncertainties in the world that were "challenging the calculations of recent decades, pro and con, about what institutional arrangements a great country ought to have for its diplomatic interaction with the rest of the world in the coming age."[65] Changes brought about by computer technology, the communication revolution, and the broad diffusion of authority, Kennan said, "make it extremely difficult to predict the future of diplomacy or prescribe its conduct."[66] In adjusting to these uncertainties, Kennan said, rather than create new entities to carry out its diplomatic functions, the United States would "do well to make the best of the foreign service it has."[67]

Kennan's message is to approach the privatization of U.S. public diplomacy thoughtfully and cautiously—and to recognize the importance of shoring up the government's own public diplomacy operation. Clearly, the private sector has an important role to play in protecting and promoting U.S. interests abroad. However, the private sector should not be viewed as a cure-all for U.S. public diplomacy's current ailments.

The innovations needed for U.S. public diplomacy to be successful over the long term must come from within—not outside—government. As *New York Times* columnist Paul Krugman observed about the outsourcing of government functions, "[T]he presumption that the private sector can do no wrong and the government can do nothing right prevents us from coming to grips with some of America's biggest problems."[68]

Notes

1. "Business Leaders Make Major Commitment to Support American Public Diplomacy," News Release, U.S. Department of State Office of the Spokesman, January 11, 2007.

2. "Changing the Nature and Scope of Public Diplomacy," News Release, Office of the Under Secretary for Public Diplomacy and Public Affairs, November 1, 2007.

3. See, e.g., Paul R. Verkuil, *Outsourcing Sovereignty* (New York: Cambridge University Press, 2007); Graeme A. Hodge, *Privatization: An International Review of Performance* (Boulder, CO: Westview Press, 2000); Jeffrey D. Greene, *Cities and Privatization: Prospects for the New Century* (Upper Saddle River, NJ: Prentice-Hall, 2002).

4. Verkuil, *Outsourcing Sovereignty*, 196.

5. See, e.g., Gary W. Bowmant (Ed.), *Privatizing Correctional Institutions* (Somerset, NJ: Transaction, 1992); Nicole B. Casarez, "Furthering the Accountability Principle in Privatized Federal Corrections: The Need for Access to Private Prison Records," *University of Michigan Journal of Law Reform* 28, no. 2 (1995): 249.

6. See, e.g., Sarah E. Gollust, "Privatization of Public Services: Organizational Reform Efforts in Public Education and Public Health," *American Journal of Public Health* 96, no. 10 (2006): 1733–1739.

7. See, e.g., Sarah Garland, "Bloomberg Moves Schools toward Corporate Model," *New York Sun*, January 19, 2007, 3.

8. See, e.g., Peter W. Singer, "Corporate Warriors: The Rise of the Privatized Military Industry and Its Ramifications for International Security," *International Security* 26, no. 3 (2001/2002): 186–220.

9. See, e.g., Deborah Avant, "The Privatization of Security and Change in the Control of Force," *International Studies Perspectives* 5 (2004): 153–157.

10. See, e.g., Peter W. Singer, "Peacekeepers, Inc.," *Policy Review* 119 (2003): 59–70; Doug Brooks and Gaurav Laroia, "Privatized Peacekeeping," *National Interest* 80 (2005): 121–125.

11. Verkuil, *Outsourcing Sovereignty*.

12. See, e.g., Susan B. Epstein and Lisa Mages, "Public Diplomacy: A Review of Past Recommendations," Congressional Research Service, September 2, 2005, which summarizes recommendations from twenty-nine articles and studies on post-9/11 U.S. public diplomacy.

13. Karen P. Hughes, *Major Public Diplomacy Accomplishments*, U.S. Department of State report, 2006.

14. Crocker Snow, Jr., "The Privatization of U.S. Public Diplomacy," *The Fletcher Forum of World Affairs* 32, no. 1 (Winter 2008): 189–199.

15. "Business Leaders Make Major Commitment," U.S. Department of State Office of the Spokesman.

16. Bruce Gregory, *Public Diplomacy and Governance: Challenges for Scholars and Practitioners*, in *Global Governance and Diplomacy: Worlds Apart?* ed. Andrew F. Cooper, Brian Hocking, and William Maley (Houndmills: Palgrave Macmillan, 2008).

17. Ibid.

18. Barry Fulton, "Taking the Pulse of American Public Diplomacy in a Post-9/11 World," unpublished paper, March 18, 2004, 4.

19. E. S. Savas, *Privatization and Public-Private Partnerships* (New York: Chatham House, 2000), 4.

20. See, e.g., Geoffrey Allen Pigman and Anthony Deos, "Consuls for Hire: Private Actors, Public Diplomacy," *Place Branding and Public Diplomacy* 4, no. 1 (2008): 85–96.

21. Brian Hocking, "Privatizing Diplomacy?" *International Studies Perspectives* 5 (2004): 151.

22. Ibid., 148.

23. Nicholas Henry, "Is Privatization Passé? The Case for Competition and the Emergence of Intersectoral Administration," *Public Administration Review* 62, no. 3 (2002): 374–378.

24. Ibid., 377.
25. Michael B. Goodman, "The Role of Business in Public Diplomacy," *Journal of Business Strategy* 27, no. 3 (2006): 5–7.
26. Ibid.
27. http://www.businessfordiplomaticaction.org/who/
28. Ibid.
29. Business for Diplomatic Action Fact Sheet, undated.
30. Jacques Steinberg, "American Road Trip through Arab Eyes: TV Series Aims to Change How Arabs View This Country," *New York Times*, January 31, 2007, B1/7.
31. Alan K. Henrickson, "Diplomacy's Possible Futures," *The Hague Journal of Diplomacy* 1 (2006): 3–27.
32. Ibid.
33. Ibid.
34. Michael Holtzman, "Privatize Public Diplomacy," *New York Times*, August 8, 2002, A25.
35. Ross Douthat, "Rebranding America," *Atlantic Monthly* 294, no. 4 (2004): 47.
36. Goodman, "The Role of Business in Public Diplomacy," 7.
37. David E. Morey, "Q: Should the United States Invest Heavily in New Efforts to Advance Public Diplomacy? YES: The State of World Affairs Demands Nothing Less than a New Public Diplomacy Paradigm," *Insight on the News*, September 30, 2002, 40.
38. Peter G. Peterson, "Privatising U.S. Public Diplomacy," *Financial Times*, January 21, 2004, 19.
39. Morey, "Q: Should the United States Invest."
40. www.edelman.com/news/ShowOne.asp?ID=146
41. Holtzman, "Privatize Public Diplomacy."
42. Ibid.
43. Douthat, "Rebranding America."
44. Peterson, "Privatising U.S. Public Diplomacy."
45. Peter G. Peterson, "Public Diplomacy and the War on Terrorism: A Strategy for Reform," *Foreign Affairs* 81, no. 5 (2002): 74–79.
46. Editorial, "The Powell Lesson," *Wall Street Journal*, November 16, 2004, A24.
47. Matthew Grimm, "Now, the Loser: Brand America," *Brandweek* 44, no. 38, October 20, 2003, 19.
48. Ibid.
49. Fulton, "Taking the Pulse of American Public Diplomacy," 9.
50. See, e.g., Paul Krugman, "Outsourcer in Chief," *New York Times*, December 11, 2006, A29.
51. Editors preface, "Council on Foreign Relations, 'Improving U.S. Public Diplomacy,'" *Middle East Quarterly*, IX, no. 3 (2002): 1.
52. Ibid.
53. Hocking, "Privatizing Diplomacy?" 147–152.
54. Ibid.
55. Fulton, "Taking the Pulse of American Public Diplomacy," 7.
56. See, e.g., Kathy Fitzpatrick and Tamara Kosic, "The Missing Public in U.S. Public Diplomacy: Exploring the News Media's Role in Developing an American Constituency," in *Media and Conflict in the Twenty-First Century* ed. Philip Seib (New York: Palgrave Macmillan, 2005), 105–125.
57. See, e.g., Joel Campbell, "Government Outsourcing Leads to Cloaked Figures," *Quill* 94, no. 9 (2006).
58. See, e.g., Craig D. Feiser, "Privatization and the Freedom of Information Act: An Analysis of Public Access to Private Entities under Federal Law," *Federal Communications Law Journal* 52, no. 1 (1999): 21–62.
59. Neil King, Jr., "Goodwill Hunting: Trying to Turn Its Image Around, U.S. Puts Top CEOs Out Front; State Department's Ms. Hughes Rallies Companies to Play Bigger Role in Diplomacy; Mr. Lane Survives a Mud Slide," *Wall Street Journal*, February 17, 2006, A1.

60. Ibid.
61. See, e.g., George Kennan, "Diplomacy without Diplomats?" *Foreign Affairs* 76 (1997): 198–212.
62. New World Dictionary of the American Language (Second College Edition) (Cleveland, OH: William Collins, 1979), 398.
63. See, e.g., University of Southern California's Center on Public Diplomacy Web site discussion of public diplomacy at http://uscpublicdiplomacy.com/index.php/about/whatis_pd.
64. Michael A. Cohen and Maria Figueroa Kupcu, "Privatizing Foreign Policy," *World Policy Journal* (2005): 34–52, 50.
65. See, e.g., Kennan, "Diplomacy without Diplomats?"
66. Ibid.
67. Ibid.
68. Krugman, "Outsourcer in Chief."

CHAPTER NINE

A Cultural Public Diplomacy Strategy

NEAL M. ROSENDORF

Cultural diplomacy must be a significant element of a comprehensive program to retool American foreign policy and thereby repair America's global reputation. At core is the need for a fundamental shift in both the substance and tone of American foreign policy, in both the realms of strategic statecraft and cultural and other public diplomacy efforts. This shift is critical to restoring our ability to play an effective leading role in international affairs. There is no easy fix to America's damaged international image, but a diplomatic effort that represents the best of American culture and society—one that reflects the qualities of openness, cooperation, generosity, broadmindedness, and yes, humility—will over the long term be a great asset to U.S. foreign relations.

The United States needs to revive, adapt, and expand cultural diplomacy programs that have worked in the past and can be effective today and to devise bold new approaches to meet the challenges unique to the current foreign relations environment. Cultural diplomacy, when conceived of creatively, is about both outreach and intake, a point completely missed by the George W. Bush administration. Foreign policy formulators need to conceptualize, as the Harvard diplomatic historian Akira Iriye has put it, "international relations as intercultural relations."

As we discuss cultural diplomacy strategies, we should keep in mind a tripartite definition of "culture": (1) the animating ideas and ideals that undergird American politics and society, make it at its best a magnet, beacon, and exemplar around the world; (2) mechanisms of exchange, learning, and relationship-building, such as tourism and education; and (3) artistic, entertainment, and information producers and vectors and their output, both high and popular.

Cultural diplomacy is of course not a magic bullet. A cardinal rule is Garbage In, Garbage Out—bad input can never cause a good result. Cultural diplomacy cannot undo or paper over poorly conceived, poorly implemented, and/or poorly received policies. Moreover, even with the most astute and nuanced overall foreign policy, there will be times that the United States must make hard decisions for its own vital interests that will not sit well with others. There will be the unavoidable jealousies that come with being the global economic, military, and cultural colossus. And there will be those individuals, regimes, and organizations that are unpersuadable because their opposition to the United States is so profound.

Nonetheless, a cultural diplomacy based on the best the United States stands for can help America regain its moral authority and ability to inspire and lead. American cultural diplomacy can help show the world a nation that is courageous, hopeful, and open, not frightened, pessimistic, and xenophobic—as long as the rest of U.S. foreign policy is appropriately congruent. A widely admired, less anxiety-provoking United States will have a far easier time developing and expanding international institutions that promote global stability and benefit American vital interests; and we will find it easier as well to assemble broad, committed coalitions when those interests are threatened.

America's Grave Prestige Problem—Eight Years of Bad Policies at Home and Abroad

Retired diplomat Richard T. Arndt, author of a magisterial study of American cultural diplomacy, has decried an unwillingness of analysts and decision makers to discuss the linkages between U.S. foreign policies that alienate other peoples and countries and the potential efficacy of U.S. cultural diplomatic efforts. Arndt asks, "What drained the reservoirs of good will?" He complains that even the best of the post-9/11 studies on how to repair America's international standing, the 2003 Djerejian Report *Changing Minds, Winning Peace*, refused to deal head-on with the issue. "At four different points," he writes, "the report leads up to, then scurries away from U.S. foreign policy— beyond their mandate, the authors explain."[1]

This chapter evinces no such qualms. I categorically hold that the United States is on balance a strong force for good in the world. Nonetheless, at various times over the past several decades American foreign policies on both global and regional issues have produced or greatly exacerbated negative attitudes toward the United States. Although the United States had some preexisting image problems before the inauguration of George W. Bush, they were minor compared to what the Bush administration inflicted through many of its foreign and domestic policies. As 2008 drew to a close, America's global prestige was at a historic low, battered over the years by, among other things, a poorly executed (and to many, poorly conceived) war in Iraq; the clumsy federal response to Hurricane Katrina's devastation of New Orleans; domestic infrastructure neglect symbolized by the widely reported collapse of a bridge in Minneapolis that killed and injured dozens of motorists; and the meltdown of the U.S. financial sector, which threatened to take much of the global economy down with it. Under George Bush, the United States devised a doctrine of preventive war that flew in the face of both established U.S. policy and international norms and tore up international agreements like the 1972 ABM treaty and the Kyoto Protocol. The United States vociferously preached democratization in the Middle East and Southwest Asia while continuing longstanding uncritical support of allied dictatorial regimes in Pakistan, Saudi Arabia, and Egypt. The administration fretted about winning Muslim hearts and minds while engaging in prisoner abuse at Abu Ghraib and Guantanamo Bay, and while abandoning any pretense of even-handedness in dealing with the Israel-Palestinian issue.

During its tenure the Bush administration compounded its wounding of America's reputation by practicing a spectacularly misguided cultural diplomatic program that was the product in equal parts of a misapprehension of what made for an effective approach, ideological rigidity, monofocus on one region and problem set. The administration adopted as its premise that the problem facing America was that the world, and especially the Muslim Middle East, did not know the real America, and that the solution was to better explain U.S. policies and values. One undersecretary of state for public diplomacy and public affairs pursued a widely derided overseas TV advertising campaign designed to show the Islamic world that the United States embraced its Muslim-Americans.[2] Her successor, convinced the personal touch was what was needed to get America's message across, went on an equally ill-fated series of "listening tours" in Muslim countries that annoyed locals, who rightly perceived far more talking than listening on the undersecretary's part (the *New York Times* reported that "[t]raveling with her was at times like being trapped in a cable television infomercial, with an emphasis on values like family and faith"[3]). The final Bush appointee spoke in explicitly militant terms of "the war of ideas" and "the arsenal of persuasion" in the service, first and foremost, of "counterterrorism."[4] This approach gave short shrift, for example, to the sharp uptick in muscular nationalism and anti-Americanism in such strategically apex locales as China, Russia, and India on the one hand, and the corrosion of America's standing with such staunch allies as Britain and Germany and even neutral, conservative Switzerland on the other.[5]

Strategizing American Global Cultural Engagement

Fortunately, although America's global reputation has taken a beating during the George W. Bush years, the United States still has by far the world's best array of assets with the potential to build "soft power," the power of persuasion and attraction, as opposed to the "hard power" of coercion. These include the ideals created in America's founding documents, our example of a tolerant, diverse society, our culture of opportunity and innovation, a tradition of United States' design and participation in international institutions, America's attractiveness as a tourist destination, and our world-leading high and popular culture and higher education. But these soft power assets will not realize their potential to contribute to cultural diplomacy if they are not marshaled thoughtfully.

A bottom-line issue is that *cultural diplomacy is not propaganda*; it is a process of outreach, relationship-building, and a mutual increase in understanding over time. Although America possesses one of the most valuable series of shorthand associations in recorded history (e.g., "All men are created equal"; "Life, Liberty, and the Pursuit of Happiness"; freedom of speech and worship), American values cannot be sold overseas in the manner of a consumer product. Moreover, an honest appraisal of U.S. history and policy makes clear that while the United States has in many ways been a remarkable force for good at home and in the larger world, there are many dark episodes that cast a shadow over America's past and feed resentments in the present. An American cultural diplomacy program that acknowledges these realities—for example, by sponsoring showings of American art or films that cast a critical eye, or by welcoming to the United States strong if responsible foreign critics to speak and debate under official auspices—is far more likely to be successful than a Panglossian presentation of America as the best of all possible worlds.

What follows is not an exhaustive program, which would take much longer to enumerate and elaborate than is possible within the confines of a book chapter. Rather, I offer some key ideas that are geared toward helping to communicate to the world an America that is open, cooperative, generous, broadminded, and possessed of a healthy dose of humility. Some of the prescriptions build on established policy; but others are novel, and a couple arguably counterintuitive. Readers will note an aversion to terminology that connotes bellicosity. Since 2006, the State Department office of the undersecretary for public affairs and public diplomacy has proceeded on the basis of a "war of ideas" aimed at countering terrorism, a stance particularly emphasized since 2006. This approach is misdirected for several reasons. First, the very phrase is redolent of the neoconservative emphasis on force as a first resort rather than last. It is critical to avoid sounding gratuitously aggressive; lest an approach designed to rehabilitate America's prestige and help create a safer international environment have the perversely opposite effect. In addition, unlike during the twentieth century, there is no serious philosophical or ideological competitor to the model of liberal democracy that embraces some variant of capitalism (consider this a modest rehabilitation of Francis Fukuyama's much maligned and poorly understood "End of History" thesis).[6] Nationalism and authoritarianism are realities in a number of states, but they do not provide universal models capable of being emulated to achieve success—there is, for example, little attractiveness to a "Chinese way," and no coherent definition of the term in any event.[7]

The violent Muslim jihadists and terrorists are not responding to an ideology or philosophy in any secular sense of the terms, but to a warped theological interpretation. Thus there is no common battleground for a war of ideas, unlike the competition between democratic capitalism and totalitarian communism, a dual of competing Western political economy models, which took place during the cold war. As a number of commentators have argued, the battle over the theological direction of Islam must take place within the Muslim community— the United States, and for that matter other Western states, can only be an interested bystander, because efforts at sponsoring intra-Muslim opponents of anti-Western jihad risk besmirching their credibility in the eyes of intended audiences.[8] There is merit to considering how to use cultural diplomacy in a *non-propagandizing fashion* to help efforts to delegitimize the al Qaeda jihadist approach. But to make such efforts central would be counterproductive, just as monofocusing on the Arab/Muslim world in cultural diplomacy efforts ignores the other five billion people out there whose support or hostility toward the U.S. matters greatly to our ability to lead and maintain both American and international security.

The State Department: Avatar of an American Culture of Diplomacy

Nothing is more important to both rehabilitating America's tattered global prestige and presenting a more accurate picture of American values than demonstrating that the United States is determined to address the enormous imbalance between spending on the military and diplomacy. The disparity is so great that Secretary of Defense Robert Gates called for a "dramatic increase in spending on the civilian instruments of national security—diplomacy, strategic communications, foreign assistance, civic action and economic reconstruction and development."[9] The budget for the Department of State in 2008 was $35 billion, versus total U.S. military spending that same year of just less than $700 billion—some twenty times more than that for State.[10] In 2008, the requested budget for all public diplomacy-related activities was approximately $1.5 billion—and that does not include areas such as oversight of visas and tourism that should be treated as integral to cultural diplomacy strategy.[11]

Money talks, and what it currently tells the world is that America is a militarized society.

America is not a new Sparta and should not allocate resources like one. The United States needs to recommit to a culture of diplomacy, underlining our core commitment as a nation to global stability and the peaceful arbitration of disputes whenever possible. Thus, the next administration should double the budget of the State Department and be prepared to concomitantly increase spending on cultural and other public diplomacy initiatives. To make this revenue-neutral at a time of severe economic downturn, the money should be drawn directly from the Defense Department.

This does not mean that the United States should let down its guard in either conventional or strategic preparedness. But the next president must be ruthless and brave about targeting pork-barrel programs like the V-22 Osprey, the infamously balky tilt-rotor aircraft that then-Defense

Secretary Dick Cheney repeatedly tried to eliminate as wasteful and ineffective, but which was saved every time by congressional patrons. Killing Osprey alone would free up at least $35 billion.[12] And there is plenty more to be found, if the will is there.

Cultural diplomacy should be made an integral part of foreign policy strategy by having it represented by mandate on the State Department Policy Planning Staff and elsewhere at senior levels within the foreign policy establishment, including the National Security Council. Appropriate candidates for these positions should be well-versed at once in general foreign policy strategy, popular and high culture, media and technology, tourism and higher education, ideally in historical perspective. Past experience at either the practical or scholarly level with the media and technology industries would be especially useful, given the transmitting boost they provide on behalf of American soft power.

Embassies and Missions, Tourism, and Education

U.S. embassies and consulates are the nation's front line of contact with the peoples around the world. In the wake of the 1998 terrorist attacks in Africa, and especially after 9/11, facility security has understandably become an overriding concern. But while the safety of U.S. diplomatic employees is very important, the locking down and fortifying of American diplomatic facilities has made them forbidding and inaccessible places. This sends out a terrible symbolic message of a hunkered down and fearful United States. We must balance security with access. Embassies and missions must become, and be perceived as, open and inviting places for visitors. A concerted effort must be made to keep the hand of security as invisible as possible. There should be ongoing cultural offerings offered onsite, with the public made to feel like welcome and valued guests.

Related to this point, the United States needs to reestablish a valuable program of the postwar era that was allowed to fall into a state of neglect: American-sponsored libraries, both onsite at U.S. embassies and missions and freestanding structures along the lines of Germany's Goethe Haus and Spain's Instituto Cervantes. These libraries should feature both U.S.-subject and local/regional-subject books and magazines in both English and local languages, as well as open Internet access through dedicated portals that are resistant to blocking by local authorities (thus, these may have to be confined in authoritarian regimes to U.S. embassies and missions).

Also related to the issue of embassies and missions, within the State Department we must disaggregate oversight of tourism from that of immigration, both of which are currently controlled by the Bureau of Consular Affairs, and give ultimate policy authority to the Undersecretary for Public Diplomacy and Public Affairs. Having international tourism under State's Public Diplomacy office will refocus policy on the benefit, not the threat, of visitors from abroad. As noted earlier, tourism has extraordinary soft power benefits to offer. We need to be making it easier, not harder, for tourists from abroad to visit America, while developing better and more efficient security measures to weed out the few true malefactors who are trying to get in. There is a dispiriting consistency to the newspaper headlines that have promised change for the better: in February 2006, USA Today reported, "USA Tries to Be Less Daunting to Foreign Visitors"; in September 2007, the International Herald Tribune reported, "US Tries to Ease Entry for Foreign Travelers." Nothing much has been altered. The United States is still "America the Unwelcoming," as foreign policy commentator Fareed Zakaria put it recently.[13] The conservative journalist Andrew Sullivan has reported,

> Getting any kind of visa can be a nightmare of bureaucracy; being finger-printed and treated like a criminal is the first actual experience many foreigners have of entering the US, and the process of getting through customs and immigration can be, even in completely incident-free circumstances, frightening. My elderly mother arrived for my wedding and started sobbing in my arms after the rough treatment she had received from airport security.[14]

It is costing the United States international goodwill, and money as well—foreign tourism is a very important source of revenue to help the American balance of payments, especially in a period of economic recession. By the same token, we should also be encouraging more Americans to travel abroad. Properly prepared, they can function as marvelous goodwill ambassadors. In learning first-hand about the larger world, they will be better-informed citizens to boot. A program to consider is a nominal federal tax credit to low- and middle-income American overseas tourists, if before heading off they complete a brief online State Department course on being responsible international travelers.

Finally, there should be a total end to encumbrances on travel by U.S. citizens, whether tourists, students, or scholars, to targeted overseas destinations—in fact, there should be official efforts made to facilitate American tourism to adversary states (unless travel would pose a clear risk to tourists' physical safety). In addition, the federal government should as a matter of policy quash mischievous attempts by state governments to impose any restrictions on U.S. citizens' overseas travel, as Florida recently attempted to do.[15] It is true that American currency can provide short-term succor to regimes that oppose U.S. policy interests. But this is completely overshadowed by the historical evidence that U.S. tourism is a poisoned chalice to repressive states—for example, United States and other Western tourism played a significant role in the early postwar era in pressuring Spain's Franco dictatorship to loosen its political and social controls, which in turn paved the way for the advent of democracy in Spain.[16] The greatest nightmare for odious governments like Cuba's or Iran's is a flood of American travelers with cash in hand, demanding access to high-quality services and freedom of movement and information, and making numerous people-to-people connections during their visits. We should similarly be making it easier, not harder, for students and visiting faculty, from abroad to come to American colleges and universities, and for American students and scholars to spend time in residence in any and all states, even—in fact especially—adversary states.

Pull the Plug on Propaganda Transmitters; Preserve, Extend and Reflag the VOA

There is little credible evidence that the overtly propaganda–oriented networks like Radio Marti, Al Hurra, and Radio Free Europe/Radio Liberty (RFE/RL) are effective in their stated goals of democracy promotion. Worse, their slanted presentation undermines the authentic American value of free and fair information.[17] The RFE/RL concept was established in the context of the cold war, in which the Communist bloc did its level best to control all of the levers of domestic information. American propaganda media broadcast into an information vacuum and were generally trusted more by peoples living under communist rule than their own governments' media. The situation today throughout much of the world is very different. There are very few current regimes that have achieved more than limited success is cutting their states off from the global information glut; citizens even in repressive states can access far more information and entertainment from outside than communist subjects could ever have imagined during the cold war. In a changed international context, these American propaganda networks do not adequately serve U.S. interests and hence should be summarily disbanded; and the networks that gear themselves toward entertainment and nonhortatory information presentation, like Radio Sawa and Radio Farda, should be absorbed into a repurposed, reflagged Voice of America (VOA).

Although a product of the early cold war-era war of ideas, the VOA has historically operated on the basis of a more straightforward, honest mandate for the presentation of information and cultural offerings. Nonetheless, the United States needs to make a clean, high-profile break with the propagandistic past. Thus, the VOA should be redesigned and reflagged as the American International Network (AIN) on the model of BBC News/BBC World Service, with an unambiguous, well-publicized mandate for unfettered, incisive critical reporting on both the United States and the world at large. This new AIN should be insulated from government editorial oversight, including any pressure to focus on United States' good news or to downplay bad news. The new network should be chartered to operate on radio, TV, and the Internet both internationally and within the United States. Some may dismiss the idea as "an NPR for the World,"[18] but let it be noted that the BBC has long had credibility with international audiences far in excess of that enjoyed by American broadcast efforts.

Hence the AIN should operate on the basis of a charter drawn up explicitly to comply with the Smith-Mundt Act's prohibition on the domestic distribution of government propaganda aimed at overseas audiences. (And given the fact that all of the existing networks and their Web sites are freely accessible in the United States via the Internet, there is probably no legal alternative to bringing material into compliance in any event.) The AIN should not prepare or present anything that is not suitable for consumption by American audiences; in fact it should aggressively seek strong (albeit responsible) dissenting voices from home or abroad for a spirited ongoing colloquy on the United States, its society and policies. The medium—a network devoted to truth, the capacity for national self-criticism, and underwritten by but not shaped by the U.S. government—will be the message as much as the specific content. The Broadcasting Board of Governors, which has oversight of overseas media and information efforts, should amend its mission appropriately away from the simplistic and, as events have demonstrated, freighted mandate to "promote freedom and democracy"[19] (let us not forget that Hamas's electoral triumph in Gaza is a product of this effort) in favor of providing a nuanced, multifaceted view of an America that values spirited colloquy and debate at home and abroad.

Renewed Support for the UN: Global Human Capital Development through the Arts

It is essential for the United States to renew its full participation in the international community and play a leading role in developing human capital around the world. Despite its flaws, the United Nations is the standard bearer of global governance, and, we should not forget, it is largely an American creation. The UN is headquartered not by accident in the United States, and it provides an ongoing potent symbol of the American virtues of tolerance and free speech—would China, or Iran, or Russia regularly provide a forum for their adversaries to criticize their host in the most virulent terms? Moreover, as former U.S. ambassador to the UN Bill Richardson noted, it was possible to expose international diplomats to American culture by showing them the pleasures of New York, America's biggest and most diverse city.[20]

Thus, the United States must recommit itself to supporting the UN and its affiliated institutions. Most basically, this means ending the embarrassing state of dues arrears, which by mid-2008 was well more than $2 billion.[21] In specific cultural diplomacy terms, the United States should enhance its participation in the United Nations Educational, Scientific and Cultural Organization (UNESCO). To give credit where it is due, the Bush administration renewed U.S. membership in UNESCO in 2003, two decades after the Reagan administration pulled out of the organization. But more, much more, needs to be done.

I propose the establishment of a new global culturally based human capital program for the less-developed world for the United States to establish and largely fund under the auspices of UNESCO: an adaptation of the highly successful and lauded Venezuelan children's music education program, *El Fundacion del Estado para el Sistema Nacional de las Orquestas Juveniles e Infantiles de Venezuela*, or simply "el Sistema," established in 1975 by José Antonio Abreu, an economist-cum-musician, to bring the benefits of instrument instruction and performance to poor and troubled Venezuelan children.[22] El Sistema provides lessons and youth orchestras to some 250,000 youngsters and, in doing so, it provides an alternative to crime and self-abuse.

The program's most illustrious alumnus, the brilliant young conductor Gustavo Dudamel, has been named music director of the Los Angeles Philharmonic. Dudamel, born poor, attests that "[t]he music saved me. I'm sure of this."

El Sistema also offers a conduit for the most talented young musicians to find their way up through competitive regional ensembles to the apex Simon Bolivar Youth Orchestra, which has toured the world to rave reviews. With the imprimatur of figures like Berlin Philharmonic conductor Simon Rattle, who has called el Sistema "the most important thing happening in classical music in the world today," a number of spin-off programs have been set up in various Latin American and Caribbean locales, as well as Scotland and even the United States, where Dudamel will play a leading role in the Philharmonic's new Youth Orchestra LA, a public-private initiative in Los Angeles "devoted to providing quality instrumental music education for children with the greatest needs, fewest resources and little or no access to instrumental music education."

For Venezuela's strongman Hugo Chavez, el Sistema represents a critical exception to the lackluster performance at home and abroad of his so-called Bolivarian revolution, and unsurprisingly he gives the program far more financial support than did his predecessors. Unlike petrodollar-driven foreign aid programs like free eye operations in Venezuela for impoverished Latin Americans, el Sistema is soft power that does its job effectively. It represents more than a crass, ineffective attempt to buy good public relations. Rather, it is a grand, universally lauded idea for the development of human capital.

Herein lies a powerful lesson for U.S. foreign policy formulators as they look to rehabilitate America's currently tattered international prestige. The program that José Antonio Abreu dreamed up three decades ago is tailormade for cultural diplomacy outreach by the United States to underprivileged peoples and regions that have in many cases seen violence, ideological extremism, and concomitant anti-Americanism. The United States could co-opt and adapt the el Sistema program, carefully emphasizing that the program long predates Chavez in Venezuela. And America should go beyond music in its human capital aid efforts, to encompass the performing and creative arts in general, including acting, dance, painting and sculpture, photography, and writing (in combination with literacy programs).

El Sistema is based in part on the idea that The Devil Finds Work for Idle Hands—fill those hands with musical instruments, paint brushes, cameras, or pens, and they are far less likely to grasp weapons or drugs.

Those whose lives are improved will be citizens better equipped to participate in local and global society, and they will know whom to thank for their improved horizons. Moreover, the world can only be grateful if the United States helps identify and cultivate more prodigies like Gustavo Dudamel from developing regions. By developing the program through UNESCO, the United States will demonstrate both its commitment to multilateralism and its generosity, while making the program more palatable to countries and peoples who may be suspicious of American intentions—although we should persistently, if quietly, underline the U.S. sponsorship of the program.

American Media and Cultural Diplomacy

Hollywood and, more broadly, American media and entertainment are among the most important elements of American soft power; but they require special understanding and handling as a potential cultural diplomacy asset. One of the most telling quotes about Hollywood's potential to influence hearts and minds comes from one of Hollywood's biggest fans: Josef Stalin, who once said, "If I could control the medium of the American motion picture, I would need nothing else to convert the entire world to communism." This may seem like a less than confidence-inspiring endorsement for the international outreach virtues of Hollywood, but autocratic figures like Stalin, China's Jiang Zemin, and the Spanish dictator Francisco Franco, among others, who admired Hollywood and sought to emulate American film, harness it for their own uses, or were simply envious, were keenly attuned to power issues and assets, both soft and hard.[23]

Thus the desirability of American media as a cultural diplomacy partner is obvious. However, there are complications. The media take the First Amendment very seriously on both artistic and business grounds, zealously guarding their right to free expression and bridling at any effort to make them a tool of U.S. propaganda. Moreover, particularly the motion picture-television industry has worked at cultivating a global image detached as much as possible from too-close identification as American, which is why the Motion Picture Export Association of America rebranded itself simply as the MPA.

This does not mean that there is a lack of opportunities for cooperation. One of the most important functions of the high-level appointees for cultural diplomacy that I have proposed be added to the foreign policy apparatus should be to liaise with the media/entertainment sector and establish a formal consultative body, through which the government would seek their advice and feedback on cultural policy. Although the media have a "don't tread on me" attitude toward infringements on their independence and content production, there can be an ongoing dialogue with producers concerning how their work is perceived abroad, to encourage their sensitivity to the national security implications of their own work as they portray Muslims, Arabs, Latinos, and others who have too often been perniciously stereotyped.

Beyond dialogue and advice, there is a very practical means of encouraging the media to act in ways that are salutary to United States' outreach efforts: money. Although it is highly unlikely that most studios or producers would accept an outright cash grant from the U.S. government because of the risk of seeming politically co-opted, there are many indirect forms of financial aid that could be attractive to studios and other popular culture producers that are eternally preoccupied with minimizing costs and maximizing earnings. Any number of cities and states provide tax and other incentives, including free use of official buildings and other property to attract film and TV production (and some provide loans as well). Their goal is partly economic, of course, but it is also about image-building, especially but not exclusively as a spur to tourism. The Department of Defense (DOD) and the individual service branches have long offered aid-in-kind to film and TV producers, such as access to military facilities, use of troops and equipments either free or at low rates, and expert advice to enhance veracity.[24] Both DOD and states and municipalities have enforced script review and approval as the sine qua non for receiving financial breaks or aid-in-kind, and it has been only rarely that producers have refused to going along with the requirement.

Similarly, the State Department could offer the film and TV industry facilities, aid-in-kind, and access to tax breaks (in conjunction with the Treasury Department), as an inducement to producing work that advances American interests and values in the international sphere. This may seem on the face of it an effort to encourage the production of propaganda. However, the criteria for gaining—or not—access to incentives should not be a crude metric of best face forward, as was the case in an early cold war-era program of indirect aid to the film industry, the International Media Guaranty (IMG) scheme, in which such landmark films as *Rebel without a Cause*, *Sweet Smell of Success*, and *All the King's Men* were denied subsidies because they were deemed deleterious to America's overseas image.[25] A new program of incentives will avoid the propaganda taint as long as the stated criteria are artistic quality, a serious engagement with contemporary issues, and an eschewal of harmful stereotypes (e.g., Muslims are automatically terrorists, or Latinos automatically *narcotraficantes*), and if there is a stated openness to subject matter that critiques U.S. society, politics, and policy.

We must be clear, though, that there is an element of alchemy when it comes to the media and the global image of America, which is not entirely understood even by cultural producers themselves. It is not hard to discern when a film like *True Lies* or the TV series "24" sends the world unpleasant messages of American stereotyping of Muslims or of torture touted as an instrument of American policy. What is harder to predict or accurately measure is an unexpected hit with a positive international image message like Disney's *High School Musical* and its sequels. *High School Musical* is a worldwide smash hit, with some 200 million mostly nine- to fourteen-year-old "tweener" female viewers spread across some 100 countries. There is no blood, no stereotyping, except perhaps of "mean girls," no prurience to offend children or their parents, even quite conservative ones. America (the Southwest, in particular) and its younger citizens come off as attractive and utterly nonthreatening, no small feat in the current era of heightened global distrust of American power and policy. It all sounds brilliant, but *High School Musical*'s blockbuster success took Disney completely by surprise, as is so often the case in Hollywood.[26]

Nonetheless, what a cultural diplomacy program can do concerning film and TV is to be animated by a faith that on balance, now as in the past, America's popular culture is a reflection of something powerfully positive about the United States. It makes sense to foster its international dissemination.

Cultural Diplomacy and IT Media

Finally as we consider cultural diplomacy and media, the United States must consider it a top priority to work toward the goal of freeing the World Wide Web, the "global electronic commons," from political censorship. The Internet has developed into one of the most remarkable venues for the global dissemination of ideas, information, and entertainment. Although it still has something of a Wild West flavor, the Web holds enormous soft power potential for the United States in particular. However, this potential is undermined when authoritarian regimes are able to buy sophisticated software that enables them to censor content and track down dissidents and would-be reformers. The aid that some

U.S. software giants have been giving to Chinese censorship efforts is nothing short of an outrage, and it is completely at cross-purposes with United States a cultural diplomacy based on the free flow of ideas. Yahoo, Cisco, and Microsoft are all widely known as U.S. companies, and their help to Beijing besmirches America's image.[27]

On the other hand, the United States should be helping to preserve, and doing nothing to impair, the positive international reputations established by some American software companies, particularly Google, with its globally known informal motto, "Don't Be Evil." For example, Google has not allowed Web surfers in Cuba, Syria, North Korea, Iran, and Sudan to download the company's new browser, Chrome, because of U.S. export controls and economic sanctions in force against these states. One knowledgeable Syrian blogger has expressed disappointment in Google, which had "earned a reputation here and elsewhere to be the good guys....They gave the impression that they depart from the big corporation mentality and attitude, which gave them credit in this part of the world. For that reason you don't hear of someone boycotting a Google service or product." He writes that the U.S. sanctions only help the Ba'athist regime to maintain control.[28] It should never be difficult for users anywhere to get their hands on the latest Web browsers, especially in places where the United States wishes to see holes punched in government control of the Internet; and the State Department's cultural diplomatic strategists should take the lead in advocating a rewriting of the rules.

Drawing in as well as Reaching out via Media and Journalism

It is imperative for the United States to put behind it the post-9/11 image of a nation hunkered down, fearful of outsiders and of criticism, and unilateral in the broad sense of the term. The world should see the historically accurate image of an America that has been open to and positively influenced by peoples and ideas from around the world. Beyond encouraging the entry of tourists and students regardless of place of origin and scholars and other intellectuals regardless of intellectual stripe, America should welcome and, in some cases, even provide financial incentives for visits and work in the United States by foreign media producers. In addition, foreign journalists should in general have unfettered right to entry and free movement in the United States, even those who are from hostile states or who are strong critics of U.S. policy.

Although it might annoy the American film/TV industry, the United States should provide generous incentives beyond those made available by individual states and municipalities to encourage foreign filmmakers from developing countries to produce movie and television content in America. The incentive package, like the one proposed to aid Hollywood producers, should include the combination of tax breaks, access to government-owned property, and logistical and other aid-in-kind; but it should, in addition, offer streamlined, high-priority visa and related visitor processing, waivers of duties and travel taxes, and the elimination of other costs ordinarily associated with foreign production in the United States. Script review and approval to participate in the program should be on the same grounds as those for Hollywood: artistic quality, serious engagement with contemporary issues, and an eschewal of pernicious stereotypes, with openness to subject matter critical of American society, culture, and politics. This is one more way for the United States to announce that it is generous, open, and secure enough in its values and society to welcome potentially critical observers from abroad. Moreover, some if not all of the film and TV creative artists who come to America to take advantage of such a program are likely to be positively impressed and speak up at some point in their home countries (e.g., "I gave the Americans a script that slammed the United States on its treatment of undocumented immigrants, and they didn't bat an eye!"). The combination of respect on the part of producers and the recasting of the U.S. image concerning criticism from abroad will pay long-term prestige dividends, even if some individual efforts might pose problems in the short run.

As has been stressed repeatedly in this chapter, freedom of speech and of the press is a core American value, and as such should be front and center in any policy that deals with foreign journalists. There should be an end to restrictions on the entry into the United States and on domestic freedom of movement currently directed at journalists from adversary states, as well as other reporters who are deemed critics of U.S. policy. To bar or restrict reporters from states we do not like, or whose reportage we do not like, runs counter to the American ethos and sends out a terrible message concerning the gaps between values and practice. A telling exchange in 2006 between a U.S. reporter and a State Department spokesman epitomizes the utter wrongheadedness of current policy:

> *Reporter*: [I]n recent months, you've talked about the need to increase cultural exchanges and try and forge more understanding

about the Iranian people and the United States. Do you think it would be wise to . . . give Iranian journalists more of a license to travel the country so as to bring that greater understanding of America back home?

Spokesman: You're certainly right that we are seeking ways to speak directly to the Iranian people. Officials from the State Department and other government agencies on a regular basis do interviews with Persian language media outlets that broadcast into Iran. As for the government journalists, I don't—I'm not aware of any move at this point to reexamine these—any restrictions that may be placed upon their movement. I would assume that there are good reasons for those restrictions. . . . [I]t doesn't really matter who's doing the interview. I know it matters to some of you. But the important point for us is the ability to speak directly to the Iranian people and the message that we send in certainly the hope that the Iranian people are listening.[29]

In fact, the identity of the reporting or interviewing journalist matters greatly; and it impairs the credibility of the message U.S. officials are trying to propound when it is offered up by an evident shill at one of the U.S. Farsi-language broadcast outlets rather than by a local journalist, even one who is employed by an official news service.[30] The United States should give journalists from adversary states free rein to travel freely within the United States, report without encumbrance, and gain interview access to high-level American officials. Doing so will not legitimate regimes with whom we are at odds; rather, it will serve as a rebuke and challenge to extend the same privilege to American reporters in their countries. And publics in these countries and elsewhere will take positive note. Of course, if there is legitimate suspicion that a journalist is engaging in espionage or fomenting violence against the United States, then all appropriate legal steps should be taken to deal with the issue.

At least as important, the American government should never—repeat, never—bar from U.S. entry foreign journalists from nonadversary states who have written or commented critically about America or its policies, as happened in 2005 to Robert Fisk, long-time Middle East correspondent for the respected UK *Independent* and a strong critic of the Iraq war, who was prevented from traveling to a speaking engagement in Santa Fe, New Mexico and instead made his appearance via remote hookup from Toronto.[31] As an ACLU representative testified before Congress several years back, " 'Ideological exclusion' is a term of art but its impact is real. The federal government is excluding people to prevent American citizens and residents from participating in conferences or exchanges of ideas with people whose ideas the administration dislikes."[32] Such actions serve to confirm the worst foreign criticism of the United States as a hypocrite that extols the marketplace of ideas in theory and punishes it in practice.

Some Final Thoughts on Cultural Diplomacy Strategy

The truer a cultural diplomacy program is to America's core values, the better our relations and prestige with the world will be. "Sunshine is the best disinfectant," as Supreme Court Justice Louis Brandeis once said, and the wounds inflicted on America's global standing will be most effectively treated by a cultural diplomacy that is predicated upon the American qualities of honesty, forthrightness, openness to varying perspectives, and a willingness to concede that while America is overall a force for good, it has sometimes fallen short.

Here are a several final points cultural diplomacy policy formulators should keep in mind:

You Can't Please Everyone with American Culture. There are millions of *Americans* who are offended or otherwise dismayed by elements of American culture, both high and popular, whether on moral, ideological, or aesthetic grounds—and sometimes a mixture of all three. So it is unrealistic to expect a less complex reaction from foreign observers. Ultimately, America has to reconcile itself to the perceived (and actual) good and bad of its culture via The Popeye principle: "I Yam What I Yam," as the cartoon sailor famously proclaimed.

Keep the Faith: There Is No Easy Metric of Cultural Diplomacy Success. Polls like the Pew Global Attitudes Survey are helpful in getting a sense of how people around the world perceive the United States. But they cannot directly measure the effectiveness of specific U.S. cultural diplomacy efforts beyond the most limited sorts of queries. And related to this point,

There is No Quick Return on Effort. Cultural diplomacy programs will not change hearts and minds on a dime. They are not a riposte. Over the long term, however, cultural outreach and communication can have a subtle, accretive, but ultimately highly beneficial effect on America's reputation abroad.

Some of the cultural diplomacy prescriptions presented in this chapter, such as courting criticism to demonstrate confidence, are counterintuitive. Some prescriptions may ultimately prove to be unworkable, if only for pedestrian political or turf-protection reasons. But if we are not bold in the strategies we devise to reestablish America's prestige and attractiveness, we will not be able to lead effectively during a time of profound challenge, an outcome that would be disastrous for the United States and the world. Cultural diplomacy cannot do the job of remaking America's image by itself; but the job of remaking America's image cannot be done without cultural diplomacy.

Notes

1. Richard T. Arndt, *The First Resort of Kings: American Cultural Diplomacy in the Twentieth Century* (Dulles, VA: Potomac Books, 2005), 545; the Djerejian report, *Changing Minds, Winning Peace: A New Strategic Direction for U.S. Public Diplomacy in the Arab & Muslim World* (Advisory Group on Public Diplomacy for the Arab and Muslim World, Edward P. Djerejian, chairman, 2003), is available at http://www.state.gov/documents/organization/24882.pdf.
2. Bush's Muslim Propaganda Chief Quits," CNN, March 3, 2003, at http://www.cnn.com/2003/US/03/03/state.resignation/.
3. "On Mideast 'Listening Tour,' the Question is Who's Hearing," *New York Times*, September 30, 2005, at http://www.nytimes.com/2005/09/30/international/middleeast/30hughes.html.
4. Undersecretary of State for Public Diplomacy and Public Affairs James Glassman, "U.S. Public Diplomacy and the War of Ideas," press conference transcript, July 15, 2008, at http://fpc.state.gov/fpc/107034.htm
5. For China see e.g. Evan Osnos, "Letter from China: Angry Youth: The New Generation's Neocon Nationalists," *New Yorker*, July 28, 2008, at http://www.newyorker.com/reporting/2008/07/28/080728fa_fact_osnos; for India see e.g., Chintamani Mahapatra, "Anti-Americanism in India: Obfuscation on US Hyde Act," *India News and Feature Alliance*, July 28, 2008, at http://www.sarkaritel.com/news_and_features/infa/july08/28anti_americanism.htm; for Russia see e.g., Alistair Gee, "Rising Anti-Americanism in Russia, *U.S. News and World Report*, January 18, 2008, at http://www.usnews.com/articles/news/world/2008/01/18/rising-anti-americanism-in-russia.html; for Britain see "Anglo-Saxon Attitudes: Not Such Special Friends," *Economist*, March 27, 2008, at http://www.economist.com/daily/news/displaystory.cfm?STORY_ID=10927596; for Germany see "Politiker reiten heftige Attacken auf Bush" ["politicians mount brutal attack on Bush"], *Die Welt* (Germany), at http://www.welt.de/politik/article2082017/Politiker_reiten_heftige_Attacken_auf_Bush.html; for Switzerland see "Swiss Envoy Warns of Anti-American Sentiment," *swissinfo*. *ch*, September 9, 2008, at http://www.swissinfo.ch/eng/front/Swiss_envoy_warns_of_anti_American_sentiment.html?siteSect=105&sid=9683342&cKey=1221475615000&ty=st.
6. Francis Fukuyama, *The End of History and The Last Man* (New York: Free Press, 1992, 2006).
7. China has sought to increase its soft power relative to the United States, especially in the developing regions, but it has done so primarily through a pocketbook diplomacy in which Beijing purchases materials and supplies services and logistics gratis or at low cost, without regard to the international or domestic behavior of intended client states. The most notorious example has been China's relationship with Sudan, which proved a soft power debacle for China in 2008 when political activists launched a series of high-profile protests during the lead-up to the Beijing Olympics against China's acquiescence in Sudan's genocidal policies in the Darfur region. For China's soft power efforts in relation to the United States, see e.g., report, *A Smarter, More Secure America* (CSIS Commission on Smart Power, Joseph S. Nye and Richard Armitage,

co-chairs, 2007), 25–26, at http://www.csis.org/media/csis/pubs/071106_csissmartpower-report.pdf. For the Darfur Olympics protest effort, see e.g., "Darfur Collides with Olympics and China Yields," *New York Times*, April 13, 2007, at http://www.nytimes.com/2007/04/13/washington/13diplo.html.

8. See e.g., Thomas Friedman, "If It's a Muslim Problem, It Needs a Muslim Solution," *New York Times*, July 8, 2005, at http://www.nytimes.com/2005/07/08/opinion/08friedman.html; Shiraz Maher, "Extremism Is Going Unchallenged," *New Statesman* (UK), April 3, 2008, at http://www.newstatesman.com/politics/2008/04/government-impact-young; Ed Husain, *The Islamist: Why I Joined Radical Islam in Britain, What I Saw Inside and Why I Left* (New York: Penguin, 2007).

9. "Defense Secretary Urges More Spending for U.S. Diplomacy," *New York Times*, November 27, 2007, at http://www.nytimes.com/2007/11/27/washington/27gates.html.

10. Travis Sharp, "US Defense Spending 2001–2009," Center for Arms Control and Non-Proliferation, at http://www.armscontrolcenter.org/policy/securityspending/articles/defense_spending_since_2001/index.html.

11. "Appendix to Nye and Armitage Testimony before U.S. Senate Foreign Relations Committee," April 24, 2008, 7, at http://www.csis.org/media/csis/congress/ts0804024Armitage-Nye_Appendix.pdf.

12. "V-22 Osprey: A Flying Shame," *Time*, September 26, 2007, at http://www.time.com/time/politics/article/0,8599,1665835,00.html.

13. Fareed Zakaria, "America the Unwelcoming," *Newsweek*, November 26, 2007 at http://www.newsweek.com/id/70991.

14. Andrew Sullivan, "America the Unfriendly," "Daily Dish" blog, *Atlantic Online*, November 2, 2007, at http://andrewsullivan.theatlantic.com/the_daily_dish/2007/11/america-the-unf.html.

15. "Florida Law Banning Cuba Travel, Research Struck Down," *New York Daily News*, August 30, 2008, at http://www.nydailynews.com/latino/2008/08/30/2008–08-30_florida_law_banning_cuba_travel_research.html.

16. See Neal M. Rosendorf, "Be El Caudillo's Guest: The Franco Regime's Quest for Rehabilitation and Dollars after World War II via the Promotion of U.S. Tourism to Spain," *Diplomatic History*, June 2006; Sasha D. Pack, *Tourism and Dictatorship: Europe's Peaceful Invasion of Franco's Spain* (New York: Palgrave Macmillan, 2006).

17. Robert McMahon, "Backgrounder: The Changing Scope of U.S. International Broadcasts," Council on Foreign Relations, March 23, 2007, at http://www.cfr.org/publication/12930/changing_scope_of_us_international_broadcasts.html; "Broadcasting Ideas Most Cubans Can't See," NBC News Report, October 9, 2007, at http://www.msnbc.msn.com/id/21206872/.

18. Robert McMahon, at http://www.cfr.org/publication/12930/changing_scope_of_us_international_broadcasts.html.

19. Broadcasting Board of Governors Mission and Strategic Guidance: BBG Strategic Plan 2008–2013, at http://www.bbg.gov/about/bbg_strategic_plan_2008–2013.pdf.

20. Clyde Haberman, "New York Type at the U.N.? Look Out," *New York Times*, April 19, 2005, at http://www.nytimes.com/2005/04/19/nyregion/19nyc.html.

21. "U.S. Funding for the U.N.: An Overview," Better World Campaign, at http://www.betterworldcampaign.org/issues/funding/us-funding-for-the-un-an-overview.html.

22. For source materials for this section's discussion of El Sistema, see Neal Rosendorf, "Maestro Dudamel, Venezuelan Soft Power, and Lessons for America," blog article, University of Southern California Center on Public Diplomacy Web site, March 6, 2008, at http://uscpublicdiplomacy.com/index.php/newsroom/pdblog_detail/maestro_dudamel_venezuelan_soft_power_and_lessons_for_america/.

23. See Rosendorf, "Social and Cultural Globalization: Concepts, History, and America's Role," in *Governance in a Globalizing World* ed. Joseph S. Nye and John D. Donahue (Washington,

DC: Brookings, 2000), 117–121; as well as Rosendorf, "'Hollywood in Madrid': American Film Producers and the Franco Regime, 1950–1970," *Historical Journal of Film, Radio and Television*, March 2007.

24. See e.g., Lawrence Suid, *Sailing on the Silver Screen: Hollywood and the U.S. Navy* (Annapolis, MD: Naval Institute Press, 1996).

25. Kerry Segrave, *American Films Abroad: Hollywood's Domination of the World's Movie Screens* (Jefferson, NC: McFarland, 1997), 204.

26. For sources related to this paragraph, see Rosendorf, "Send in the Mousketeers!" blog article, University of Southern California Center on Public Diplomacy Web site, August 22, 2007, at http://uscpublicdiplomacy.com/index.php/newsroom/pdblog_detail/ send_in_the_mousketeers1/.

27. "U.S. Lawmakers Scold Tech Companies for China Censorship," *PC World*, February 15, 2006, at http://www.pcworld.com/article/124733/us_lawmakers_scold_tech_companies_ for_china_censorship.html.

28. Jessica Dheere, "Google Blocks Chrome User in Syria, Iran," *MediaShift*, October13, 2008, at http://www.pbs.org/mediashift/2008/10/google-blocks-chrome-browser-use-in-syria- iran287.html.

29. U.S. State Department Press Briefing, April 7, 2006, at http://www.state.gov/r/pa/prs/ dpb/2006/64251.htm.

30. See comments by U.S. Rep. David Obey, VOA News, "Rice Defends US Broadcast Plans for Iran," April 4, 2006, at http://www.voanews.com/english/archive/2006–04/2006–04- 04-voa84.cfm.

31. Soledad Santiago, "A Battle-Tested Pen," *Santa Fe New Mexican*, September 16, 2005. See http://www.copvcia.com/free/ww3/092805_world_stories.shtml.

32. "ACLU Testimony Before the [House] Subcommittee on National Security, Emerging Threats, and International Relations Regarding Censorship at the Borders," March 28, 2006, at http://www.aclu.org/safefree/dissent/24776leg20060328.html.

CHAPTER TEN

Public Diplomacy in an Age of Faith

JENNIFER A. MARSHALL AND
THOMAS F. FARR

Henry Kissinger's 1994 magnum opus *Diplomacy* presents a grand sweep of world affairs from Richelieu to Reagan. It documents the history of monarchies, tyrannies, and republics, and their rise and fall through the centuries. Dynasties, political parties, and hundreds of statesmen find their place in the narrative but, excepting a brief treatment of Catholic universalism and its replacement by the state system, the subject of religion is strangely absent.[1] In fact, the word "religion" does not appear in the detailed index of the massive 900-page work.[2] Surprisingly, Kissinger's exploration of the period from the late 1960s through the 1990s, during which he was a major diplomatic player himself, gives no hint that there were religious actors or ideas at work in the world. There is virtually no mention of Pope John Paul II or the contributions of religious communities to the growth of democracy. Grand Ayatollah Ruhollah Khomeini and the 1979 Shiite revolution in Iran merit only a casual reference. Virtually nothing is made of the impact of Wahhabism in Saudi Arabia or its export around the world, the rise of Islamist extremism, or the growth of Pentacostalism. In this telling, religion had almost no impact on international affairs.

A decade later, however, foreign affairs thinkers had begun to engage more systematically the subject Kissinger had avoided.[3] Madeleine Albright and Walter Russell Mead, for example, wrote books that not only included religion in the index, but also put God in their titles.[4] These works are emblematic of increasing attention in the post-9/11 era to the intersection of religion and foreign affairs. Foundation grants have begun to encourage the study of religion and international relations at major universities such as Georgetown.[5] The National Endowment for Democracy has some promising new initiatives that focus on Islamic communities.[6] In July 2008, the State Department's Human Rights and Democracy Fund put out its first request for proposals on programs to advance religious freedom.[7]

A 2007 report by the Center for Strategic and International Studies (CSIS) notes some minor improvements over the past decade in the foreign policy establishment's awareness of religion, noting, for example, nineteen mentions of religious issues in the 2006 National Security Strategy compared to four in the 2002 NSS.[8] The report also detects progress in certain corners of America's foreign policy agencies:

> Parts of the intelligence community address religion as a transnational concern; the military services are increasingly developing doctrine and training on approaching religious leaders and communities in stability operations; USAID works with faith-based organizations and incorporates religious sensitivities into some development programming; and State Department officials promote international religious freedom and are focused on improving relations with the Muslim world.[9]

Such attention to religious dynamics is a welcome development as the United States struggles to come to grips with the ideological clash at the heart of the war on terrorism. Unfortunately, the cases in which American foreign policy successfully engages religious ideas and actors are atypical and isolated. Ad hoc in nature, they have not been part of a systematic formulation of policy, strategy, and tactics for waging and winning a war of ideas. Overall, the response of U.S. diplomacy to the religious scaffolding that bestrides the international order has been at best inconsistent and often incoherent. The same CSIS study concludes,

> Current U.S. government frameworks for approaching religion are narrow, often approaching religions as problematic or monolithic forces, overemphasizing a terrorism-focused analysis of Islam and sometimes marginalizing religion as a peripheral humanitarian or cultural issue.[10]
>
> American interests will be better met through increased awareness and recognition of how religion affects international affairs, including through the faith and religious beliefs of politicians and

elites; the belief structures that underlie national and international views; and the impact of religious organizations. Religious leaders, organizations, institutions and communities can mobilize religion to sanction violence, draw on religion to resolve conflicts, or invoke religion to provide humanitarian and development aid. To engage successfully, government analyses, policy, training, and programming must fully incorporate an understanding of the varied roles for religion in conflict-prone settings.[11]

Religion's Persistence Worldwide

The reality is that the world is overflowing with religious ideas, actors, communities, and movements—with very public consequences. There is little reason to believe that this state of affairs will change anytime soon. Polls from across the globe show a growth in religious affiliation and in the desire for religious leaders to be more involved in politics. Two demographers of religion, Todd Johnson and David Barrett, have concluded, "Demographic trends coupled with conservative estimates of conversions and defections envision over 80 percent of the world's population will continue to be affiliated to religions 200 years into the future."[12]

The implications of religion's resurgence are multifaceted. Islamist radicalism draws the most attention, but the issue is hardly confined to Muslim majority countries or the Muslim diaspora. An explosion of religious devotion among Chinese citizens increasingly worries communist officials—a phenomenon on public display during the recent Beijing Olympics. Religious ideas and actors affect the fate of democracy and public policy in Russia, relations between nuclear powers India and Pakistan, and the consolidation of democracy in Latin America. In sub-Saharan Africa, religion plays an important role in issues from economic growth to political stability and public policies on HIV/AIDS.

Some would conclude from the evidence that religion's persistence bodes ill for the future of liberty—that public manifestations of religion by their nature stand in the way of democracy and modernization. Such conclusions, however, overlook a wealth of data indicating that religious practice can yield significant goods for society. Rather than being inimical to the advance of freedom, religious ideas and actors can buttress and expand ordered liberty. Outcomes associated with religious practice include higher levels of civic engagement, health, and material welfare.[13]

At the same time, religion's role on the world stage has complex political implications. Religious belief has both bolstered and undermined political stability. It has not only advanced political reform and human rights but has also induced persecution, extremism, and terrorism. Engaging religious communities in developing the habits of liberal democracy is essential to promoting ordered liberty in much of the world. The advance of freedom in highly religious societies requires policy makers to address the overlapping authorities of religion and state and how religiously grounded norms might legitimately influence public policy. The United States' experience is highly relevant in this regard. Explaining the success of America's model—the reconciliation of faith and freedom through religious liberty—is one of the most pressing tasks for public diplomacy today.

U.S. Policy's Religious Reticence

Ambivalence toward religion, however, has long been a weakness of U.S. foreign policy. In public and private diplomacy, foreign aid and democracy programs, U.S. policymakers and diplomats have been plagued by confusion about what role, if any, religion should play. Most analysts lack the vocabulary and the imagination to fashion remedies that draw on religion, a shortcoming common to all the major schools of foreign policy. Modern realists see authoritarian regimes as partners in restraining radical Islamism and consequently, when they focus on religion at all, view it primarily as an instrument of power. Liberal internationalists are generally suspicious of religion's role in public life, seeing it as a restraint on human autonomy and too divisive to contribute to democratic stability. Neoconservatives emphasize American exceptionalism and the value of democracy, but few have paid serious attention to religious actors or their beliefs and how these contribute to or detract from the formation of cultures in which democracy can flourish. The U.S. "freedom agenda" has been seriously weakened as a result.[14]

America's International Religious Freedom policy provides a case in point. That policy, established by the 1998 International Religious Freedom Act (IRFA), has made laudable strides toward relieving the plight of individuals persecuted for their religious beliefs. The United States has roundly condemned nations that most egregiously violate religious liberty and helped to free individual prisoners. But opposing religious persecution and freeing religious prisoners is the beginning, not the end, of religious liberty.[15]

A more expansive religious freedom agenda should seek to promote policy regimes that consistently apply religious liberty tenets rooted in constitutional government. Religious persecution is generally associated with egregious abuse of people—torture, rape, unjust imprisonment—because of their religious beliefs and practices or those of their tormentors. A political order centered on religious liberty does not tolerate persecution, to be sure, but it also protects the rights of individuals and groups to *act publicly* in ways consistent with their beliefs. Those rights include, most importantly, the freedom to influence public policy within the bounds of liberal norms. Addressing this aspect of religious liberty is a critical step in creating stable self-government in societies with powerful religious groups.[16]

To the extent that U.S. policy has taken religion seriously as a driver of culture and politics in Muslim societies, it has at times appeared more intent on diluting religion's effect than encouraging a political culture of accommodation. Some efforts have reflected the United States' own moral confusion and poll-driven culture. Attempts to "reach out" to Muslim youth have often centered on American pop music; a chair of the U.S. Broadcasting Board of Governors once suggested that the pop star Britney Spears "represents the sounds of freedom."[17] Such an impoverished notion of freedom is counterproductive if the United States is to engage effectively in the war of ideas with the Muslim world. Lasting solutions will require the involvement of religious actors who can speak from the heart of their respective communities about how religion and ordered liberty can be mutually reinforcing.

Effective ideological engagement requires an accurate concept of the role of religion in the United States as well as accurate perceptions about the beliefs that motivate foreign populations. That begins with mustering the full force of the ideas on which the United States is founded. The United States is a religious nation, but the religious roots of the American order and the role of religion in the continued success of the American experiment are poorly understood by the general public and policy makers alike. A lack of appreciation for how religion can buttress and expand ordered liberty leads to a lack of vocabulary, imagination, and remedies that draw on religious ideas, individuals, and institutions. When U.S. policy communicates an official position of awkwardness and reticence on these matters, and ambivalence about the significance of religion in people's lives, it hinders U.S. policy makers from reaching and winning hearts and minds abroad.

Effective public diplomacy must recognize religion as a powerful driver of culture, including political culture. Religion is one of the strongest determinants in both the life of an individual and the life of the community; it defines the worldview of many whom U.S. policy seeks to influence. Public diplomacy must therefore include strategies for communicating with deeply religious audiences. Specifically, U.S. policy makers should

- understand the role of religion and religious freedom in the American constitutional order;
- highlight the success of the United States in reconciling the dual authorities of state and religion, providing insight about how religiously grounded norms might legitimately influence public policy;
- present a positive vision for religion's contribution to a liberal order, advancing a robust vision of religious liberty as the foundation of democratic order;
- engage civil society resources, including religious individuals and institutions, in this battle of ideas.

The "Separationist" Problem

The inadequate consideration of religion in public diplomacy results from the habits of thought pervasive within policy circles generally and the foreign policy community in particular. Specifically, notions of the strict separation-of-church-and-state and assumptions about secularization act as blinders to social and political realities at home and abroad. The U.S. foreign policy establishment is not necessarily antireligious or irreligious. Even religious people can fall into the habit of thinking that religion is a private matter, or that it is not normative in human behavior, or that it is by its nature an obstacle to democracy. Such attitudes are broadly dispersed within the foreign affairs community and reinforce the resistance to thinking about religion as a policy issue.

One cause of hesitancy is the perception that religious engagement is unconstitutional. There is among foreign policy officials a generalized belief that the Establishment Clause prohibits any government activity dealing with religion.[18] Like many graduates of American higher education, U.S. officials have often been schooled in a strict separation-of-church-and-state philosophy. This encourages an expansive "separationist" mentality, the perspective that the constitutional idea of nonestablishment of religion requires the government to have nothing to do with religion. It also encourages the belief that religion is such a personal, private affair that it ought to be inconsequential in matters of public policy and of negligible significance to society as a whole.

Although some U.S. official actions in the realm of religion and foreign policy may raise constitutional issues, the Constitution neither mandates ignorance about religion nor proscribes its public practice. As former secretary of state Madeleine Albright has written, "the constitutional requirement that separates state from church in the United States does not also insist that the state be ignorant of the church, mosque, synagogue, pagoda, and temple."[19] What the Constitution unambiguously requires, however, is the defense of religious freedom.

Confusion about religion's place in foreign policy also stems from prevailing assumptions about the direction of history and the meaning of modernity. Specifically, the so-called secularization theory holds that societies will inevitably become less religious over time as scientific knowledge displaces faith. In this view, religion is inherently emotive and irrational, and thus opposed to modernity, an obstacle to political and economic progress. As modernity advances, religion will shrink to the irrelevant margins of human behavior and ultimately will disappear. Data on religious belief and practice in the United States[20] and evidence from around the world, however, suggest that the secularization theory is obsolete.[21]

The late Adda B. Bozeman, whose work focused on the interrelation of culture and statecraft, observed, "[T]he most critical aspect of American disposition toward non-Western societies...is a pronounced inability or unwillingness to come to terms with religions, philosophies, ideologies, and other bodies of beliefs that have decisively shaped the foreign mind-sets but which continue to baffle Americans."[22] In short, a lack of understanding of religion's continued relevance in America's constitutional order precludes clear thinking about the relationship between religion and liberty abroad. Overcoming this deficit will require restoring a more robust concept of religion's role, beginning with the cultural and legal framework established at the American founding.

America's Religious Character: Theory and Practice

The American model of religious liberty, in combination with its thriving religious culture, is unique in the world. These features characterize the American order as much as its democratic political system or market economy. The religious traditions of America serve to sustain both limited government and a free, vigorous economy. As Michael Novak puts it, democratic capitalism is a system of three parts: "Not only do the logic of democracy and the logic of the market economy strengthen one another. Both also require a special moral-cultural base."[23]

A useful way to conceptualize the Founders' understanding of religion and religious freedom is to visualize three basic principles that underlay their approach. The first is a claim about the theistic foundation of American liberty. This claim was most famously articulated by Thomas Jefferson in the Declaration of Independence. All men, he wrote, were created equal and endowed with inalienable rights by their Creator. While Jefferson's first principle is no longer universally assumed in American politics, opposition is of recent vintage. As late as the 1950s, Justice William O. Douglas wrote that "we are a religious people whose institutions presuppose a supreme being."[24]

This claim about God and man yielded a theory of human nature, that is, that each man owes a duty to the Creator because God imparts life and is the source of natural rights. But this observation did not yield laws mandating the performance of man's duty toward God. To the contrary, it fed the conviction that human nature and good government require liberty. James Madison, the father of the Constitution and the primary architect of the religion clauses of the First Amendment, made the critical intellectual pivot that energized the American understanding of religious liberty and democratic government. No man, he wrote, may exercise for another the duty owed to God. To fulfill one's obligations to God, each human being must have freedom.[25]

From these understandings of God, natural rights and religious freedom flows a theory of the state. The state's responsibility to its citizens and to its religious communities is to protect and nourish freedom, especially the free exercise of religion. This is the focus of the religion clauses of the First Amendment—at least as it was interpreted for the first 150 years of this country's existence. The First Amendment's ban on the establishment of religion is designed to protect free exercise by protecting religion from the state. The Founders believed fervently that establishment would corrupt religion.

All of the Founders believed, from the most religious to the least, that morality is necessary for the health of democracy and religion is necessary for morality. Because religious freedom derives from God, it is a natural right that is not created by the state, but must be protected by the state. But, because democracy requires moral citizens and morality requires religion, religious freedom was considered more than a matter of justice and human dignity. It was also a fundamental pillar of the American democratic experiment.[26]

These principles reflected a major theme in American history, that is, the vigorous practice of religion and the influence of religious ideas, actors, and communities on civic life. From the earliest seventeenth-century settlements to the great social justice causes led by religious congregations in the late nineteenth century to the current day services provided by congregations and faith-based organizations (which reach far beyond U.S. borders), religion has been and remains a vibrant force in America.

The American Jesuit John Courtney Murray noted that the Protestant characteristic of religious plurality—a vigorous and contending diversity—was the native condition of colonial America. At the founding, the idea of God as Creator, author of a transcendent moral law, and Judge of all men, was a fundamental insight incorporated into America's founding principles. The religious system that developed from this principle at the time of the founding generation was one of pluralism, or—as Murray put it—creeds contending intelligibly within the civil sphere.[27] Pluralism, he argued, was an achievement of the American political order that reconciled civil and religious authorities and regulated competition among religious groups. This achievement has been a major factor in the success of our democracy.

In recent decades, however, the successes of American religious pluralism have come under challenge from strict separationism and from a secularist conviction among U.S. elites that "comprehensive doctrines," especially those of religion, do not belong in the democratic public square.[28] As a result, religion has played a diminishing role in determining social norms and dictates of law in the United States. A reduced understanding of religion's relevance domestically contributes to the failure to recognize religion's importance as a motivating factor in world politics. This has resulted in a greater psychological distance between America and societies dominated by religious institutions, ideas, and actors. Without the capacity to conceive the beliefs and motivations of highly religious societies, policy makers have been, and will continue to be, ill-equipped to communicate with such audiences effectively.

Yet, more than half of American adults consider religion very important in their lives, and 86 percent say that it is at least somewhat important.[29] Approximately six in ten American adults report membership in a local religious congregation, and nearly four in ten attend at least once a week.[30] Faith-based organizations are extremely active in providing social needs in America, as well as sending aid abroad. In 2000, religious Americans gave away 3.5 times more money than and volunteered with more than twice the frequency of their secular counterparts.[31] Clearly there is a gap between the religious practices of American citizens and the confusion and disarray of U.S. policymakers when it comes to articulating in our public diplomacy the continuing importance of religion to American democracy.

Ten Prescriptions for U.S. Public Diplomacy

U.S. public diplomacy aims to advance U.S. interests and security by imparting to foreign audiences an understanding and appreciation of American founding principles, ideals, institutions, and policy. It must, therefore, begin with an adequate conception and articulation of the American constitutional order, particularly "the first freedom" of religious liberty. The challenge for public diplomacy is to distinguish essential elements of the American order from incidental features of twenty-first-century American culture. Self-government demands a high degree of social consciousness about the ideas that sustain the order. Despite this imperative, Americans have not been consistently diligent in defending the ideas at the heart of the American order.

This shortcoming has "gradually made for a crippled, decidedly unconvincing national self-image," according to one international relations scholar, exposing America's defining attributes to mischaracterization at home and abroad.[32] Such a vague, "unconvincing" national identity makes it difficult to communicate purposefully and coherently abroad.[33] If we are to convince others of our bona fides and our good will, we must know who we are.

The failure to appreciate the definition and role of religious liberty in the American order is particularly problematic. Debates over the extent of religious liberty domestically also lead to a narrow understanding of what the concept means and how it should be implemented abroad. To overcome these deficits in the war of ideas, U.S. public diplomacy should advance a robust vision of a religious freedom that provides a foundation for liberty, preserves religious integrity, enables religious pluralism, and reconciles the dual authorities of religion and state. Specifically, public diplomacy should incorporate the following strategies:

1. Communicate America's successful reconciliation of dual authorities.

The American constitutional order produced a constructive tension between church and state—not the radical separation some assert. One of the major reasons for the success of the American experiment is that it reconciled the dual authorities of religion and secular government. The genius of the American founding was that it balanced citizens' dual allegiances to God and to earthly authorities without forcing believers to abandon or to compromise (or "to moderate") their primary loyalty to God. Indeed, in its fundamental principles of limited government and popular sovereignty, the American system encourages its citizens to have loyalties above the state and to draw on those transcendent loyalties in making moral arguments about the common good. This stands in marked contrast to the French Revolution, which sought to detach public morality from religion and led to an understanding of "religious freedom" as the state-enforced privatization of religion.[34]

U.S. public diplomacy should carefully articulate America's mode of religious liberty and explain how it creates a climate conducive to religious practice both in private and in public. This is critical for projecting an accurate image of America, as well as for communicating an appreciation for religion as a motivating factor in world politics.

2. *Adequately define and defend religious liberty.*

Religious freedom exists when the rights of individuals and religious communities are properly protected and ordered within a constitutional state. Religious freedom is based on a culturally sustainable political balance between religion and state in which individuals and religious communities (both majority and minority) as well as state officials and entities accept reciprocal accommodations.[35]

In such a system, the state's use of force is limited. It may not use its power either to coerce or disallow belief. The state also accepts the "prophetic" role of religion in society, in which religious individuals, motivated by the belief in a higher authority, call the state to account for its actions, or fashion publicly accessible moral arguments consistent with their beliefs. At the same time, religious believers accept limits in return for rights. Acceptance of limits by majority communities is of particular importance (as is their understanding of reciprocal benefits). Historical evidence and contemporary social science data suggest that societies benefit as a whole when religious freedom is observed.[36]

Religious freedom requires religious individuals and institutions to renounce violence and access to the police powers of the state to coerce adherence to their beliefs. This includes a rejection of criminal laws that prohibit apostasy or conversion. Religious communities must learn to deal with the challenges presented by apostasy and conversion through better teaching and peaceful persuasion, not by access to civil authority.

Revealed truth claims about the common good must be submitted to public reason and public debate, rather than imposed through force.

Religious groups may not seek preferential treatment in policy or law to privilege membership in their community. They may not seek, for example, religious tests for public office. Religious majorities may neither invoke civil law against religious blasphemy or defamation, nor impose laws requiring certain forms of worship, belief in particular scriptures or religious creeds or codes.

In exchange, all individuals and communities are guaranteed civil liberties without regard to their religious profession. All have the freedom to worship, privately and in community with others; to teach and raise children in the religious tradition of the parents; to build houses of worship and train clergy consistent with tenets of the faith; to persuade peacefully of the truths of their religious claims and to invite converts. Most importantly, all have the right to enter into public policy debates with religious and religion-based moral arguments about the common good. Such arguments should be permitted on the same basis as nonreligious arguments about the common good.

3. Communicate the benefits of religious liberty for both religion and state.

U.S. public diplomacy should develop strategies to help convince majority religious communities (e.g., Russian Orthodox, Iraqi Shiite, Afghan Sunni) that religious freedom will benefit them. The prospect of religious liberty is often perceived as a threat to majority religious communities that have enjoyed cultural and political dominance. It can, however, offer substantial benefits for those communities, while benefiting individuals, minority groups, and society as a whole.

The case can be made on at least two levels. First, modern history demonstrates that in countries seeking transition to democracy, majorities cannot succeed in maintaining a religious monopoly by the use of civil authority and the law. The post-Soviet example of the Russian Orthodox Church provides a case in point. Its alliance with political authoritarianism in an attempt to maintain its privileged position has detracted from the stabilization of Russian democracy and, at the same time, reduced its credibility as a religious entity. History strongly suggests that democracy requires majority groups to accept and engage in religious competition if they are to succeed, rather than seek laws to outlaw apostasy, conversion, blasphemy, defamation, and the like.

Second, social science data appear to confirm what history suggests. A growing body of work in several disciplines is providing evidence of the value of religious freedom for all elements of society. Sociologists Rodney Stark, Roger Finke, and Brian Grim, and international relations scholar Dan Philpott have shown that religious freedom is linked to the well-being of societies and religious communities.[37] Societies that have adopted religious liberty tend to be marked by an absence of religious violence and conflict, better health outcomes, higher literacy, and more social harmony. Economists Robert Barro and Rachel McCleary at Harvard have shown the correlation between religious practice and economic development and growth.[38]

Together, these data suggest that religious freedom is highly correlated with outcomes conducive to the consolidation—that is, the maturation and longevity—of democracy and increased prosperity. There seems to be a "bundled commodity" of fundamental freedoms, with religious freedom at the center.[39] Religious liberty acts like a lynchpin; the whole framework relies on it and would collapse without it. In short, stable democracies require religious freedom.

4. Better integrate the ongoing work of promoting religious
freedom into U.S. democracy promotion strategies.

The 1998 International Religious Freedom Act states, "It shall be the policy of the United States...to condemn violations of religious freedom, and to promote, and to assist other governments in the promotion of, the fundamental right to freedom of religion."[40]

The agenda advocated here calls for a wider view of the mandate of the International Religious Freedom office at the State Department. Created by the 1998 IRFA, the office annually reports on religious freedom around the world, identifying those countries that are the worst offenders in persecuting religious believers. This role as human rights monitor is an important step, but foreign policy engagement on religious liberty should go further.

A decade after its creation the International Religious Freedom office has not been integrated into the overall democracy promotion strategy of the United States. Ideally the office should serve as a resource and offer strategic input in the essential task of establishing freedom of religion as the foundation of democracy. Instead, religious persecution is treated primarily as a sequestered, humanitarian problem. In the State Department, international religious freedom policy is functionally and bureaucratically quarantined. The office is burrowed in the human rights bureau, itself outside the mainstream of foreign policy. The ambassador at large who heads the religious freedom office is subordinate to a lower-ranking official and, unlike other ambassadors at large, does not attend senior staff meetings. This communicates—to American diplomats, foreign governments, and religious communities alike—that advancing international religious freedom is not a mainstream element of U.S. foreign policy.[41]

The case of the Afghan convert to Christianity Abdul Rahman illustrates the problem when an exclusive focus on opposing persecution neglects the relationship between religious freedom and democracy. After the United States deposed the Taliban in 2001, the Afghans elected a democratic government and ratified a constitution. The terrible religious persecution of Afghan women and minority Shiites slowed dramatically. But these developments did not bring about religious freedom. The Afghan government no longer tortures people on the basis of religion, but it continues to bring charges against apostates and blasphemers, including officials and journalists seeking to debate the teachings of Islam. Instead of seeing such cases as serious obstacles to the consolidation of Afghan democracy, the State Department has treated them as humanitarian problems. U.S. pressure rescued Rahman from an apostasy trial, permitting him to flee the country in fear of his life and escape certain execution. This was hailed as a victory for U.S. international religious freedom policy.

But while U.S. intervention may have achieved a humanitarian success in this instance, the Rahman case was in fact a defeat for the overall religious liberty policy. U.S. action did not address the fundamental long-term problem: Afghanistan's democracy is unlikely to endure unless it defends the right of all Afghan citizens to full religious liberty, especially the right of Muslims to debate freedom and the public good, the role of sharia, and the religion-state nexus. This kind of sustained discourse is vital to the success of any Islamic democracy.[42]

5. Appoint public diplomacy leadership with a strong understanding of the significance of religious liberty and religious culture.

Public diplomacy leadership calls for more than communications and marketing credentials. The message itself is even more critical than the modes and techniques for projecting it to the world, and that demands strong grounding in American constitutional thought. In the twenty-first-century war of ideas, it is absolutely critical that U.S. public diplomacy rely on the bedrock of the American founding principles. Pop culture and commercialism do not do justice to American ideals; they are flimsy and inadequate in the fight against potent ideologies that present strong and coherent—and deeply misguided—explanations of the nature and purpose of human existence.

Prerequisites for senior and mid-level positions in the field of public diplomacy should include experience and demonstrated ability in articulating the enduring significance of American founding principles. In particular, public diplomacy officials should be able to explain and defend the U.S. religious liberty model. They should demonstrate an understanding of the vigorous role of religion in American society today.

Assigning public diplomacy personnel in regional bureaus at the State Department has helped integrate public diplomacy with mainstream diplomatic concerns. The same must be achieved for religion and public diplomacy so that evaluating religious dynamics of target cultures becomes a regular function of analysis and articulating the role of religion in the United States becomes a consistent feature of communications strategy.

6. Reform Foreign Service Officer training and career options.

Foreign Service Officer (FSO) training should include basic education in the U.S. Constitution's principles concerning religious liberty and the Founders' understanding of the role of religion in American society. Further training should offer social science evidence on the correlation of religious liberty and political/economic stability in America and abroad. Further, FSOs should have options to pursue coursework that would equip them with the means to address the overlapping authorities of religion and state, and the historic American success in this area, as well as in-depth exploration of religious dynamics in key regions of the world.

Existent training on religion is minimal. When religious issues are addressed in training, there is little accountability or opportunity for application of the knowledge gained. This conveys to diplomats that religion is not a priority concern for the Foreign Service. For years the training school for FSOs, the Foreign Service Institute (FSI) in Arlington, Virginia, had not paid significant attention to religion as an aspect of foreign policy. To FSI's credit, this has begun slowly to change with, for example, the hiring of a faculty specialist in Islam. Moreover, there has been some discussion among FSI course directors of a more rigorous approach to religion in the international order. One of the co-authors has delivered a series of talks at FSI and has been engaged informally in these discussions. But these welcome steps remain ad hoc, driven by individual course directors rather than broad policy change. Without systemic changes to training and broader American public diplomacy applications, these individual efforts are unlikely to have appreciable effect.

All FSOs, and public diplomacy specialists in particular, should understand and be able to articulate the significance of religion in the American constitutional order and civil society. They should also be equipped to appreciate the role of religion in the individual lives and societies of foreign audiences. Previous experience working for or alongside religious or civil society groups should be viewed as a strong credential. Individuals who understand the character and influence of religious belief in individual and community life are well-equipped to grapple with the challenges of reconciling dual authorities of religion and state.

Specific recommendations:

- Create a religion subspecialty for FSOs. This subspecialty could be created under the current economic, political, and public diplomacy career tracks. In regions of the world where religion is a significant force in society and politics, U.S. diplomatic posts should be staffed by individuals who have a deep understanding of the particular religious dynamics and are grounded in the importance of religious liberty and practice in the American order. From ambassadors to FSOs in their first assignments, the selection of individuals with training on the significance of religion will enhance communications potential and contribute to the credibility of U.S. foreign policy.

Incentives should be created to attract FSOs to this subspeciality. Specialists should be recruited in particular to the State Department's geographic bureaus, where resources, assignments, and promotions are often concentrated.[43] Incentives should include awards and promotions for excellence in reporting and in recommending and implementing policies concerning religion. There must be significant career opportunities for religion specialists, especially assignments to countries of major importance to the United States, such as Iraq, Afghanistan, Saudi Arabia, Egypt, Pakistan, Iran (should the United States reestablish relations), Russia, China, India, and others. Junior FSOs who excel in such positions should be promoted to career track positions within the State Department, such as desk officers for these countries, office directors, and deputy assistant secretary positions. Ultimately, FSOs with demonstrated expertise on religion should be assigned as ambassadors to key countries and assistant secretaries of state. Political appointees to foreign policy positions should also reflect these priorities.

- As a temporary transitional strategy, designate personnel to provide analysis of religious dynamics to U.S. missions. A religion subspecialty will take time to develop and implement. In the meantime, religion attachés could fill a critical void in current staffing in regions where religious issues are particularly complex. Douglas Johnston of the International Center for Religion and Diplomacy estimates that approximately thirty U.S. missions—including those in the Middle East, Southeast Asia, and the Balkans—would benefit from a religion specialist. The qualifications of the attaché would include an expertise in the religious complexities of the location and an understanding of religious belief on the individual and societal levels. The attaché would build relationships with local religious leaders to gain knowledge and trust for dealing with the particular situation at hand.[44] It will be important, however, not to permit this temporary expedient to become a surrogate for FSO training, including in public diplomacy.

7. Tap various religious traditions for principles that support civil society and limited, constitutional government.

Religious principles have contributed to the shaping of the American republic and society, including the Catholic principle of subsidiarity,[45] the Protestant work ethic, the Lutheran concept of sphere sovereignty, and the general Christian principle of "just war," which defines the legitimate use of force.[46] Muslim principles have been used, in America and abroad, to promote charity and other democratic virtues that support the growth of civil society. These are examples of religious contributions to liberal democracy and civil society that should be understood and integrated by FSOs in general, and public diplomacy specialists in particular, as key to America's engagement with a world of public religion.

8. Seek the counsel of religious individuals and groups with experience in target cultures.

Individuals with experience serving foreign communities through religious schools, hospitals, and other mercy ministries are one example of largely harmonious interaction between the United States and non-Western cultures.[47] Those who have participated in such outreach efforts glean valuable insights into the culture and religious beliefs that continue to confound many U.S. officials.

U.S. religious NGOs have successfully networked with Muslim NGOs at the United Nations in issues related to family. Western religious believers can understand and appreciate Muslims' belief in a supernatural reality, adherence to a comprehensive moral code, and the concept of a well-ordered interior life. This appreciation, often lacking in foreign policy circles, could provide valuable insights.

9. Encourage and build upon the idea of "faith-based diplomacy."

Faith-based diplomacy is a type of Track II unofficial diplomacy that combines insights drawn from religious faith with the practice of international relations.[48] The private sector faith-based "diplomat" has moral authority and engages in conflict resolution by appealing to transcendent spiritual resources, including sacred texts and prayer. At the same time, such diplomacy recognizes "the profound and irreconcilable differences between religious traditions";[49] to minimize these differences would threaten the credibility of faith-based diplomats. Effective conflict resolution requires that the faith-based diplomat appeal to a religious tradition's particular tenets. Of particular importance for conflict resolution is the capacity of religious traditions to "(1) reflect on their history in a redemptive manner, (2) bring meaning and dignity to the suffering, and (3) to hold out the promise of genuine healing."[50] For example, the International Center for Religion and Diplomacy has conducted such conflict resolution projects in places like Sudan and Pakistan.

10. Encourage and promote the actions of religious leaders who reject violence and coercion in the name of faith.

Democracy promotion cannot proceed in a highly religious world without a plan to address highly religious societies. Religious communities are a powerful source of identity and culture. Their authority structures often dictate social and legal norms and influence political culture.

If the United States is to encourage the spread of democracy, it must learn to engage and influence powerful religious communities. The struggle over the direction of Islam goes on within each Muslim country. U.S. policy and public diplomacy should continue to seek out and strengthen voices in the Muslim world that condemn violence and coercion in the name of religion.[51] Religious leaders can speak with spiritual authority that will command far more attention among believers than pronouncements from political leaders. It is the hearts and minds of these believers—caught between calls for political moderation and violent extremism—that are particularly at stake, and religious leaders can carry significant weight with them. U.S. officials and their surrogates should work with leaders who are urging temperance to encourage and reinforce their repudiation of force.

In this effort, it is important to make a distinction between political moderation and religious or doctrinal moderation. The two are not necessarily synonymous, though a secularization perspective tends to conflate them. For the purposes of international politics, the political expression of a religious group's beliefs is the major concern, not the mere fact that they profess deeply held beliefs. A society can be strongly religious and politically moderate—the United States is a prime example.

Conclusion

America is a religious nation that has dealt over time quite successfully with the religion-state relationship. The American Founders established a system that not only effectively balanced these dual authorities, but also welcomed religious practice and its contribution to the common good. This harmony of interest was well accepted—at least until the latter half of the twentieth century.

Since the 1950s, new interpretations of the establishment clause have promoted a "separationist" mentality that suggests the state and religion should have nothing to do with one another. U.S. foreign policy has reflected this confusion and ambivalence over the role of religion in America, a characteristic that has translated into a lack of facility in dealing with religious societies abroad. Religion is often understood as a force that will or should be marginalized as societies modernize and democratize. Rather than wrestling through the difficult but essential task of reconciling state and religious authority in highly religious societies, religious liberty—in its fullest sense—has been left aside in too many discussions of promoting democracy.

In recent years, the State Department and other agencies have become more attuned to the importance of religion in foreign affairs. Exchanges among religious leaders, the establishment of an office for international religious freedom, and some ad hoc additions to FSO training represent positive developments. However, these are far from the systematic changes that must take place for U.S. foreign policy in general, and public diplomacy in particular, if it is to address the critical significance of religion in public life and in the foundation of free societies.

The United States needs an overarching policy that communicates a consistent message about the importance of religion and religious liberty in a constitutional order. International religious freedom efforts should promote this vision. Foreign service training and career advancement should incorporate it as well. Public diplomacy should focus on communicating these foundational principles of the American order.

Notes

1. Henry Kissinger, *Diplomacy* (New York: Simon and Schuster, 1994), 56–58.
2. Ibid., 877–912.
3. See Pavos Hatxopoulos and Fabio Petito, eds., *Religion in International Relations: The Return from Exile* (New York: Palgrave Macmillan, 2003); Scott M. Thomas, *The Global Resurgence of Religion and the Transformation of International Relations: The Struggle for the Soul of the 21st Century* (New York: Palgrave Macmillan, 2005); Jonathan Fox and Shmuel Sandler, *Bringing Religion into International Relations* (New York: Palgrave MacMillan, 2004); John D. Carlson and Erik C. Owens, eds., *The Sacred and the Sovereign: Religion and International Politics* (Washington, DC: Georgetown University Press, 2003); Ted G. Jelen and Clyde Wilcox, eds., *Religion and Politics in Comparative Perspective: The One, the Few, and the Many* (Cambridge: Cambridge University Press, 2002); Timothy Samuel Shah and Monica Duffy Toft, "God Is Winning," *Foreign Policy* (2006): 39–43.
4. Madeleine Albright, *The Mighty and the Almighty: Reflections on America, God, and World Affairs* (New York: HarperCollins, 2006); Walter Russell Mead, *God and Gold: Britain, America and the Making of the Modern World* (New York: Vintage, 2008).
5. See the Henry R. Luce Initiative on Religion and International Affairs, accessed at www.hluce.org/hluceinitiative.html.
6. The National Endowment for Democracy (NED) has begun to fund a variety of Muslim reformers. NED funds the International Forum for Islamic Dialogue, including its "Islam 21" project, which is building a core of educators among Muslim youth and a network of liberal Islamic intellectuals and activists. The related Muslim Civic Participation Project is developing a generic civic curriculum to conceptualize and articulate a pluralist and modernist Islamic discourse, using a "training the trainers" approach to create a network of educator activists in Bahrain, Egypt, Iraq, Jordan, Morocco, and the UK. NED grantees also include the Center for the Study of Islam and Democracy, specifically for its work in developing the Network of Democrats in the Arab World.
7. This request for proposals, however, came 10 years after the passage of the International Religious Freedom Act and as a result of congressional pressure.
8. Liora Danan et al., *Mixed Blessings: U.S. Government Engagement with Religion in Conflict-Prone Settings* (Washington: Center for Strategic and International Studies, 2007), 10.
9. Ibid., 2.
10. Ibid., 3.
11. Ibid.,1.
12. David B. Barrett and Todd M. Johnson, "Quantifying Alternative Futures of Religion and Religions," *Futures* 36 (2004): 959.
13. Patrick F. Fagan, "Why Religion Matters Even More: The Impact of Religious Practice on Social Stability," *Backgrounder No. 1992*, The Heritage Foundation, December 18, 2006, at *www.heritage.org/Research/Religion/BG1992.cfm* (February 13, 2008).
14. See Thomas F. Farr, *World of Faith and Freedom: Why International Religious Liberty Is Vital to American National Security* (New York: Oxford University Press, 2008); also Farr, "Diplomacy in an Age of Faith: Religious Freedom and National Security," *Foreign Affairs*, March/April 2008. Farr, *World of Faith and Freedom*, esp. Chapter 2.
15. Ibid, passim.
16. Ibid., chapters 8–10.

17. Robert R. Reilly, "Britney vs. the Terrorists," *The Washington Post*, February 9, 2007. http://www.washingtonpost.com/wp-dyn/content/article/2007/02/08/AR2007020801679.html

18. Danan et al., *Mixed Blessings*, 39.

19. Madeleine Albright, "Faith and Diplomacy," *The Review of Faith & International Affairs* 4 (2006): 8.

20. "American Piety in the 21st Century: New Insights to the Depth and Complexity of Religion in the US," Selected Findings from the Baylor Religion Survey (Baylor: Baylor Institute for the Study of Religion September 2006), 7–8, 12.

21. See, e.g., Peter L. Berger, ed., *The Desecularization of the World: Resurgent Religion and World Politics* (Washington, DC: Ethics and Public Policy Center, 1999); Jose Casanova, *Public Religions in the Modern World* (Chicago: University of Chicago Press, 1994); David Martin, *A General Theory of Secularization* (New York: Harper and Row, 1978) and *On Secularization: Towards a Revised General Theory* (Aldershot, England: Ashgate, 2005); For an early theological perspective on desecularization, see Harvey Cox, *The Secular City: Secularization and Urbanization in Theological Perspective* (New York: Macmillan, 1965). On secularization in American culture, see Christian Smith, ed., *The Secular Revolution: Power, Interests, and Conflict in the Secularization of American Public Life* (Berkeley: University of California Press, 2003).

22. Adda B. Bozeman, "Knowledge and Method in Comparative Intelligence Studies," in *Strategic Intelligence & Statecraft* (New York: Brassey's, 1992), 191.

23. Michael Novak, *The Spirit of Democratic Capitalism* (New York: Madison Books, 1991), 16.

24. Zorach v. Clauson (1952). Douglas writing for the court majority.

25. On Madison's views concerning the importance of religion, and the role of the First Amendment, see John T. Noonan, *The Lustre of Our Country: The American Experience of Religious Freedom* (Berkeley: University of California Press, 1998), 61–91; James T. Hutson, *Religion and the Founding of the American Republic* (Washington, DC: Library of Congress, 1998), 70–76; Philip Hamburger, *Separation of Church and State* (Cambridge, MA: Harvard University Press, 2002), 105–106, 165–166, 181–185; Michael Novak, *On Two Wing: Humble Faith and Common Sense at the American Founding* (San Francisco, CA: Encounter Books, 2003), 52–61, 131–141. For a contrary view on Madison and the founders, see Walter Berns, "Religion and the Founding Principle," in *The Moral Foundations of the American Republic*, 3rd edition, ed. Robert H. Horwitz (Charlottesville: University of Virginia Press, 1987).

26. Hutson, *Religion and the Founding of the American Republic*, 79–80.

27. John Courney Murray, S. J., *We Hold These Truths: Catholic Reflections on the American Proposition* (New York: Sheed and Ward, 1960), 125.

28. John Rawls, *Political Liberalism* (New York: Columbia University Press, 1996), 10. Rawls was the most influential American public philosopher of the late twentieth century.

29. "U.S. Religious Landscape Survey. Religious Beliefs and Practices: Diverse and Politically Relevant" (Washington: Pew Research Center 2008), 22.

30. Ibid., 36, 39.

31. Author C. Brooks, *Who Really Cares: The Surprising Truth about Compassionate Conservatism* (New York: Basic Books, 2006), 34.

32. Adda B. Bozeman, "American Policy and the Illusion of Congruent Values," in *Strategic Intelligence*, 216.

33. Samuel P. Huntington, *Who Are We? The Challenges to America's National Identity* (New York: Simon and Schuster, 2004), 10–20.

34. See Mustafa Akyol, "Render Unto Atatürk," *First Things*, March 2007. The French model, on which Kemal Ataturk based his reforms in twentieth-century Turkey, is well known to the Muslim world. Somewhat ironically, the French marginalization of religion is conflated by Islamist extremists with American democracy promotion policy, the goal of which, they argue, is to destroy Islam.

35. Alfred Stepan, "Religion, Democracy and the 'Twin Tolerations,'" in *World Religions and Democracy,* ed. Larry Diamond et al., (Baltimore: The Johns Hopkins University Press, 2005), 3–23.

36. Brian Grim, "Religious Freedom: Good for What Ails Us," *The Review of Faith and International Affairs,* June 18, 2008. http://www.cfia.org/ArticlesAndReports/ArticlesDetail. aspx?id=10368

37. See, e.g., Rodney Stark and Roger Finke, *Acts of Faith: Explaining the Human Side of Religion* (Berkeley: University of California Press, 2000); Brian J. Grim and Roger Finke, "Religious Persecution in Cross-National Context: Clashing Civilizations or Regulated Religious Economies," *American Sociological Review* 72, no. 4 (2007); and Daniel Philpott, "Explaining the Political Ambivalence of Religion," *American Political Science Review* (August 2007): 522–523.

38. Robert J. Barro and Rachel M. McCleary, "Religion and Economic Growth," Harvard University, April 8, 2003, http://www.economics.harvard.edu/faculty/barro/files/ Religion_and_Economic_Growth.pdf.

39. Grim and Finke, "Religious Persecution in Cross-National Context."

40. The International Religious Freedom Act of 1998, Public Law 105–292, Sec. 2(b)(1).

41. Farr, "Diplomacy in an Age of Faith," 118.

42. Ibid., 118–124.

43. Danan et al., *Mixed Blessings*, 50.

44. Douglas M. Johnston, "The Case for a Religion Attaché," *Foreign Service Journal* (February 2002): 33–38. Johnston puts a $10 million price tag on the training, payroll, and operating costs of such an effort.

45. Peter L. Berger and Richard John Neuhaus, *To Empower People: From State to Civil Society,* 20th Anniversary Edition, Michael Novak, ed. (Washington DC: American Enterprise Institute, 1996), 139.

46. See, e.g., James Turner Johnson, *Morality and Contemporary Warfare* (New Haven, CT: Yale University Press, 1999) and Jean Bethke Elshtain, *Just War against Terror: The Burden of American Power in a Violent World* (New York: Basic Books, 2003).

47. See Walter Russell Mead, "God's Country," *Foreign Affairs* (September/October 2006): 42.

48. Douglas Johnston, *Faith-Based Diplomacy: Trumping Realpolitik* (New York: Oxford University Press, 2003), xii, 15.

49. Ibid., 17.

50. Ibid., 16–17, 19.

51. See Thomas F. Farr, "Islam's Way to Freedom," *First Things,* November 2008.

CHAPTER ELEVEN

The U.S. Military and Public Diplomacy

ABIODUN WILLIAMS

Can and should the U.S. military, which wields the tools of "hard power," engage in "soft power" initiatives such as the practice of public diplomacy? The U.S. Department of Defense's (DOD) mission is to organize, train, and equip the nation's military forces to prevent war and protect the security of the country. However, the geopolitical realities of a long asymmetric war against extremism, and the emerging threats from ungoverned and undergoverned areas around the globe, pose important challenges for protecting U.S. national security. Ensuring national security is no longer merely a matter of defending borders and patrolling oceans and skies, but requires reconstruction and stabilization efforts, building partnerships, and improving the U.S. image abroad. Moreover, the traditional tools of hard power are insufficient to meet the foreign policy demands of the twenty-first century, and soft power is reemerging as a vital component of foreign policy. Indeed, the challenge is to integrate hard and soft power—"smart power"[1]—to achieve foreign policy goals.

This chapter argues that the military has an important role to play in the promotion of soft power, such as through public diplomacy initiatives. Public diplomacy is too important to be left entirely to civilian agencies, particularly as the actions of the U.S. military critically affect the way other countries and their citizens view the United States. The military cannot afford to ignore public diplomacy or treat it as an afterthought. This chapter also contends that civilian and military public diplomacy efforts will be important factors affecting the success or failure of the U.S. Africa Command (AFRICOM). Since the announcement of its creation in February 2007, AFRICOM has aroused concerns and suspicions about its mission both within the United States and in Africa. These include fears that AFRICOM will lead to a militarization of U.S. foreign policy, will expand the U.S.-led war on terrorism, and will become a tool to secure greater access to Africa's vast oil resources. What Africans and Americans think of AFRICOM is important, and public opinion will be a powerful force that will help or impede AFRICOM's mission.

This chapter also provides a brief overview of U.S. public diplomacy efforts. It discusses the evolution of the military's role in public diplomacy, the strategic and operational advantages it possesses with regard to this tool of foreign policy, and the current public diplomacy initiatives the military is pursuing in other Combatant Commands (COCOMs), and on the African continent. Finally, this chapter addresses the rationale for the creation of AFRICOM, the apprehensions of the command that still persist, and proposes the elements of a public diplomacy strategy to overcome these challenges.

Overview of Public Diplomacy

Public diplomacy, defined as the "promotion of the national interest by informing, engaging, and influencing people around the world,"[2] has long been an important element of U.S. foreign policy. The term was coined in the mid-1960s by the former Dean of the Fletcher School of Law and Diplomacy at Tufts University, Edmund A. Gullion,[3] and signifies a range of educational, informational, and cultural programs, activities, and broadcasts.[4] Broadly, the concept of public diplomacy is an integral component of what Joseph Nye termed "soft power," or the "ability to attract others by the legitimacy of U.S. policies and the values that underlie them."[5] Whereas traditional diplomacy relies on government-to-government interaction, public diplomacy supplements that communication with government-to-people interaction.[6]

Under the auspices of the U.S. Information Agency (USIA), the U.S. government developed a constellation of cultural and educational tools—ranging from Voice of America broadcasts to educational grants—to foster goodwill toward the United States behind the iron curtain. Public diplomacy was seen as an essential tool of U.S. foreign policy to counter the spread of Communism.[7] With the end of the cold war, the decade of the 1990s saw a "process of unilateral disarmament in the weapons of advocacy."[8] Policy makers neglected public diplomacy efforts and few new initiatives were specifically created to engage and influence global audiences. The nadir of public diplomacy's importance in U.S. foreign policy occurred in 1999 when the USIA was subsumed into the Department of State (DOS) and the Broadcasting Board of Governors. As a result of this realignment, the DOS's under secretary for public diplomacy and public affairs became the lead for the U.S. government's public diplomacy efforts.

The attacks of September 11, 2001, prompted a renewed interest in the role of public diplomacy in U.S. foreign policy. Numerous academic articles, government reports, and journalistic accounts highlighted the causal relationship between the absence of public diplomacy efforts in the Middle East and the growing distance with Muslim communities.[9] In particular, experts noted that "the waning of American cultural presence abroad left a gap in public perception eagerly filled by those with political agendas diametrically at odds with ours—particularly extremists in the Islamic world."[10] Winning the "war on ideas" was now seen as an essential tool in the war on terrorism. In an address to the country exactly one month after the attacks of September 11, President Bush articulated the views of many Americans when he stated:

> I'm amazed that there is such misunderstanding of what our country is about, that people would hate us. I am, I am—like most Americans, I just can't believe it. Because I know how good we are, and we've got to do a better job of making our case.[11]

Recognizing this need to "make our case" through public diplomacy, the September 2002 National Security Strategy (NSS) stated that the government will use "effective public diplomacy to promote the free flow of information and ideas to kindle the hopes and aspirations of freedom of those in societies ruled by the sponsors of global terrorism."[12] The 2002 NSS notably does not limit public diplomacy promotion to merely one agency or department. It rather refers to this goal as being one that "we"—the U.S. government as a whole—must undertake. The threat posed to the United States from extremism rather than from traditional nation-state enemies in a traditional battlespace prompted a reconsideration of the "clean division[s] between war and peace"[13] and a reexamination of the importance of public diplomacy throughout the military and civilian organs of the government.

The recognized need for all government agencies to engage in public diplomacy did not originate with the 2002 NSS, however. During President Clinton's tenure, the secret Presidential Decision Directive

(PDD) 68 released on April 30, 1999, stated that public diplomacy needed to be expanded beyond its traditional stakeholders due to the demands of the information revolution. PDD 68 stipulated that—though the DOS was the lead agency for this effort—all agencies have a duty to communicate with foreign audiences to project U.S. foreign policy abroad.[14] Thus, public diplomacy became characterized as "everyone's business"[15] almost one decade ago.

The global effort to combat terrorism, including *Operation Enduring Freedom* in Afghanistan and *Operation Iraqi Freedom*, generated questions about the appropriate balance of hard and soft power. In 2003, the U.S. military began to engage in activities that were typically the purview of the civilian organs of the government, such as the U.S. Agency for International Development (USAID) and the DOS. The hard power required to combat insurgencies in the Middle East became intertwined with the soft power necessary to promote stabilization. As a result of these activities and in recognition of the lessons learned in this new battlespace, Secretary of Defense Robert Gates recently stated:

> Military success is not sufficient to win [the fight against extremism]: economic development, institution-building and the rule of law, promoting internal reconciliation, good governance, providing basic services to the people, training and equipping indigenous military and police forces, strategic communications, and more—these, along with security, are essential ingredients for long-term success.[16]

Secretary of State Condoleezza Rice echoed this view that no single U.S. government agency could single-handedly defeat extremism. Only by integrating elements of hard and soft power can the United States adequately be equipped to meet the strategic challenges of the future. According to Secretary Rice, twenty-first-century foreign policy requires "better 'jointness' too between our soldiers and our civilians."[17] The next section assesses the challenges and opportunities of developing the soft side of the military's power and forging stronger links between the military and civilian agencies.

Should the U.S. Military Conduct Public Diplomacy?

Even with the commitment to "jointness" by the Secretaries of Defense and State, and the recognized need to promote the U.S. image abroad, some critics charge that the DOD should not play a role in the promotion of soft power initiatives. These critics argue that including the Pentagon in public diplomacy "militarizes" foreign policy and exacerbates the current imbalance in resource allocation between the civilian and military government agencies. Underlying these criticisms is the broader question of how U.S. power is articulated and projected around the globe.

The charge of U.S. foreign policy "militarization" stems from the prominent role that the Pentagon has taken in the realm of soft power programs—particularly in aid and development activities—in the Middle East. With "field artillerymen and tankers building schools and mentoring city councils"[18] in Iraq and Afghanistan, the U.S. military has performed missions and adopted skills sets that many policy makers, journalists, and international observers argue are counter to the traditional missions of the armed forces. Critics further cite that this shift is reflected in the growing resource asymmetry between the military and civilian agencies, with the Pentagon's share of Official Development Assistance expanding from 3.5 percent in 1998 to approximately 22 percent in 2005. In contrast, USAID's share shrunk from 65 percent to 40 percent in this same period.[19]

Although civilian leadership in soft power programs is important, the military's participation in public diplomacy initiatives does not necessarily militarize foreign policy nor mean that the military engages in activities in which it lacks doctrine or experience. The charges of militarization overlook the reality that the deployed members of the armed forces are often already the public diplomacy face of the U.S. abroad in more than sixty countries. Rather than deny the existence of the DOD in the "immediate battleground in the struggle of ideas,"[20] civilian and military practitioners need to craft a strategy to achieve diplomatic and security results that capitalize on the strengths of the various organs of the U.S. government. The U.S. image can be improved in tangible ways by putting the DOS and USAID back in their "lane of the road" and providing them the resources, personnel, and infrastructure to fulfill their legal mandate to set the agenda for U.S. foreign and development policy. This strategy would not seek to remove the foreign policy mandate from DOS, but would acknowledge the effect of the military on U.S. public diplomacy. Defeating extremism can only be achieved through the patient application of civilian capabilities in the areas of economic development, education, rule of law, and public health, as well as through attention to the important public diplomacy role that the U.S. military currently plays—and should play—in the promotion of soft power.

Can the U.S. Military Conduct Public Diplomacy?

In addition to the normative question of whether the military should engage in public diplomacy, critics have raised the practical question of whether the military can engage in public diplomacy. From the Berlin airlift during the cold war to *Operation Unified Assistance* following the 2004 tsunami, the military has demonstrated adeptness in engaging in soft power promotion. The Pentagon can engage in soft power promotion in a way that capitalizes on its institutional strengths without diminishing the central role of the civilian agencies of the government.

The DOD has historically subsumed the practice of public diplomacy under the umbrella term "strategic communications," which generally refers to information assets. Strategic communications encompass:

> The synchronized coordination of statecraft, public affairs, public diplomacy, military information operations, and other activities, reinforced by political, economic, military, and other actions, to advance U.S. foreign policy objectives.[21]

The essential elements of strategic communications include public diplomacy, public affairs, civil–military operations, information operations, and international broadcasting.

The military defines public diplomacy as

1. Those overt international public information activities of the United States Government designed to promote United States foreign policy objectives by seeking to understand, inform, and influence foreign audiences and opinion makers, and by broadening the dialogue between American citizens and institutions and their counterparts abroad.
2. In peace building, civilian agency efforts to promote an understanding of the reconstruction efforts, rule of law, and civic responsibility through public affairs and international public diplomacy operations. Its objective is to promote and sustain consent for peace building both within the host nation and externally in the region and in the larger international community.[22]

The DOD plays a supporting role in the practice of public diplomacy, as the under secretary for public diplomacy and public affairs in the DOS leads the U.S. public diplomacy effort. The DOS is charged with making "public diplomacy an integral component in the planning and execution of United States foreign policy."[23]

Military Doctrine on Public Diplomacy

The importance of strategic communications to the U.S. military, and specifically public diplomacy, can be seen through its incorporation in strategic doctrine. Doctrine refers to a set of principles, methods, and standards that are codified in official or unofficial documents. Doctrine informs the military's practices, mission, and organization and defines how the military thinks about its role in the world.[24] The month after the attacks of September 11, the Defense Science Board Task Force released their report on "Managed Information Dissemination." This task force—jointly staffed by staff members of the Office of the Secretary of Defense and the DOS—concluded that the "U.S. Government does require a coordinated means to speak with a coherent voice abroad." In light of the proliferation of information in the global sphere, it found that

> Coordinated information dissemination is an essential tool in a world where U.S. interests and long-term policies are often misunderstood, where issues are complex, and where efforts to undermine U.S. positions increasingly appeal to those who lack the means to challenge American power.[25]

The task force determined that military hard power alone was insufficient to manage current geopolitical challenges. It recognized that coordinated civilian and military efforts at public diplomacy were powerful assets to national security in the information age. More recently, Secretary of Defense Robert Gates affirmed this evolution in thinking in the DOD about the limits of hard power by stating "we cannot kill or capture our way to victory."[26] He has further argued,

> We must focus our energies beyond the guns and steel of the military, beyond just our brave soldiers, sailors, Marines, and airmen. We must also focus our energies on the other elements of national power that will be so crucial in the coming years.[27]

Additional military doctrine affirms that soft power plays an important role in U.S. national security. The DOD's 2006 Quadrennial Defense Review (QDR) articulates the national defense strategy of the United States, including the proposed force structure, budget, and force modernization plans for the U.S. military. The 2006 QDR identifies strategic communications as an essential component of the military's strategy to address the national security challenges of the twenty-first century. According to the 2006 QDR, "The Department will work closely with interagency partners to integrate strategic communication into U.S. national security policy planning and operations."[28] In addition, the QDR states,

> Victory in the long war ultimately depends on strategic communication by the United States and its international partners. Effective communication must build and maintain credibility and trust with friends and foes alike, through an emphasis on consistency, veracity and transparency both in words and deeds. Such credibility is essential to building trusted networks that counter ideological support for terrorism.[29]

To guide the implementation of the Department's QDR goals, additional military doctrine was released, including the 2006 Roadmap for Strategic Communications. To improve the military's strategic communications, the 2006 Roadmap recognizes that military culture needs to be adapted to recognize the value of communications. It states that the military must align communications with other traditional aspects of military strategy, such as policy formulation and operational planning.

COCOM Public Diplomacy Initiatives

In accordance with the goal of integrating strategic communications into military planning and culture, several public diplomacy initiatives are currently being pursued in the unified COCOMs. Each regional Combatant Commander[30] is charged with the direction and implementation of all U.S. military activity within their geographic region, including public diplomacy initiatives. A broad range of public diplomacy initiatives are currently pursued in each COCOM in the form of joint missions, humanitarian assistance, disaster preparedness, military training and education, and civic action programs to help national militaries become more effective and professional.

In addition to general public diplomacy initiatives, the COCOMs also pursue very specific public diplomacy missions. CENTCOM, for example, has contracted for issue-specific polling in its area of responsibility (AOR) to determine the needs and interests of the local publics.[31]

CENTCOM also maintains a Strategic Effects Cell in Baghdad, a similar cell with NATO in Kabul, and works with the Defense Intelligence Agency and the Open Source Center to generate regionally focused media.[32] EUCOM works with the DOS's Bureau of Intelligence and Research to contract for opinion polling in nine Trans-Saharan countries in support of counterterrorism information operations.[33] In addition, EUCOM conducts a range of strategic communication initiatives under the aegis of *Operation Assured Voice*.[34] This operation includes a series of web-based initiatives (in the languages spoken in the EUCOM area of responsibility), collaborations with local newspapers, and private industry.[35] Under the auspices of *Operation Unified Assistance*, PACOM facilitated the cooperation of humanitarian NGOs and multinational militaries in the relief operations in December 2004.[36] Lastly, SOUTHCOM has created an office for "launching ideas, not Tomahawks."[37]

The functional commands also perform public diplomacy activities. STRATCOM provides a summary of foreign media to regional commanders to assist their strategic communication initiatives. Importantly, STRATCOM also has the responsibility to coordinate information capabilities across the specific combatant command boundaries.[38] Lastly, SOCOM plans and hosts multinational workshops on psychological operations (PSYOP). SOCOM also is responsible for the integration and coordination of PSYOP capabilities across the DOD.[39]

Public Diplomacy Activities in Africa

For most of the past fifty years, public diplomacy has been an integral part of U.S. policy toward Africa. Public diplomacy programs have identified and cultivated emerging leaders and promoted educational and cultural exchanges. The military also currently conducts a range of public diplomacy efforts on the continent.

Combined Joint Task Force Horn of Africa (CJTF-HOA)

CJTF-HOA, created after the attacks of September 11, was intended to prevent terrorism from fomenting in the Horn—in the countries of Djibouti, Ethiopia, Eritrea, Kenya, Somalia, Sudan, and Yemen—and to promote regional stability through humanitarian assistance. Based at Camp Lemonier in Djibouti, CJTF-HOA uses "military training, humanitarian aid and intelligence operations to keep northeastern

Africa and Yemen from becoming the next Afghanistan."[40] This joint task force, run out of CENTCOM, was originally established with a counterterrorism mandate to prevent the flow of jihadists across the Horn, but it later evolved to incorporate humanitarian goals and security promotion.[41] Recent CJTF-HOA public diplomacy initiatives have included distributing shoes and toys to orphans in Djibouti,[42] aiding crash victims,[43] inoculating more than 20,000 animals in Ethiopia,[44] building schools,[45] and providing instruction on the laws of war.[46] In addition to military personnel, the CJTF-HOA's more than 1,400 staff includes civil engineers, doctors, nurses, and veterinarians.[47]

Trans-Sahara Counter-Terrorism Partnership (TSCTP)

Similar to the goals pursued by CJTF-HOA, the TSCTP is an initiative designed

> To enhance the indigenous capacities of governments in the pan-Sahel (Mauritania, Mali, Chad, and Niger, as well as Nigeria and Senegal) to confront the challenge posed by terrorist organizations in the region and to facilitate cooperation between those countries and our Maghreb partners (Morocco, Algeria, and Tunisia) in combating terrorism.[48]

The TSCTP not only institutionalizes cooperation in the area of counterterrorism, but it expands existing public diplomacy campaigns in North Africa, promotes democratic governance, and provides development assistance to address the underlying social and economic inequalities that often foment terrorism.[49] In this way, the TSCTP seeks to use military and civilian resources to govern the ungoverned spaces on the continent and to provide a "comprehensive approach to regional security."[50] Under the TSCTP, the DOD primarily provides military counterterrorism training, intelligence training, and military infrastructure. These activities all fall under the auspices of *Operation Enduring Freedom—Trans-Saharan*. In fact, since its inception, TSCTP has disbursed approximately $353 million for military training and equipping, diplomacy, and development.[51]

The TSCTP has developed specific public diplomacy messages to ensure that the local citizens recognize that these training and assistance programs are sponsored by the United States. To that end, the TSCTP has created Military Information Support Teams (MIST) and

Civil Military Support Elements (CMSE) to craft public diplomacy messages that underline the depth and longevity of U.S. commitment to North Africa. MIST and CMSE promote moderate political messages,[52] provide textbooks for local schools, and seek to generate support for both the United States and for moderate Islamic viewpoints.[53] Through the TSCTP, the DOS also works to foster a sense of commonality between local populations' values and American interests. DOS further leads the effort to "communicate messages among vulnerable populations to isolate and marginalize violent extremists."[54] In particular, the DOS supports the Anti-Terrorism Assistance (ATA) program and the Terrorist Interdiction Program (TIP) under the auspices of the TSCTP.[55] In addition to the Pentagon and the DOS, the Department of the Treasury, USAID, and the Department of Justice also contribute to this interagency approach to the region.

With the DOS as the program lead, the TSCTP was actually developed as an extension of the success of the Pan Sahel Initiative (PSI), which was launched in 2003 as a DOS Security Assistance Program.[56] PSI sought to provide Chad, Mali, Mauritania, and Niger with the skills, training, capacity building, and equipment needed to secure their borders.[57] Notably, the PSI was not the first training and assistance program sponsored by the U.S. government on the continent. Previous initiatives included Africa Crisis Response Force, African Crisis Response Initiative, Operation Focus Relief, African Contingency Operations Training and Assistance, African Coastal and Border Security Program, and the Global Peace Operations Initiative.[58]

Many of the criticisms of the TSCTP and PSI address the potential consequences if the funding backfires, by fueling existing tensions on the continent, generating anti-Americanism,[59] allowing national leaders to use the military funding against internal opposition groups, turning the arrested populations into martyrs, and even crippling the economics that have relied on smuggling networks for decades.[60] In fact, some critics of these programs argue that recipient governments are manipulating the reporting of terrorist activities to justify the receipt of arms and funding.[61] Other observers have countered that the TSCTP and the PSI have institutionalized counterterror cooperation and provided the recipient governments with the means and the methods to combat domestic terrorism.[62] Ultimately, the effectiveness of all of these programs inevitably rests with the cooperation and reliability of the participating governments,[63] and the development of a comprehensive, integrated approach for TSCTP and other soft power instruments.[64]

U.S. Africa Command

On February 6, 2007, President Bush and Secretary of Defense Robert Gates announced the creation of AFRICOM, in recognition of Africa's growing strategic and economic importance. U.S. military involvement in Africa had previously been shared by three commands: CENTCOM, EUCOM, and PACOM.[65] This splintered approach created inefficiencies and undermined the ability of the United States to address key continental issues. AFRICOM was officially launched on October 1, 2007 and became a separate, independent combatant command on October 1, 2008. It has the responsibility for U.S. military activities on the African continent and its offshore islands, except Egypt, which will remain under CENTCOM. As initially envisaged by the Bush administration, AFRICOM would represent an interagency—"whole of government"—approach to the promotion of U.S. strategic objectives in Africa, integrating DOS and USAID staff into the DOD command. Since the initial announcement in February 2007, the administration has refocused its rhetoric regarding the command and has not stressed its "experimental" innovation. In the words of AFRICOM's commander, four-star Army General William "Kip" Ward, AFRICOM is about "doing the same things the U.S. military was doing already, but doing them in a better coordinated and a more cohesive way."[66]

The creation of AFRICOM could be viewed as the culmination of the Bush administration's push for a strategic approach to the continent as attention to Africa increased throughout the first term of President Bush's presidency. In 2004, an advisory panel of Africa experts was convened by Congress and determined that greater interest in Africa had emerged due to the convergence of five factors: terrorism, armed conflicts, HIV/AIDS, global trade, and oil.[67] In addition, the 2006 NSS further states,

> Africa holds growing geo-strategic importance and is a high priority of this Administration. It is a place of promise and opportunity, linked to the United States by history, culture, commerce, and strategic significance. Our goal is an African continent that knows liberty, peace, stability, and increasing prosperity. Africa's potential has in the past been held hostage by the bitter legacy of colonial misrule and bad choices by some African leaders. The United States recognizes that our security depends upon partnering with

Africans to strengthen fragile and failing states and bring ungoverned areas under the control of effective democracies.[68]

Despite the recognition of the strategic importance of Africa—and the recognition that a unified command for the continent would address a significant lacuna in the DOD's bureaucratic structure—AFRICOM has encountered a number of challenges. AFRICOM was immediately faced with questions about the timing and rationale for its creation; its location; its impact on third-party countries, such as China; the costs for operation; the possibility of unintended security consequences; and the challenges of integrating interagency personnel and missions. These questions have contributed to AFRICOM's image problem. A number of analysts have noted that the DOD "significantly mismanaged"[69] the creation of the command[70] and conveyed mixed messages about its mission and goals. One on hand, AFRICOM was described as a "new model for interagency integration"[71] and an "experimental" "whole of government" approach to foreign policy.[72] On the other hand, its role was also described as simply "support[ing] and complement[ing] our civilian-led initiatives"[73] and as "bureaucratic headquarters reorganization within the Department of Defense."[74] There was a lack of an effective public diplomacy strategy at the "take off" that fostered uncertainties and allowed fears and misperceptions to take root. African governments and African publics, in particular, feared that the creation of AFRICOM signaled the resurgence of colonialism on the continent, the subjugation of humanitarian assistance to military prerogatives, a frontier in U.S. energy exploitation, and a new theater for the war on terrorism.

This resistance to AFRICOM is striking in light of the overall positive U.S. image on the continent. Two recent opinion polls reveal that—though distrust of the United States has intensified around the globe—Africa is one of the few areas that maintains a favorable view of the United States. In the July 24, 2007, *Pew Global Attitudes Survey*, the United States tops the list of dependable allies in eight of ten African countries surveyed.[75] Ethiopia, Ghana, Kenya, Mali, Nigeria, South Africa, Tanzania, and Uganda listed the United States as their most dependable ally.[76] In addition, an April 8, 2008, article by *Gallup International* reveals that approval of U.S. leadership in sub-Saharan Africa is approximately twice as high as it is in other areas of the world. This poll of 139 countries shows a 62 percent approval rating of U.S. leadership among the countries of sub-Saharan Africa, compared to the 32 percent world median.[77] Fundamentally, the United States has a reservoir of goodwill on the African continent that is threatened by AFRICOM's image problem.

Given the existing environment of mistrust, one of the most pressing tasks facing U.S. civilian and military officials is to develop an effective public diplomacy strategy through not only a concise explanation of U.S. goals, but also through listening and interaction with African governments, civil society, and publics. The U.S. military and civilian personnel working in AFRICOM must create a public diplomacy strategy to reduce the misperceptions of AFRICOM that complicate the relations between the United States and Africa and will impede the success of the command. In this effort, the military needs to utilize its unique capabilities and resources. To be effective, this public diplomacy strategy must listen to the views of African leaders and publics about AFRICOM, communicate a clear and consistent message, analyze the way that message is being interpreted in Africa, and manage expectations.

Listen Carefully

AFRICOM needs to understand the complexities of a diverse continent, composed of fifty-three countries with various languages, cultures, societies, and traditions. Perceptions of AFRICOM vary from region to region, country to country, and village to village. To that end, U.S. officials must listen carefully to these different groups to determine what their aspirations and realities are and to create an "interactive relationship between senders and receivers."[78] AFRICOM must be sensitive to local needs and regional differences. For example, opposition to AFRICOM has been virulent in the southern region of the continent, particularly among the fourteen countries comprising the Southern African Development Community (SADC). Many SADC members are suspicious about U.S. intentions on the continent due to the history of the United States backing colonial regimes in Mozambique, Angola, and Rhodesia during the cold war and the minority government in South Africa during the apartheid.[79] In addition, countries such as South Africa may fear losing regional influence with the emergence of AFRICOM.[80] AFRICOM leaders need to gain a comprehensive understanding of the various perceptions that exist through active listening and interacting with the various societies.

Credibility in this effort can only be achieved by establishing a dialogue with African military chiefs, African NGOs, the media, and the public. The military can play an active role in listening by partnering with the DOS to go on "listening" tours around the continent. Scheduling public events, university symposiums, and joint public forums in which both civilian and military personnel have an opportunity to address the concerns of the public is imperative. Only after listening to the fears and misunderstandings that exist can AFRICOM civilian and military personnel began to rebuild trust on the continent and communicate their message.

Communicate a Message

The second step in a successful public diplomacy strategy is explaining how AFRICOM will add real value to African security, how it will build effective security mechanisms that are beneficial to African countries and the African public, and how it intends to promotes peace and stability. AFRICOM must be perceived as a command that addresses African interests as fully as it does U.S. interests. AFRICOM's mission must reflect African realities, such as the desire for "democratic consolidation, the continuing quest for sustainable development, the need to enhance state capacity, the craving for good governance, promotion of human security."[81] To communicate this message, AFRICOM officials must first confront the misperceptions and fears that exist regarding the command and must communicate its mission in a way that does not breed resentment. AFRICOM officials must provide answers to African concerns about AFRICOM, including the charges about the militarization of foreign policy and development assistance; the access to resources, including energy supplies; the move to counter China's growing influence; and the fear that the United States will quickly withdraw when faced with hardship or difficulty. Second, AFRICOM must leverage the power of personal relationships. Many fears and misperceptions of AFRICOM can be alleviated through personal relationships formed with local citizens. Lastly, AFRICOM must recognize the challenges and opportunities in public diplomacy promotion posed by emerging technology. Given the democratization of information dissemination, AFRICOM needs to capitalize on all of these forms of communication to engage with African civil society. "Ineffective and often antiquated methods"[82] of listening and engaging with African publics will impede the effectiveness of the U.S. message. To that end, AFRICOM must adapt to the local information environments on the African continent. Civilian and military personnel should investigate what media are being used in different countries and regions, how are they used, and which population groups use predominantly which media. Public diplomacy is a vital tool with which to engage many diverse elements of a society, but only if those elements in society are receiving the message.

Analyze the Message

The third step in promoting an effective public diplomacy strategy is the research and analysis of how the messages are being received by the continent. Public diplomacy strategies require efforts to understand the efficacy of messaging, through public opinion polling, census data, studies, and focus groups. Developing metrics for success through the use of these media monitoring tools will allow the U.S. government to tangibly gauge public opinion. Currently no public opinion polls or surveys exist that have measured public reaction to AFRICOM and thus government officials have been forced to rely on anecdotal evidence regarding public opinion about the command on the continent.

With its experience in other COCOMS, the military can provide ample support to this aspect of AFRICOM's public diplomacy strategy. According to a 2007 GAO Report on U.S. public diplomacy, the DOD uses a "campaign style" approach to public diplomacy in which each step in public diplomacy efforts is supported by goals, guidelines, and constant research and evaluation.[83] The military's systematic approach to measuring communications includes "developing clear objectives, testing messages, identifying targeted and complex dissemination strategies, and measuring effectiveness."[84] These GAO findings conversely argue that the DOS generally does not use this type of actionable research to support public diplomacy goals. By supporting public diplomacy activities with actionable research to assess public opinion, the military can determine which messages are effective to tailor communications to the receiving public.

Manage Expectations

An important goal of AFRICOM's public diplomacy should be to manage expectations of the command. AFRICOM will provide no quick fix to Africa's security challenges. To that end, AFRICOM's military and civilian personnel need to consider that "The best and most skillful public diplomacy cannot save a flawed policy, but a flawed policy can compromise the best-established public diplomacy."[85]

Conclusion

Unlike traditional diplomacy, which focuses on government-to-government communications, effective public diplomacy is a dialogue that involves the communication of a government's foreign policy to different segments of a nation. Whereas public diplomacy was marginalized as a tool of foreign policy following the collapse of the Soviet Union—culminating in the adoption of the USIA into the DOS—the terrorist attacks of September 11 and their aftermath have underlined its importance and relevance. The central assumption of public diplomacy—that opinions matter—needs to play an increasingly important role in the formation and implementation of U.S. foreign policy. The U.S. military has long incorporated strategic communications, and specifically public diplomacy, into its doctrine, policy, and actions. Given the significant role that the U.S. military plays in the formation of world public opinion about the United States, it must take public diplomacy seriously.

Although an effective public diplomacy strategy is critical to the success of AFRICOM's mission, it is important to remember what public diplomacy cannot do. It cannot be a substitute for clear strategic goals. It cannot substitute for a lack of coherence and unity of effort in implementing U.S. security policies and programs. And it cannot replace the political will and commitment that ultimately is required for its success. A major weakness in U.S. foreign policy toward Africa has been the lack of a long-term sustained and steady commitment, including addressing security challenges. The creation of AFRICOM is an indication that this might finally be changing.

Notes

I would like to thank Elizabeth Grimm, my research assistant at the U.S. Institute of Peace, for her invaluable help in preparing this chapter.

1. CSIS (2007). "Center for Strategic & International Studies Commission on Smart Power: A Smarter, More Secure America." Retrieved October 1, 2008, from http://www.csis.org/media/csis/pubs/071106_csissmartpowerreport.pdf.

2. E. P. Djerejian, Changing Minds, Winning Peace: A New Strategic Direction for U.S. Public Diplomacy in the Arab and Muslim World, Report of the Advisory Group on Public Diplomacy for the Arab and Muslim World (October 1, 2003): 1–80

3. P. D. A. Association, "What Is Public Diplomacy?" Retrieved August 28, 2008, from http://www.publicdiplomacy.org/1.htm.

4. U. S. A. C. O. P. Diplomacy, "Building America's Public Diplomacy Through a Reformed Structure and Additional Resources." Retrieved August 28, 2008, from http://www.state.gov/documents/organization/13622.pdf.

5. Joseph S. Nye, "The Decline of America's Soft Power," *Foreign Affairs* 83, no. 3 (2004): 16–20.

6. N. Cull, *The Cold War and the United States Information Agency: American Propaganda and Public Diplomacy, 1945–1989* (Cambridge, UK: Cambridge University Press, 2008).

7. L. Beehner (2005), "Perceptions of U.S. Public Diplomacy," Retrieved August 28, 2008, from http://www.cfr.org/publication/8934/perceptions_of_us_public_diplomacy.html.

8. J. K. Glassman, "U.S. Public Diplomacy and the War of Ideas," *Foreign Press Center Briefing*, Retrieved August 28, 2008, from http://fpc.state.gov/107034.htm.

9. For a small sampling of this body of scholarship, please see: *The 9/11 Commission Report: Final Report of the National Commission on Terrorist Attacks upon the United States* (New York: Norton, 2004); "The Need to Communicate: How to Improve U.S. Public Diplomacy with the Islamic World," *The Brookings Institution* (January 2004); "Strengthening U.S.-Muslim Communications," Center for the Study of the Presidency (July 2003): http://www.thepresidency.org/pubs/US-MuslimCommunications.pdf; Public Diplomacy Council. "Engaging the Arab/Islamic World—Next Steps for U.S. Public Diplomacy," Summary of Public Diplomacy Forum (February 27, 2004): http://pdi.gwu.edu/merlin-cgi/p/downloadFile/d/6504/n/off/other/1/name/SummaryoftheFeb27Forumdoc/; and "Finding America's Voice: A Strategy for Reinvigorating US. Public Diplomacy," Report of an Independent Task Force sponsored by the Council on Foreign Relations (September 2003): http://www.cfr.org/pdf/public_diplomacy.pdf).

10. Diplomacy, A. C. O. C. (2005), "Cultural Diplomacy: The Linchpin of Public Diplomacy "Retrieved August 28, 2008, from http://www.state.gov/documents/organization/54374.pdf.

11. G. W. Bush, (2001), "President Holds Prime Time News Conference," Retrieved August 28, 2008, from http://www.whitehouse.gov/news/releases/2001/10/20011011–7.html#status-war.

12. NSS (2002). The National Security Strategy of the United States of America.

13. E. Edelman, "Testimony Statement: Defense Undersecretary for Policy Edelman Urges Strengthening of Civilian Capacities," Retrieved September 16, 2008, from http://www.africom.mil/getarticle.asp?art=1963.

14. PDD, "International Public Information (IPI): Presidential Decision Directive PDD 68." Retrieved September 22, 2008, from http://www.fas.org/irp/offdocs/pdd/pdd-68.htm.

15. Cull, *Cold War and the United States Information Agency*, 502.

16. R. M. Gates, (2007), "Landon Lecture (Kansas State University)," Retrieved August 28, 2008, from http://www.defenselink.mil/speeches/speech.aspx?speechid=1199.

17. C. Rice, (2006). "Transformational Diplomacy," Retrieved August 28, 2008, from http://www.state.gov/secretary/rm/2006/59306.htm.

18. Gates, "Landon Lecture," 2007.

19. M. Malan, *U.S. Civil-Military Imbalance for Global Engagement: Lessons from the Operational Level in Africa* (Washington, DC: Refugees International, 2008), 1–48.

20. Djerejian, Changing Minds, Winning Peace, 2003.

21. J. B. Jones, Strategic Communication: A Mandate for the United States, *Joint Force Quarterly* Issue 39, (2005): 108–114.

22. DOD (2001), Joint Publication 1–02: Department of Defense Dictionary of Military and Associated Terms.

23. Code, U. S. Title 22: Foreign Relations and Intercourse, Chapter 38: Department of State § 2732: Public Diplomacy Responsibilities of the Department of State.

24. D. Petraeus and J. Mattis, Field Manual 3–24 Counterinsurgency. D. O. T. Army and U. S. M. Corps, 2006.

25. DOD 2001, 2.

26. R. M. Gates, "Speech to the United States Global Leadership Campaign," Retrieved August 28, 2008, from http://www.usglc.org/index.php?option=com_content&task=view&id=228&Itemid=26.

27. Gates, "Landon Lecture," 2007.

28. DOD (2006). Quadrennial Defense Review Report. D. O. Defense.
29. Ibid.
30. The regional Combatant Commanders currently include the Commanders of the U.S. Central Command (CENTCOM); U.S. European Command (EUCOM); U.S. Northern Command (NORTHCOM); U.S. Pacific Command (PACOM); and the U.S. Southern Command (SOUTHCOM). The other four unified COCOMs are functional commands and include U.S. Joint Forces Command (JFCOM); U.S. Special Operations Command (SOCOM); U.S. Strategic Command (STRATCOM); and the U.S. Transportation Command (TRANSCOM).
31. GAO, U.S. Public Diplomacy: Actions Needed to Improve Strategic Use and Coordination of Research, 2007.
32. DOD, (2008). Report of the Defense Science Board Task Force on Strategic Communications.
33. GAO 2007.
34. DOD 2008.
35. C. F. Wald, "New Thinking at USEUCOM: The Phase Zero Campaign," *Joint Forces Quarterly* 43 (2006): 74–75.
36. A. S. Natsios, "Testimony of Andrew S. Natsios, USAID Administrator, on US relief efforts to tsunami-affected countries, Testimony before the Subcommittee on Foreign Operations Appropriations Committee," 2005. Retrieved August 27, 2008, from http://www.pacom.mil/special/0412asia/index.shtml.
37. DOD 2008.
38. DOD, (2006). Joint Publication 3–13: Information Operations.
39. Ibid.
40. S. M. Maloney, "How can Somalia really be fixed?" *Maclean's* 120, no. 3 (2007).
41. R. G. Berschinski, "AFRICOM's Dilemma: The 'Global War on Terrorism,' 'Capacity Building,' 'Humanitarianism,' and the Future of U.S. Security Policy in Africa." *Strategic Studies Institute Monograph,* from http://www.strategicstudiesinstitute.army.mil/pdffiles/PUB827.pdf.
42. J. Hulle, "CJTF-HOA Give Shoes, Toys to Orphans," 2008. Retrieved September 7, 2008, from http://www.hoa.centcom.mil/ArticleArchive/July2008/Orphanage070108.asp.
43. K. Garcia, "U.S. Soldiers use CLS skills to aid crash victims," 2008. Retrieved September 8, 2008, from http://www.hoa.centcom.mil/ArticleArchive/June2008/Accident062708.asp.
44. "Ambassador Joins CJTF-HOA Team to Promote Ethiopian Livestock Health," U.S. Embassy Addis Ababa, Ethiopia, News Release (May 21, 2008), from http://www.hoa.africom.mil/getArticle.asp?art=1768&lang=
45. D. I. Dean, "School dedication celebrates Ethiopian, U.S. partnership," 2008. Retrieved September 17, 2008, from http://www.hoa.centcom.mil/ArticleArchive/June2008/KelamiSchool061008.asp.
46. K. Garcia, "UPDF schooled in Laws of War," 2008, Retrieved September 8, 2008, from http://www.hoa.centcom.mil/ArticleArchive/June2008/UPDFLOAC060808.asp.
47. D. J. Danelo, "Around the Horn," *U.S. Naval Institute Proceedings* 132, no. 6 (2006).
48. DOS, (2007). "Country Reports on Terrorism." Retrieved August 28, 2008, from http://www.state.gov/s/ct/rls/crt/2006/82730.htm.
49. W. P. Pope, "Statement of William P. Pope, Acting Coordinator for Counterterrorism, US Department of State, before the Committee on International Relations, Subcommittee on International Terrorism, Non-Proliferation and Human Rights of the U.S. House of Representatives," 2005. Retrieved from http://www.eucom.mil/english/Transcripts/20050310a.asp.
50. D. Miles, "New Counterterrorism Initiative to Focus on Saharan Africa," 2005. Retrieved August 28, 2008, from http://www.defenselink.mil/news/newsarticle.aspx?id=31643.
51. GAO (2008). Combating Terrorism: Actions Needed to Enhance Implementation of Trans-Sahara Counterterrorism Partnership.

52. Ibid.

53. L. K. Boudali, "The North Africa Project: The Trans-Sahara Counterterrorism Partnership," 2007. Retrieved August 28, 2008, from http://stinet.dtic.mil/cgi-bin/GetTRDoc?AD=A DA466542&Location=U2&doc=GetTRDoc.pdf.

54. GAO 2008, 14.

55. J. P. Pham, "Strategic Interests: Al Qaeda's Franchise in Africa," 2007. Retrieved September 17, 2008, from http://worlddefensereview.com/pham062107.shtml.

56. Miles 2005.

57. P. Ulmer, "Special Operations Command Europe Trains African Soldiers," 2004. Retrieved August 28, 2008, from http://www.eucom.mil/english/FullStory.asp?art=367.

58. ICG, "Islamic Terrorism in the Sahel: Fact or Fiction," *International Crisis Group Report* 92 (2005): 1–42.

59. C. Thomas-Jensen and M. Fick, "Foreign Assistance Follies in Niger," *CSIS Africa Policy Forum* (2007). Retrieved September 22, 2008, from http://forums.csis.org/africa/?p=59.

60. ICG 2005.

61. T. Archer and T. Popovic, The Trans-Saharan Counter-Terrorism Initiative: The US War on Terrorism in North Africa, The Finnish Institute of International Affairs (2007): 1–82.

62. Pham 2007.

63. R. Khatchadourian, "War in the Greatest Desert: The U.S. Military's $500 Million Gamble to Prevent the Next Afghanistan," 2005. Retrieved September 17, 2008, from http://www. internationalreportingproject.org/stories/algeria/algeria_war2.htm.

64. GAO 2008, 20.

65. U.S. European Command previously had the responsibility for forty-two African countries; U.S. Central Command had responsibility for Djibouti, Egypt, Eritrea, Ethiopia, Kenya, Seychelles, Somalia, and Sudan; and U.S. Pacific Command had the responsibility for the Comoros, Madagascar, and Mauritius.

66. E. Blunt, "Uncertainty over US Africa Force," *BBC News*, 2007 from http://news.bbc. co.uk/2/hi/africa/7085775.stm.

67. L. Ploch, "Statement before the U.S. House of Representatives Committee on Oversight and Government Reform, Subcommittee on National Security and Foreign Affairs," 2008. Retrieved August 28, 2008, from http://www.africom.mil/getarticle.asp?art=1902.

68. NSS (2006)., "The National Security Strategy of the United States of America."

69. K. H. Hicks, "Africom: Vision and Prospects," 2008. Retrieved August 28, 2008, from www.csis.org/media/csis/congress/ts080723hicks.pdf.

70. Though the creation of AFRICOM emanated from the DOD, the Implementation Planning Team (IPT) established by the Pentagon in 2006 by then Secretary of Defense Donald Rumsfeld, included interagency representatives from both USAID and the DOS. IPT director was Rear Admiral Robert Moeller and the deputy director was Ambassador Robert Luftis.

71. D. Skinner, "Senior Pentagon, State Department Officials Discuss "Militarization of Foreign Policy" at Congressional Hearing," 2008. Retrieved August 28, 2008, from http:// www.africom.mil/getArticle.asp?art=1959.

72. R. Henry, "News Transcript from the DOD Special Briefing on Africa Command," 2007. Retrieved August 28, 2008, from http://www.defenselink.mil/transcripts/transcript. aspx?transcriptid=3997.

73. J. D. Negroponte, "Testimony Statement: Deputy Secretary of State Negroponte Stresses Increased Role of Civilian Agencies is Critical to National Security before the U.S. Senate Committee on Foreign Relations," 2008. Retrieved August 28, 2008, from http://www. africom.mil/getArticle.asp?art=1962.

74. D. Taylor, "Voice of America: Skepticism Abounds as AFRICOM Launch Looms— Part 3 of 5," 2008. Retrieved August 28, 2008, from http://www.voanews.com/english/

archive/2008–05/Skepticism-Abounds-as-AFRICOM-Launch-Looms-PART-3-of-5.cf
m?CFID=27434819&CFTOKEN=62435852.

75. Pew, "Global Opinion Trends 2002–2007: A Rising Tide Lifts Mood in the Developing
World," *The Pew Global Attitudes Project,* 2008. Retrieved August 28, 2008, from http://
pewglobal.org/reports/display.php?ReportID=257.

76. In this survey, the Ivory Coast listed both the United States and China as its most dependable ally and Senegal listed France as its most dependable ally.

77. J. Ray, "U.S. Leadership Approval Highest in Sub-Saharan Africa," 2008. Retrieved
August 28, 2008, from http://www.gallup.com/poll/106306/US-Leadership-Approval-
Highest-SubSaharan-Africa.aspx.

78. DOD, (2008). Report of the Defense Science Board Task Force on Strategic
Communications.

79. J. E. Frazer, "The United States," in *From Cape to Congo: Southern Africa's Evolving Security
Challenges,* ed. M. Baregu and C. Landsberg (Boulder, CO: Lynne Rienner, 2003).

80. P. Fabricius, "Flexing Our Political Muscle: Is South Africa the Emerging African power or
the Top Dog on the Continent?" *Daily News,* 2007.

81. W. Okumu, "Africa Command: Opportunity for Enhanced Engagement or the
Militarization of U.S.-Africa Relations?"2007. Retrieved August 28, 2008, from http://
www.internationalrelations.house.gov/110/oku080207.htm.

82. H. Hyde, "Speaking to our Silent Allies: Public Diplomacy and U.S. Foreign Policy,"
Retrieved August 27, 2008, from http://usinfo.state.gov/journals/itps/1202/ijpe/pj7–
4hyde.htm.

83. GAO 2007.

84. Ibid., 10.

85. Cull 2008, 496.

CHAPTER TWELVE

Conclusion: The Task for Policy Makers

PHILIP SEIB

The premise of this book is that American public diplomacy needs a thoughtful and very thorough overhaul. Mere fine-tuning will not fix it. Many U.S. public diplomacy efforts in recent years have been naïve, archaic, and largely ineffective. These problems will persist unless the new administration's policy makers are willing to acknowledge past difficulties and let imagination supersede tradition.

The Iraq War provides good evidence of the limited effectiveness of hard power. In future conflicts, should an enemy army square off with the U.S. military on a conventional battlefield, American might will easily prevail. But that kind of confrontation is unlikely to occur; most of America's enemies are smart enough to know that guerrilla warfare—urban or otherwise—offers the only hope for challenging the United States in battle. America might eventually prevail in such conflicts, but only at great cost. By now the intrinsic weakness of over-reliance on hard power should be apparent to U.S. policy makers. An alternative must be found.

Hard power coerces while soft power convinces. Decency and common sense demand greater reliance on the latter. Embracing soft power is not a sign of weakness, even if it is a less macho way of dealing with the rest of the world. If progress is truly to be made in relationships among nations, soft power must gradually displace hard power.

Should that happen, public diplomacy will become increasingly important because it is the essence of soft power and the mechanism through which this form of influence is exercised. As William Rugh points out in his chapter, the United States possesses an ample array of soft power tools. They have not, however, been put to work in a coordinated way that takes full advantage of their value. Soft power does not take effect spontaneously; it requires strategic planning and tactical deployment, just as hard power does. This must be recognized and acted upon if public diplomacy as a tool of soft power is ever to be more than a small subsidiary of America's foreign policy. So far, that has not occurred.

America has a long tradition of using public diplomacy. Nicholas Cull underscores this in his overview of the history of this field. A stellar example of the public diplomat was Benjamin Franklin, whose shrewd use of charm won European friends for an emerging nation that had no choice but to rely on diplomacy as an adjunct to its limited military capability. Since then, public diplomacy's path has been bumpy. It was notably successful in some instances during the cold war, but more recently it has been window dressing for a foreign policy that has relied more on brawn than brains. This is not to say that the world has become so calm that diplomacy—public or otherwise—will always be sufficient to ensure security and achieve policy goals, but America is certainly strong enough to be able to rely on a mix of soft and hard power, a combination of approaches that can be called "smart power." Striking a balancing of those approaches to create a successful smart power formula should be a principal task for the Obama administration.

A striking example of the flawed nature of recent American public diplomacy is Al Hurra television, the Arabic-language satellite news channel funded by the U.S. government (at great expense) to showcase American policies and values. Its unofficial objective is to compete with Al Jazeera and other Middle East news organizations that are perceived as being unfriendly toward U.S. interests. Al Hurra has been a dismal failure; surveys find that in most of the region its audience is minuscule, and abundant anecdotal evidence indicates that it is not considered a credible source of information. Al Hurra is based on a cold war model that was able to take credibility for granted when audiences in Eastern Europe, for example, desperately wanted alternatives to Soviet propaganda. In the Middle East today, however, television news viewers seem quite satisfied with the broad spectrum of indigenous news products available to them. Al Hurra tries to fill a need that doesn't exist.

Instead of trying to compete head-to-head with the likes of Al Jazeera, U.S. policymakers should develop a more sophisticated strategy for delivering the American outlook through respected Arab news organizations. Even more important, U.S. officials should try to influence the coverage being delivered by Arab journalists to their home audiences. Clear precedent for this can be found in the British strategy to affect U.S. public opinion during 1940–1941. Winston Churchill's government placed its principal emphasis not on using the BBC to advance the interventionist viewpoint, but rather actively courted and facilitated coverage by American journalists such as Edward R. Murrow, Raymond Graham Swing, Quentin Reynolds, and others. Churchill involved himself in this process, which proved enormously successful. Sympathetic portraits of Britons under siege were delivered in a steady stream to American audiences, and this helped to undermine the isolationist argument that was impeding the flow of U.S. aid and damaging Britain's war effort.

In simple terms, this approach amounts to co-opt rather than compete. At the very least, it is worth trying, particularly given the decided lack of impact that Al Hurra has had. In their chapter, Shawn Powers and Ahmed El Gody detail the flawed assumptions and inadequate operating standards that have rendered Al Hurra ineffective. The new administration should stop throwing money at Al Hurra and devise a new approach to reaching the Middle Eastern news audience.

A significant element in plotting the future course of American public diplomacy should be an appraisal of how publics around the world are responding to U.S. efforts. This volume's chapters by scholars from Russia, China, and Egypt—Viktoria Orlova, Guolin Shen, and Hussein Amin—point out that much of the tension that exists between their countries and the United States can be reduced only if American policies change; public diplomacy by itself is not a panacea. The assumption that the United States is fundamentally a bully is widespread, and in any effort to change that perception the burden of proof rests with America.

This does not mean that public diplomacy efforts are pointless. These three authors indicate that their fellow citizens are receptive to American advances because there is much about the United States that they admire—its culture, its technologies, and its fundamental freedom and character. These attributes constitute the foundation on which public diplomacy efforts can be built, but that structure will always be wobbly if it attempts to support an American worldview that is primarily hubristic.

Listening should be a cornerstone of public diplomacy, and for these three and other countries, U.S. policy makers need to listen more carefully. This does not mean embarking on "listening tours" that amount to little more than extended photo opportunities. Instead, public diplomacy should be informed by honest public opinion surveys plus on-the-ground interaction that encourages forthright exchanges of views. These efforts may produce invaluable information about perceptions of existing American public diplomacy efforts and about the United States more generally.

With a thorough appreciation of what has gone before and what the world is thinking, entering the modern era of public diplomacy will be less daunting. Then the task will become one of modernizing America's public diplomacy machinery and its products.

At the heart of this must be an understanding of the ramifications of the communications revolution that has been underway for roughly a decade. We have come a long way from Ben Franklin's letters and chats, from VOA's cold war broadcasts, and even from the original conception of Al Hurra. The world belongs to the Internet, and that must be accorded more prominence as a tool of public diplomacy.

As Amelia Arsenault points out, the "participatory ethos of the contemporary information environment" changes the public's expectations about communication. No longer will people be merely passive recipients of messages from news organizations, governments, or anyone else. The interactive capabilities of the Internet, for all their imperfections, encourage individuals to become players, to push back against messages with which they disagree, and to disseminate their own views. The results may be chaotic, but the process that produces them is fundamentally democratic and is changing the marketplace of ideas forever. For those conducting public diplomacy, the Internet fosters new levels of intellectual competition, with the din of many voices—sometimes a chorus, sometimes a cacophony—as the inescapable backdrop for making one's case.

The United States must embark on a far more realistically imaginative approach to Internet-related public diplomacy. This does not mean trying to monitor, much less respond to, the world's more than 100 million blogs or tracking every Web site that might mention U.S. policy. Rather, public diplomats should create a package of imaginative products, ranging from blogs to YouTube, that are heavily promoted as sources of information and as vehicles for conversation about American life and policy. Some of this is done now but not in a way that makes content and accessibility recognized throughout the world. "America. gov: Telling America's story" is bland and uninviting. "Change.gov," the site created by the transition team for President-elect Obama provided promising evidence of greater technological sophistication. Whatever the exact format of the public diplomacy offering, it must stress interactivity, which means having dedicated content and personnel, and this requires relying on more than leftover boilerplate and techies stuffed in a closet.

This may seem a daunting task, but to compete effectively in the new communication environment will require substantial investment and real commitment to engaging the rest of the world despite the occasional unpleasantness that will inevitably part of this process. The "public" to which public diplomacy is directed is vast, curious, and progressively less inhibited about challenging the information that they are given. This is a world far beyond the niceties of old-fashioned diplomacy that could be conducted exclusively among comfortable elites. New media have opened a reconfigured diplomatic process to much of the world, and these new participants will never allow themselves to be shut out.

To help supply the reinforcements needed in the increasingly populous world of public diplomacy, the private sector must be called upon. Given how few businesses and other private enterprises feel constrained by national borders, private players are logical participants in reaching out to the world. For a start, good global citizenship is essential. This means that the "ugly American" stereotype must be permanently retired, and some corporate partnerships with the State Department have emphasized this, educating traveling businesspeople about ways to avoid boorishness.

But instilling politeness is not ambitious enough. Championing free enterprise is a widely admired element of the American character and it can be a valuable facet of U.S. public diplomacy. Given that economic development is a crucial need in much of the world, linking private sector development assistance—in the form of counseling and training—to broader public diplomacy strategy would make sense. In her chapter, Kathy Fitzpatrick presents a strong case that nongovernmental American presence abroad can be useful, particularly if coordinated in ways that enhance constructive visibility. For instance, involvement by U.S. businesses in local charitable projects overseas is common, but it should be better woven into the larger public diplomacy context, at least on a country-by-country basis.

Perhaps an even more potent facet of public diplomacy is cultural diplomacy. This is something the United States has generally done well. Dispatching Benny Goodman to the Soviet Union or Isaac Stern to China presented a benign and popular American visage that international publics generally appreciate without question. So why is this strength not put to better, more comprehensive use?

Sending major artists abroad is the easy part of cultural diplomacy. As Neal Rosendorf points out in his chapter, more difficult are the arrangements for tasks involving definition and presentation of American ideals and establishing the mechanisms of "exchange, learning, and relationship-building." The numbers of American students studying abroad and foreign students studying in the United States have moved significantly upward during the past several years. That is excellent, but it does not obviate the need to eliminate harassment such as that which Arab academics anticipate (often correctly) they will encounter when entering the United States through a major airport. Believing this, they stay home.

Any American who travels overseas, particularly in countries less than friendly toward the U.S. government, consistently finds a significant difference in attitude between those who have spent time in America and those who know it only from afar. The former are most often friendlier and more open to further information, so to allow pointless obstruction of those who want to visit is counterproductive.

American culture offers assets of immeasurable value to public diplomacy efforts, but putting these assets to work is perhaps sometimes too easy. Setting up a concert tour, a traveling art exhibit, or a short-term student exchange is mostly a logistical matter that can stand apart from larger policy concerns. The task for the new stewards of American public diplomacy is to better incorporate cultural diplomacy into the more political schemata of U.S. foreign policy. The overall goal is to make the whole greater than the sum of its parts, which means not settling for individual successes here and there but rather integrating the best and fixing (or sometimes jettisoning) the worst elements of public diplomacy.

The significance of religious freedom in American life should also be accorded more prominence in public diplomacy. Considering religion's importance throughout much of the world, this attribute of American society should be explained fully and serve as a regular theme in public diplomacy efforts. As Jennifer Marshall and Thomas Farr point out in their chapter, commitment to separation of church and state should not lead to ambivalence about the strength of religious belief in the United States. Although the Muslim world tends to attract the most attention when the connections between religion and foreign policy are discussed, plenty of other areas merit attention.

Latin America, sub-Saharan Africa, and China are among the places where religious issues are increasingly important and where a public diplomacy message tied to religious freedom could advance American interests.

In one form or another, religion is at the heart of much of America's history and culture, and there is ample evidence that in much of the world attitudes about the United States improve as its commitment to religious freedom is better understood. It is possible to make this known without proselytizing for any particular religion. Doing so deserves a more prominent place in U.S. public diplomacy.

An offshoot of the hard power versus soft power debate is the notion of using the military as an instrument of public diplomacy. The newest U.S. military command, AFRICOM, which is responsible for Africa, has implicitly undertaken such a role. The command structure includes a civilian as deputy to the commander for civil-military activities, and much has been made about undertaking humanitarian aid missions, helping African states professionalize their own militaries, and otherwise aiding democratization. That sounds benign, but some NGOs and other civilian agencies worry about a blurring of lines between their work and that of the military. They express concern that their credibility will be threatened if publics in host countries come to believe that U.S. aid will be encumbered by unwanted U.S. military presence. On a larger scale, some see this as a further militarization of foreign policy.

In his chapter focusing on AFRICOM, Abiodun Williams observes, "Public diplomacy is too important to be left entirely to civilian agencies, particularly as the actions of the U.S. military critically affect the way other countries and their citizens view the United States." In some ways, this observation and the debate that inevitably will follow illustrates the uncertainty and complexity involved in planning the future of American public diplomacy.

The issues addressed in this book do not cover every aspect of public diplomacy, but the range of topics shows how important it will be for policy makers to adopt an at least equally broad perspective as they reappraise this part of the U.S. foreign policy process.

Plenty of other issues could become focal points of public diplomacy: advancing women's rights, facilitating microcredit programs, enhancing environmental protection, upgrading public health and public education, and more. Meeting the needs of the publics that the United States wishes to reach and influence should be given greater weight by policy planners. Pulling such efforts together will require remapping bureaucratic turf, never an easy task but an essential one if U.S. public diplomacy is to have the coherence and breadth that it requires.

All this comes back to the importance of nations becoming committed to soft power and relying on it instead of hard power. If that happens, the world will be a better place, and the door to that world can be opened by public diplomacy.

CONTRIBUTORS

Hussein Amin is professor and chair of the Department of Journalism and Mass Communication at the American University in Cairo. Among his many publications is his book *Civic Discourse and Digital Age Communication in the Middle East*.

Amelia Arsenault is a George Gerbner Post-Doctoral Fellow at the University of Pennsylvania and is a research associate at the University of Southern California Center on Public Diplomacy.

Nicholas J. Cull is professor of public diplomacy at the University of Southern California, where he directs the Masters degree program in Public Diplomacy. He is author of *The Cold War and the United States Information Agency: American Propaganda and Public Diplomacy, 1945–1989* (2008) and numerous other works on the history of the media and public diplomacy, including the UK Foreign Office Report: "Public Diplomacy: Lessons from the Past" (2007).

Ahmed El Gody is a Ph.D. candidate at Örebro University in Sweden where he teaches in the Department of Media and Communication and the Global Media Masters program. El Gody has written books and articles about new media and democracy in the Middle East and Africa.

Thomas F. Farr is visiting associate professor of religion and world affairs, and senior fellow at the Berkley Center for Religion, Peace, and World Affairs at Georgetown University. During a twenty-one-year career in the Foreign Service, Dr. Farr specialized in strategic military policy, political affairs, and religious freedom, and he was the first director of the State Department's office of international religious freedom. He is the author of *World of Faith and Freedom: Why Religious Liberty Is Vital to American National Security* (2008).

Kathy R. Fitzpatrick is professor and director of graduate studies in public relations in the School of Communications at Quinnipiac University. Recent publications include "Advancing the New Public Diplomacy: A Public Relations Perspective" in *The Hague Journal of Diplomacy* (2007) and *Responsible Advocacy: Ethics in Public Relations* (2006).

Jennifer A. Marshall is director of the Richard and Helen DeVos Center for Religion and Civil Society at The Heritage Foundation. Marshall oversees the foundation's work on education, welfare, family, religion, and civil society.

Victoria V. Orlova is head of the program planning department of Channel One Russia, and conducts research in media and international relations. She holds a Ph.D. in philology and journalism.

Shawn Powers is a visiting assistant professor at the University of Southern California's Annenberg School for Communication, London Studies Program.

William A. Rugh has served as deputy chief of mission in Syria, U.S. ambassador to Yemen, and U.S. ambassador to the United Arab Emirates. In Washington, Ambassador Rugh was Director of USIA's Near East Bureau. He is an associate at Georgetown's Institute for the Study of Diplomacy and an Adjunct Scholar at the Middle East Institute. His books include *American Encounters with Arabs: The "Soft Power" of U.S. Public Diplomacy in the Arab World; Engaging the Arab and Islamic Worlds through Public Diplomacy* (editor); and *Arab Mass Media: Newspapers, Radio and Television in Arab Politics.*

Neal M. Rosendorf has taught at Long Island University, the University of Queensland in Brisbane, Australia, and Harvard University's Kennedy School of Government. He is the author of numerous articles, book chapters, and book reviews that have been published in such venues as *Diplomatic History, International History Review, Historical Journal of Film, Radio and Television, The American Interest,* and *Foreign Service Journal.*

Philip Seib is professor of journalism and public diplomacy at the University of Southern California. His recent books include *Beyond the Front Lines: How the News Media Cover a World Shaped by War, Broadcasts from the Blitz: How Edward R. Murrow Helped Lead America into War, New Media and the New Middle East,* and *The Al Jazeera Effect.*

Guolin Shen is assistant professor of journalism at Fudan University. He focuses on American political communication and international communication. He was a Fox Fellow at Yale University and has published two books about American media and politics.

Abiodun Williams is vice president of the Center for Conflict Analysis and Prevention at the United States Institute of Peace. Previously he was associate dean of the Africa Center for Strategic Studies at the National Defense University, and from 2001 to 2007 was director of the Strategic Planning Unit in the Executive Office of the UN Secretary General. He served in peacekeeping operations in Macedonia, Haiti, and Bosnia. He has taught at Georgetown University, University of Rochester, and Tufts University and has published widely on conflict prevention, international peacekeeping and multilateral negotiations.

INDEX

ENTERParsed